EX- LIBRIS
RANDAL BINGLEY

In the Wake of a Woman

STONE AGE PIONEERING OF NORTH-EASTERN SCANIA, SWEDEN, 10,000–5000 BC,

THE ÅRUP SETTLEMENTS

EDITED BY PER KARSTEN & BJÖRN NILSSON

National Heritage Board, Sweden

SKRIFTER No 63

RIKSANTIKVARIEÄMBETET
Box 5405, SE-114 84 Stockholm, Sweden
Phone +46 (0)8-5191 8000
www.raa.se

RIKSANTIKVARIEÄMBETET UV
Internet bookstore customer service:
Phone +46 (0)31-334 29 05, +46 (0)31-334 29 04
Fax +46 (0)31-334 29 01

IN THE WAKE OF A WOMAN
Stone Age Pioneering of North-eastern Scania, Sweden, 10,000–5000 BC, the Årup Settlements

Graphic Design
    THOMAS HANSSON

Picture Design
    STAFFAN HYLL

Cover & chapter photos
    THOMAS HANSSON

Model
    HELENE WILHELMSSON

English revised by
    ALAN CROZIER

National Land Survey maps
    © LANTMÄTERIVERKET, S-801 82 GÄVLE, SWEDEN. DNR L 1999/3

Print
    GRAHNS TRYCKERI AB, LUND, SWEDEN 2006

All artefact drawings 67% of actual size

Riksantikvarieämbetet, Arkeologiska undersökningar, Skrifter No 63
ISSN 1102-187x
ISBN 978-91-7209-412-3
ISBN 91-7209-412-5

Contents

Preface

Figure 1. Those who made the fieldwork successful. Back row from left to right: Annika Jeppsson, Lisa Pålsson, Adam Bolander, Helén af Geijerstam, Björn Nilsson, Kai Persson, Conleth Hanlon, Martin Svanberg, Tony Björk, Lindsay Lloyd-Smith, Hubert (dummy). Front row from left to right: Åsa Perneby, Helene Wilhelmsson, Gunilla Olsson, Johanna Bergqvist. Absent from photo: Emma Bentz, Robert Dahl, Anna Ihr, Jonas Lidén, Rickard Lindberg, Kalle Melin, Sofia Yassin. Photo by Sven Waldemarsson.

In the north-eastern part of the province of Scania there is a large flat lowland area known as the Kristianstad Plain. This fertile agricultural land is surrounded by several lakes to the north and west and by the shores of the Baltic to the south and east. Immediately adjacent to River Skräbeån in the eastern part of the plain lies the archaeological site of Årup. Sand and silt dominate west of the river and to the east the soil is constituted by till, locally with a marked element of boulders. Thus, River Skräbeån forms a distinct geographical boundary in the landscape. This book tells the story of the fascinating archaeological discoveries made at Årup by the National Heritage Board in the summer and autumn of 2002.

Our investigation area was situated in a beautiful eighteenth-century English park on a gentle, easterly slope down towards the river. In connection

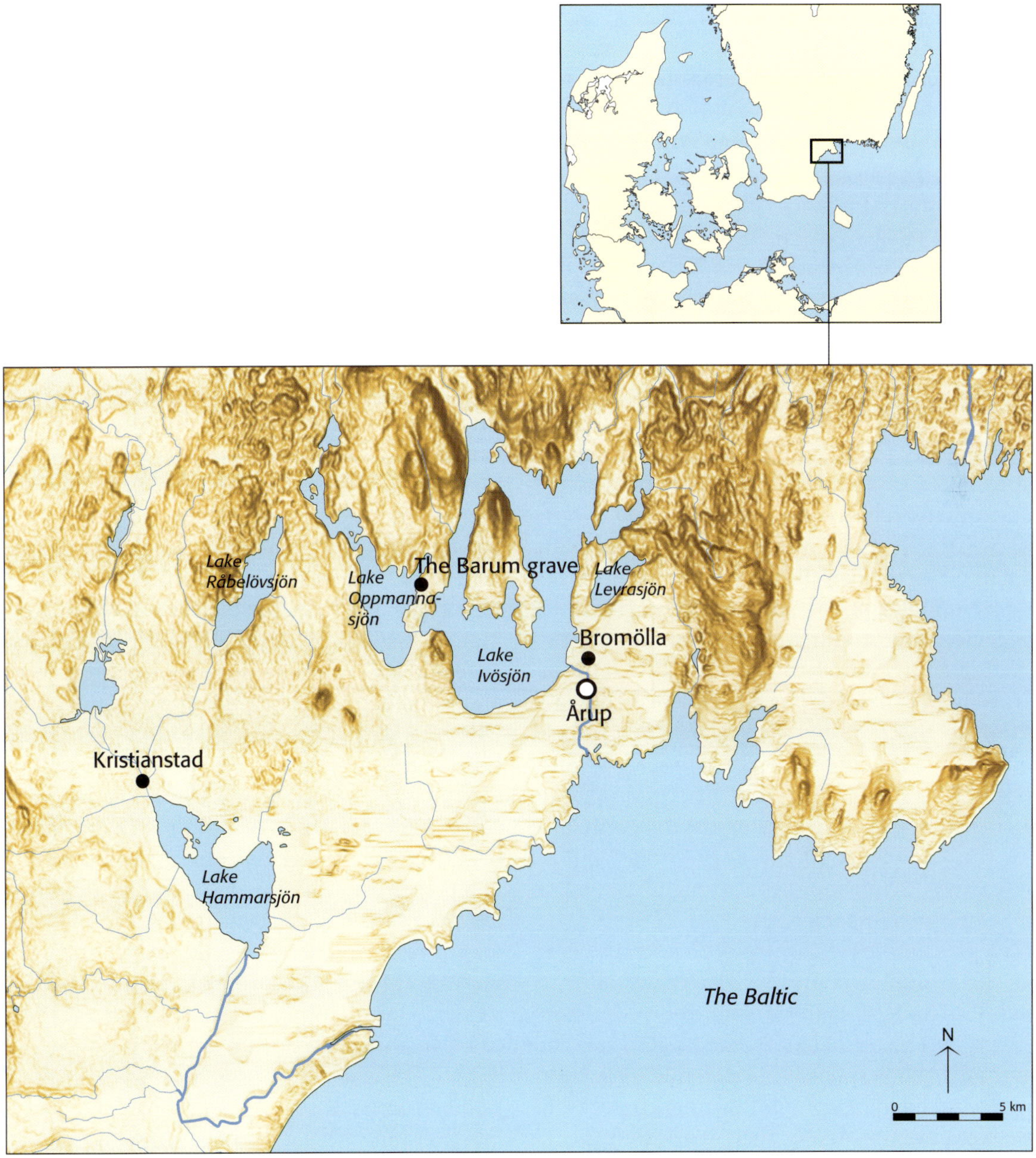

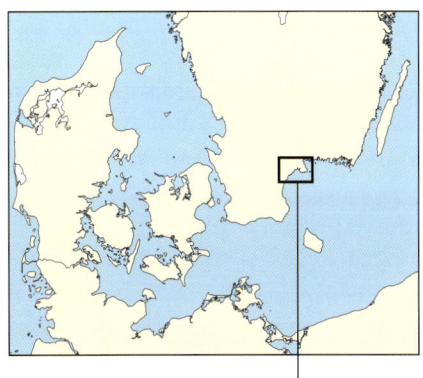

Figure 2. Maps showing the location of the Århup investigation site in north-eastern Scania. The cities of Kristianstad and Bromölla are also indicated as well as the Barum Grave.

with the construction of a new motorway large parts of the park had to go and the archaeologists were let loose. There we uncovered an Early and Middle Mesolithic settlement complex and, in addition, a well-defined Late Palaeolithic flint assemblage.

The previously known Mesolithic sites in the region have primarily been found in connection with the revision of the Cadastral Index Map and the associated field survey of ancient monuments in the area. Only a few Mesolithic archaeological investigations have been conducted, mostly performed in the first half of the twentieth century. The results of these early investigations have never been properly published. They are mostly to be found as notes in archives or as occasional references in other archaeological publications. Thus, our knowledge is poor, which to some extent can be explained by the fact that only a very few large-scale development projects have been carried out in the region. But another probably more important factor contributing to the state of affairs is that vast areas of land have been covered with sand during the repeated post-glacial sea transgressions, thus making it difficult indeed to find Mesolithic sites. Against this background the Årup site constitutes a very important contribution to the knowledge of the Early Stone Age in north–eastern Scania in both a regional and a south Scandinavian perspective.

It is a pleasure for me as project leader and editor of this volume to present the fruits of true teamwork. Conleth Hanlon and Björn Nilsson have from the start acted as archaeological project leaders with the responsibility for managing the fieldwork, archaeological analysis, and reports. It has been exciting to follow their work for a year.

Almost every week they came up with some new discoveries, including revisions of earlier archaeological "truths" and fresh interpretations on flint typology, find distributions, and hut reconstructions. They worked armed with curiosity and a highly developed source-critical sense. During their research they also became skilled use-wear analysts under the supervision of Bo Knarrström. This volume is above all Conleth's and Björn's joint work and ideas. In addition, Björn Nilsson has been co-editor of the book. He has also drawn all the artefact illustrations as well as the hut reconstructions, top-class as usual. Sofia Yassin had the responsibility of converting the often complicated digital field data into maps and distribution plans. She also undertook the topographic mapping of the site and the region, and together with Per Lagerås, the Quaternary geologist of the project, made the basis for the environmental reconstructions. Per Lagerås solved the complicated geological history of Årup. In addition Per painted the local environmental reconstructions. Both Per and Sofia had good help from Nils-Olof Svensson, who mapped the different Yoldia, Ancylus, and Littorina stage shorelines in the area. Thomas Hansson, responsible for the book layout, took active part already in the initial writing phase. His beautiful photographs and constructive ideas about text and pictures have inspired us throughout the project. Thanks also to Staffan Hyll for his magnificent picture design work and artefact photographs. Finally, a special thanks to our great model, Helene Wilhelmsson, for an excellent job of performing the Barum woman.

Lund, August 2006
Per Karsten

Prologue

By Conleth Hanlon & Björn Nilsson

IN THE WAKE OF A WOMAN

It is the summer of 1939, just outside the village of Barum, Kiaby parish, 2 km north of the castle of Bäckaskog, north-eastern Scania. Close by the eastern shore of Lake Oppmannasjön, Oscar Larsson, a local farmer, is occupied with the construction of a cow path through the steep riverbank leading down to the water. Suddenly he stops. A strange thing emerges in the light and chalky earth. The upper part of a human skull! He brushes off the soil and takes a closer look at the find spot. At the bottom of the ditch he can see parts of a skeleton. Larsson halts, and decides to phone the Historical Museum in Lund.

Later on, Folke Hansen, a skilled veteran archaeologist, gave the site his fullest attention. Hansen immediately observed that the burial had been damaged in that the cranium, some vertebrae, the right humerus, part of the right femur and parts of the right lower leg had been removed. Apparently the deceased had been placed in a pit that was about 0.6 m wide and 1.2 m deep, sitting in an upright position with retracted knees, arms folded in front of the stomach, and the back slightly arched (Hansen 1941). Apart from the unusually well preserved skeleton he also found a slotted bone point, some flints, and a bone chisel. Without

doubt this was a unique grave, the oldest burial on Swedish soil.

Despite the slender character of the skeleton researchers initially thought it was a male. In fact, in the 1940s "he" was referred to as "a perfectly normal gentleman of 40. Not a cripple in any way", by a professor in Lund (quoted in Karsten 2004). Of course this interpretation was based on the slotted bone point, an artefact associated with hunting – an activity perceived as being performed by men. Soon after the discovery the burial – now considered almost a national treasure – went up for display at the Museum of National Antiquities in Stockholm. After thirty years in the exhibition a renewed osteological investigation showed that the skeleton was in fact that of a 45-year-old woman who had given birth to several children (Gejvall 1970). In 1996, the Barum woman was subjected to yet another combination of renewed analyses consisting of osteological and odontological analyses as well as analysis of isotopic diet indicators and pollen (Sten et al. 2000). Radiocarbon dating placed the grave at 7895±75 ^{14}C-years BP, in the interval 7010–6540 cal. BC with 2 sigma. The interval spans the Maglemosian–Kongemosian transition. The results of the investigation showed that the woman had suffered from an infection that possibly had caused blood poisoning.

Figure 3. The place where the Barum grave was discovered in 1939, today marked with a memorial stone with the inscription: "The ancient fisherwoman from Barum was interred here" (authors' translation). Photo by Thomas Hansson.

Whether this had contributed to her death or not could not be deduced. Her teeth showed signs of extensive wear especially concentrated on the incisors and premolars, possibly indicating work such as softening of raw hide by chewing or twining of string. Stable isotope analysis indicated a diet of primarily terrestrial origin with a possible lacustrine component. Pollen analysis indicated that the burial took place in springtime due to a high incidence of birch (*Betula*) and hazel (*Corylus*) pollen. The occurrences of microscopic charcoal and soot particles in the samples were regarded as possibly deriving from clothing worn by the woman.

Since 1939 there have been no further field efforts. We do not know anything apart from her height, age, when she died and that she was a mother. Still, there are further pieces of information to be found regarding the life and times of the woman from Barum if one only widens ones perspective somewhat. By bringing other known Mesolithic sites and solitary finds in the region into the context of the sites of Årup and Barum, it is hoped that a greater understanding of settlement patterns and communication in the area will be reached.

Already during fieldwork at Årup, it was realised that finds such as handle cores, microblades, core axes, lanceolates, and regular blades indeed were roughly contemporary with the Barum grave. Given the location of Årup in relation to the site of the Barum burial – a distance only 9 km northwest of Årup as the crow flies – by one of very few possible waterways leading to the coast at the time in question, it was of course a splendid opportunity for us to try to shed some light on the enigmatic burial. In an attempt at drawing a picture of Mesolithic life in north-eastern Scania it was most gratifying to be able to incorporate a real human being who may very well have spent the greater part of her life in the area. She must have walked along the shores, leaving her foot-prints along the shores of the River Skräbeån and the lakes. For us, the Barum woman became the protector of the project and was constantly present in our minds.

INVESTIGATING ÅRUP

Rescue archaeology has its strengths and weaknesses. Its primary strength is the large areas that become the subject of archaeological investigation, facilitating the exploration of entire site structures, enabling questions regarding site organisation.

On the downside, however, one could argue that archaeologists do not possess any great means of influencing the choice of location or, for that matter, the object of investigation. It is society's demand for development, not archaeological research, that governs these choices. Rescue archaeology is

Figure 4. The area of investigation – once part of a beautiful eighteenth-century English park – viewed from the north-west towards the River Skräbeån. Photo by Helén af Geijerstam.

biased in the sense that the results are primarily based on investigations performed in the densely populated coastal plains of today where the pressure for infrastructural development is greater. The most considerable drawback, though, is the lack of time available during fieldwork. Developers suffer under tight budgets and even tighter time schedules, thus risking loss of large sums of money at the slightest delay or change of plan. In such circumstances, archaeology unfortunately tends to get the worst of it.

Taking note of this, the reader should understand that large-scale rescue archaeology requires special methods, methods that if practised in the context of a traditional research excavation would perhaps be perceived as coarse, brutal, and insensitive. Large areas excavated under pressure force one to decide priorities. These are weighed against the questions put in the plan of investigation; what can be carefully investigated, what is to be superficially documented and what is not to be documented at all? In consequence, time-saving methods

Figure 5. The Bronze Age layer was removed with the use of an excavator to uncover the Mesolithic level. Photo by Conleth Hanlon.

must be developed helping to give answers to questions addressed towards archaeological objects. The different methods practised during the Årup excavation should be viewed in the light of a large 12,000 m² investigation area with a highly complex archaeological picture combined with a very tight time schedule.

The two main problems to be dealt with were, on the one hand, the existence of Late Bronze Age occupation layers partly overlying Middle Mesolithic features, and on the other hand the occurrence of transgressional and aeolian deposits covering Late Palaeolithic and Early Mesolithic features and assemblages. In the light of this, the excavation relied

heavily on the use of excavators and total stations. Moreover the stripping of the topsoil was rendered difficult owing to some hundred tree stumps, which due to their sheer size had to be left standing since removal of them would have caused extensive damage. In addition, the very warm and dry summer and autumn of 2002 complicated the excavation as the soil humidity rapidly evaporated from uncovered areas, rendering the detection of features difficult. The dry weather also resulted in wind-blown sand continuously covering uncovered features, which called for recurring clear-up actions.

The choice of method practised at the site of Årup had both advantages and disadvantages. On the credit side extensive use of excavators and total stations facilitated investigation of a large area in a short period of time compared to traditional excavation of series of smaller trenches. In addition, the removal of the topsoil from the entire site gave a good overview, revealing the full extent of archaeological features and deposits. In fact, it is doubtful whether any Mesolithic features would have been found at all if the stripping method had not been used. At any rate the results would have been considerably more modest in character.

On the debit side, however, it could be argued that finds are bound to be lost when such a coarse level of recovery is applied. Furthermore, the sample which is recovered will be biased towards larger artefacts at the expense of smaller ones, and there will be a bias in favour of artefacts of colours contrasting with the background soil matrix.

Figure 6. A total station digitally registered cultural deposits and features as well as artefacts recovered in connection with the machine stripping. Photo by Helén af Geijerstam.

These are perfectly valid objections but are a part of the price one has to pay when conducting large-scale excavations. The material possibly lost should however be seen in relation to the tight time schedule. Had a much finer technique of recovery been employed, it would no doubt have increased the amount of material several times over, but the time limit ruled this out. Nevertheless, a series of squares were dug and the soil sieved before the machine stripping was initiated, thus giving an idea of the nature of the cultural deposits beforehand and where to put in the resources.

Even if the methods applied speeded things up during excavation, the extensive plotting of artefacts with total stations entailed rather time-consuming work in the form of registering of finds in the post-fieldwork phase.

TAPHONOMIC FACTORS IN THE ARCHAEOLOGY OF ÅRUP

Generally speaking the conditions for preservation of organic material in the region can be considered good due to the occurrence of cretaceous bedrock and calcareous soil (see Lagerås et al. this volume). But, contrary to what one could expect, the conditions of preservation at Årup were very poor. Unlike the western and northern parts of the region, where calcareous soil dominates, no Mesolithic osteological material was found. Wood found in the peat and gyttja deposit was also in a state of heavy decay, rendering it impossible to discern possible chop or cut marks.

This state of affairs can largely be explained by taphonomic factors in action at the site. Since the settlements at Årup are rather small and contain a relatively limited amount of finds they have largely been seen as representative of repeated occupations of short duration. This is in line with what

one would expect when dealing with more or less temporary campsites and it is also likely that the find material originally present was limited to start with. In addition, it can be assumed that the major part of the organic waste produced at Årup was carried away by the action of the river.

The repeated transgressions and regressions affecting the area would have had an impact on both sediments and groundwater level, whereby the process of repeated moisturing and desiccation may have destroyed organic materials. In addition, variations in pH values of the permeating water and groundwater may have affected organic materials negatively. These processes seem especially to have been at work at Årup. Given the permeable nature of the sandy deposits in the area, this allows water and oxygen to pass freely, thus creating aerobic conditions accelerating the process of degradation (cf. Noe-Nygaard 1987). Regarding the pH value of the soil at Årup, this should be expected to have been basic originally but over the millennia the calcareous content have leached from the soil, rendering the pH value acidic. In stark contrast, the flint objects at Årup were in a very good state of preservation, not exhibiting any visible signs of water rolling or wind polishing. This suggests that the sites must have been covered very shortly after abandonment. As a suggestion, aeolian sand deposited by wind coming from the west would have covered the sites in such a short period. That aeolian sand has been a problem in historical times in the region have been commented by Carl von Linné (Carolus Linnaeus), who when travelling in the area in 1749 remarked on the problems of aeolian sand destroying farmland on the Kristianstad Plain (Linné 1751). That this indeed is a natural force still in action was painfully experienced during fieldwork, bringing about the need for continuous clearance of newly uncovered features.

Making sense of the lithic puzzle
– methods of understanding life at Årup

With no preserved bone material whatsoever, we are stuck with lithics. To make some real sense out of Årup it seemed quite appropriate to let the pieces of flint help us to tell the story of what actually had happened at Årup.

In accordance with Karsten & Knarrström (2003) the authors share the growing opinion that one should not make uncritical assumptions about human behaviour based solely on constructed typological data. This is not to say that the authors have fallen into the trap of relativism. Nor do we think that typology is completely pointless and without virtue. On the contrary, typology in a general sense can be of great use when moderately applied as a comprehensive chronological instrument or for comparative studies of archaeological materials. It simply means that we have arrived at the conclusion that a more truthful picture of prehistoric human behaviour can be reached if one also considers purely functional attributes in statements about the past.

When concerned with questions regarding the function and use of lithic tools at archaeological sites in order to understand human behaviour, typology suddenly becomes a terribly blunt instrument (Karsten & Knarrström 2003:12ff). Essentially, typology is really only a question of form and perceived meaning that is historically and culturally dependent; it does not automatically tell us much about the original function or use of artefacts. In fact, the relationship between form and function is to a greater or lesser extent arbitrary and may vary both contextually and in time and space (e.g. Odell 1981; Hodder 1986; Nelson 1997:374f).

With the above ideas in mind the flint material of the different contexts was subjected to a series of analyses, which in addition to basic studies of technology and raw material comprised use-wear analysis, refitting analysis and finally spatial analysis. The criteria for selection of material to be analysed varied between the different contexts. Artefacts selected for use-wear analysis were obtained by a random selection of formal tools as well as blades and flakes judged as possibly having been used. For refitting analysis, a comprehensive view was applied taking into account all pieces of flint in the contexts where the method was implemented. Contexts 1 and 2 were selected for refitting and use-wear analysis while contexts 3, 4, 6 and 7 were selected for use-wear analysis only. Despite the time-consuming nature of the methods, these were deemed of fundamental importance for the interpretation and understanding of life and work at Årup.

Since time and money as a rule constitute strictly limited assets in commissioned archaeology it is quite impossible to try to refit every piece of flint on a site, just as it is equally impossible to scrutinise every single artefact for traces of use-wear. Even if it was possible, would the general picture really change that much? For these reasons questions regarding representativity become pointless. Each result is a result in its own right, providing us with a piece of valuable information contributing to the greater picture. Regarding use-wear analysis all it really tells us is the type of use certain selected individual artefacts have been subjected to. However, it does not tell us whether identical, though unanalysed, pieces were used in a similar manner. Therefore, the results of use-wear analysis should be utilised with moderation even if they still can be cited as analogies.

The background and questions justifying the employment of these methods were the following:

- *Use-wear analysis.* In the absence of organic material at Årup, it was difficult to shed light on the topics of economy and subsistence strategy.

Questions regarding these could only be illuminated by use-wear analysis. The presence of micro-wear will denote that a tool has been used to work a material of some kind. A typological identification of artefacts implying a certain use or function does not always correspond with factual use or function. To be able to discuss such questions use-wear analysis was crucial.

- *Refitting analysis.* To be able to evaluate the degree of contemporaneity of the flint material in various contexts as well as to get an idea of whether the contexts had been affected by bioturbation, repositioning or the like, refitting analysis would be a way of deciding on these matters. Did the flint material represent singular or repeated events? It would not be possible to understand or discuss lithic technology and lithic strategies without the use of refitting analysis. What was made on site? What was missing on site? Did variations in technology correspond to preferences of raw material? In addition, a crucial question was whether the material could be chronologically and culturally placed by comparative studies of working techniques and procedures.

- *Spatial analysis.* If single short phases of human occupation prove possible to distinguish at a site one can look at the distribution of artefacts to see whether any coherent patterns emerge, which can shed light on the behaviour of the group of people who occupied the site at that time. Did the observed flint assemblages correspond to features on site? To what degree was it possible to identify particular activity areas within the hut contexts? How did typologically defined activity areas correspond to activities indicated by use-wear analysis?

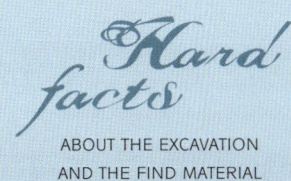

Hard facts

ABOUT THE EXCAVATION
AND THE FIND MATERIAL

- The Årup excavation was carried out by on average 10 archaeologists during 50 days, between 22 July and 27 September 2002.

- The excavation covered a total area of 12,000 m², of which 813 m² were excavated by hand.

- The retrieved material consists of 26,894 worked flints, weighing altogether 74 kilos. The total number of stone objects such as hammerstones, axe fragments, and grindstones amounts to 53 objects weighing roughly 13 kg. Of other categories we may mention 16 pieces of quartz, weighing in total 0.4 kg.

- The excavation discovered a total of eight well-defined activity areas. In all 16,079 pieces of flint are associated with the contexts, weighing in total 34 kg. Only a negligible amount of stone and quartz was found. Of this, based on number, 13% can be certainly associated with the Late Palaeolithic, while 62% can mainly be assigned to the Early Mesolithic and 25% to the Middle Mesolithic.

- Traces of habitation were found in the form of seven hut structures belonging to the Early and Middle Mesolithic, which provide us with a rare insight into the ordinary household activities of everyday life.

- Two contexts were found involving fire and water, which allow a glimpse of the usually more obscure and elusive realms of human life – the rituals.

- Plant macrofossil samples and charcoal samples were routinely collected from excavated archaeological contexts, the object not only being the dating of these but also to get a picture of the palaeo-environment in the area. For this reason charcoal samples due for radiocarbon dating were identified to species. Plant macrofossil and pollen samples were taken from gyttja and peat sequences in order to date and analyse formation and environmental change and to give a better understanding of the shoreline displacement in the area. A total of 211 samples were collected, divided into 107 carbon samples, 88 plant macrofossil, and 16 pollen samples. Thirty samples were radiocarbon dated, of which 25 were successfully dated, while five turned out to be insufficient for dating.

- During the excavation, total stations equipped with a software product by the name of Intrasis (Intra-Site Information System) were employed. The software is an extensive GIS (Geographical Information System) compatible measuring and recording program developed by the National Heritage Board especially for archaeological fieldwork (www.intrasis.com).

- Cultural deposits, features, and artefacts recovered in connection with the machine stripping were digitally registered by the total station. Extensive plotting of artefacts was carried out in order to enable later study of spatial patterning. Features in the subsoil and in the occupation layers were excavated contextually and the occupation layers were excavated in 1-metre squares. The soil from these was dry-sieved through a 3 mm mesh. Artificial vertical separation of cultural layers was carried out on a couple of occasions. Knapping floors were excavated in 0.5 metres squares, thus enabling finer spatial patterning.

- The majority of the hut contexts were excavated by hand in their entirety. The contexts were either excavated by a square-system of 0.5–1 metre squares or by free digging-units where the finds were plotted with a total station. Included features were contextually excavated.

- If you want to take a closer look, you will find the material in the keeping of Lund University Historical Museum (LUHM 31295 and 31304).

Past vegetation, topography and shore displacement

By Per Lagerås, Sofia Yassin & Nils-Olof Svensson

INTRODUCTION

The Palaeolithic and Mesolithic together represent a period of great environmental change. In southern Sweden, it spans eight millennia, from the deglaciation around 13,000 BC to the introduction of farming at 4000 BC, and it encompasses the development from late-glacial tundra to the mid-Holocene interglacial climatic optimum (all dates and ages in this book are presented in calendar years). The Early Mesolithic in particular was a period of constant change, with climatic amelioration, establishment of woodlands, and large-scale sea-level fluctuations. Connected to these changes was also a continuous adaptation of the fauna. An understanding of this complex and fascinating environmental history is fundamental for the interpretation of the archaeological record. Even without the narrow view of ecological determinism, there is no doubt that these dramatic environmental changes had a great impact on human culture and behaviour.

The interesting archaeological finds from Årup trigger our imagination and raise important questions about the palaeoenvironment. Flint artefacts, hearths, and windbreaks were documented on the site, and dated to the Late Palaeolithic and the Mesolithic. The archaeological excavation of these Stone Age remains, in the summer of 2002, took place in an old English-style park, with impressive beech and larch trees planted in the late eighteenth century. Close to the excavation site run the River Skräbeån on its short way to the Baltic coast. It was a beautiful setting, which, however, had very little to do with the conditions that prevailed during different periods of the Stone Age. What was the environment like when Late Palaeolithic hunters stopped for a rest and some flint knapping, or when Mesolithic people settled and raised their huts and windbreaks? What did the vegetation and topography look like and how close was the coast?

In an attempt to answer these questions, we present palaeoecological studies and environmental reconstructions connected to the archaeological investigations at Årup. While Nilsson and Hanlon in the next chapter present results from the excavations, the focus here is on the results and interpretations of palaeoecological analyses, stratigraphy, micro-topography, and shoreline displacement.

The River Skräbeån in north-eastern Scania, southern Sweden, marks the eastern boundary of an agricultural plain called Kristianstadslätten (the Kristianstad Plain), which is characterised by calcareous bedrock, sandy Quaternary deposits,

Figure 7. River Skräbeån at Årup. Photo by Per Lagerås.

and a very flat topography. A few kilometres to the north rises the Pre-Cambrian bedrock of granite and gneiss, with a stronger relief and covered by sandy till and coniferous forests. In a geological sense, the site is situated in an area where Continental Europe meets the old bedrock of Fennoscandia.

The area has undergone a long series of environmental changes since the last deglaciation, and it has also attracted a lot of palaeoecological and geological research. The regional vegetation development has been studied in several pollen-analytical projects, beginning with basic stratigraphical works (Nilsson 1935, 1964), and followed by studies on

past cultural landscapes (Berglund 1966b, 1991; Regnéll 1989; Göransson 1991) and woodland ecology (Björkman 1996). Fauna history has been interpreted and summarised based on a large number of subfossil vertebrate finds (Liljegren & Lagerås 1993). The late-glacial and Holocene shoreline displacement has been thoroughly studied, in particular in Blekinge to the east, which is a key area for the understanding of the history of the Baltic (Berglund 1964; Liljegren 1982; Berglund & Björck 1994).

Thanks to these earlier studies, the local analyses from Årup can be compared with regional background palaeoenvironmental knowledge. By combining local on-site analyses with this regional overview, it is possible to put the archaeological site in a wider perspective and to envisage the importance of both long-term and short-term environmental change. Another benefit from working in this area is the availability of digital elevation data, which enables realistic GIS reconstructions of ancient shorelines and topography.

The general aim is to show how the setting of the archaeological site at Årup has changed through time, and to emphasise how the regional landscape development has been decisive for the shifting local conditions.

Methods, results, and basic interpretations are presented in the following four sections *Shore displacement: regional perspective*, *Shore displacement: local perspective*, *Vegetation development and on-site stratigraphy*, and *Micro-topography of the settlement site*, while more comprehensive reconstructions are presented in the last section, *Three Stone Age environmental reconstructions*.

SHORE DISPLACEMENT:
REGIONAL PERSPECTIVE

In this section we present a series of regional maps showing shorelines and topography at different time slices. The aim here is to give a wide geographical perspective on the site, and to show how past fluctuations of the Baltic completely changed the geography of the flat plains of Kristianstadslätten.

The area chosen for reconstructions cover most of Kristianstadslätten, which is dominated by open agricultural land, together with some of the elevated hinterland, which is mostly forested. The central parts of the plains are surrounded by a number of lakes. Of these, the lakes Råbelövssjön,

Araslövssjön, and Hammarsjön in the west are drained by River Helgeån, while the lakes Oppmannasjön and Ivösjön in the north are drained by the River Skräbeån. Both rivers have their outlets in the Hanöbukten Bay of the Baltic. The Quaternary deposits on the plains are dominated by glaciofluvial sand, which has been secondarily reworked by the Baltic (Ringberg 1991a, b). Some of the sand has also been affected by aeolian activity, both during late-glacial time and in connection with later agriculture (Agrell 1980; Lagerås 2003).

Kristianstadslätten itself, with its sandy deposits and soft bedrock, is not very suitable for studies of shore displacement. However, the province of Blekinge, some kilometres to the east, is a key area in this respect (Berglund & Björck 1994). Its hard bedrock, relatively strong relief, and numerous small lakes have offered perfect conditions for this kind of research. The main method has been to investigate the sediment stratigraphies of lakes at different elevations.

The complex history of shore displacement in Blekinge, as well as in the whole of the Baltic basin, is the combined effect of eustasy and isostasy. The eustasy is characterised by global sea-level fluctuations reflecting climatic cycles, or, to be more precise, reflecting the volumetric relationship between oceans and inland ice-caps. The magnitude of the eustatic fluctuations in the oceans due to the glacial–interglacial cycle is approximately 120 m (Fairbanks 1989). Superimposed on the eustatic cycle is the effect of isostasy, which is the Earth's crust's vertical response to loading or unloading. In Sweden and in other areas that were covered by a thick ice-sheet during the Weichselian glaciation, isostasy during late-glacial and postglacial time has been characterised by land uplift. The uplift rate was high immediately after the deglaciation and has gradually slowed down. The combination of eustasy and isostasy through time has resulted in alternating periods of transgression and regression. Eustatic sea level rise that is faster than the local isostatic uplift leads to transgression, while the opposite leads to regression. In the Baltic, however, it is even more complicated, since the temporal pattern of transgressions and regressions is also related to occasional damming of the Baltic, erosion of threshold, and the breaking of new outlets.

A SHORE DISPLACEMENT CURVE FOR THE ÅRUP AREA

Since the Årup Site is situated roughly along the same land uplift isobase as the thoroughly investigated areas in middle and eastern Blekinge (e.g. Berglund 1964, 1966a, 1971; Björck 1979, 1981; Liljegren 1982; Svensson 1989; Yu 2004), the shore displacement curve from middle Blekinge published by Berglund and Björck (1994) may be extrapolated to Årup with a satisfying degree of accuracy. This was also done initially in the project (Gedda 2003). However, many of the sites used for that curve are situated quite far from Årup, and there is a fair amount of information about shorelines from sites situated closer by. An attempt is therefore made here to compile shoreline data from north-eastern Scania and western Blekinge in order to construct a new shore displacement curve. Detailed information from studies further east in Blekinge (Berglund 1964, 1971; Liljegren 1982; Yu 2004) and the Kalmarsund area (Svensson 1989, 2001) was used to fill in details of uncertain time periods. The new curve for Årup is presented in figure 8, and the background data are briefly described below.

In conclusion, the new curve is in general agreement with the earlier published ones for Blekinge, but with minor deviations. It has the benefit of being based on local background data, and, below, it will be used as a basis for shoreline reconstructions at Årup.

The sites, used to draw the Årup shore displacement curve, have when needed been corrected for differential land uplift. Observations with the same age as the isobase reconstructions (fig. 9) have been corrected to Årup isobases without further ado. Sites near Årup, for which differences in uplift are small, have not been corrected; for more distant sites details are given in the text.

To begin with, the highest shoreline in the area is well studied (e.g. Hellberg 1971; Ringberg 1991a, 1991b), and in the Årup curve it is interpolated from nearby sites to 53 m above sea level. It is dated by the deglaciation chronology to 12,500 BC (Lundqvist & Wohlfahrt 2001).

The succeeding development of the Baltic Ice Lake in south-eastern Sweden has been studied by Berglund (1966a), Björck (1979, 1981), and Svensson (1989, 1991). The results of these studies are difficult to combine and to apply at Årup, and local studies would be needed. The general shore displacement is thus just indicated as a smooth hatched line in the Årup curve. The shore level at the final stage of the Baltic Ice Lake (17 m above sea level) is interpolated from nearby sites at Listershuvud and Maglehem, which were correlated to this event by Svensson (1989, 1991).

The final Baltic Ice Lake drainage at Mount Billingen has recently been connected to the Swedish varve chronology and Greenland ice cores and given the age 9615 BC (Andrén et al. 1999). The drainage amount is estimated at about 25 m (Björck 1979, 1995; Svensson 1989, 1991) and because of its fast character it should not differ much due to different isostasy.

During the subsequent Yoldia stage of the Baltic, there was a connection to the oceans across central Sweden. This connection was rather narrow and shallow, thus relatively little saltwater entered

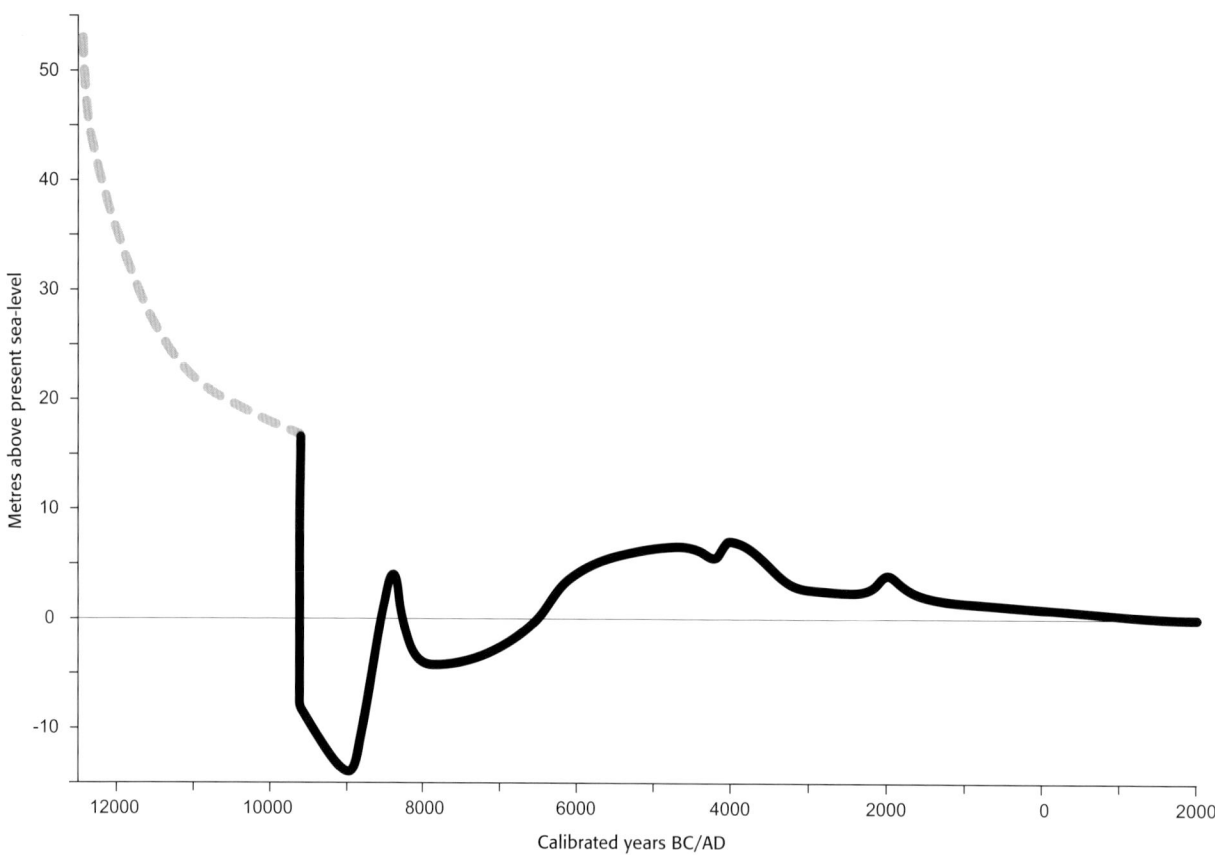

Figure 8. Shore displacement curve for the Årup area.

the Baltic. At Oskarshamn, for instance, brackish water was only noted for *c.* 150 years during the middle of the stage (Svensson 1989, 1991), and the influence of brackish water in the Hanöbukten Bay off Årup was probably even less. During the Yoldia stage the Baltic was mainly regressive due to the rather weak eustatic sea-level rise which could not counteract the isostatic uplift.

At Oskarshamn, the regression measured 17 m (Svensson 1989, 1991), while further south and away from the ice centre the regression must have been lower due to less intense isostasy. Using data

about the older and younger shorelines from the last Baltic Ice Lake stage and the Ancylus transgression from Oskarshamn (Svensson 1989, 1981), Kalmar (Svensson 2001), and the present study area, it is possible to calculate the regression during Yoldia time to about 5–8 m, thus reaching down to 13–16 m below present-day sea level.

The onset of the Ancylus transgression at about 9000 BC (Svensson 1989) shows that the Baltic once again was isolated and dammed above the ocean level. The transgression culminated around 8400 BC (Svensson 1989, 1991; Björck 1995). Its maximum level in the area is not established in detail, but in Lake Nosabysjön, near Kristianstad, a layer of Ancylus clay gyttja is observed up to nearly 1.5 m below sea level (Nilsson 1935). The maximum Ancylus Lake water level would thus be expected to be at least a couple of metres higher. Upstream, in the fen Nosabykärret, Sundelin (1922) found no stratigraphic evidence of Ancylus Lake sediments. The threshold altitude of Nosabykärret is not given by Sundelin, but a value of some 4–5 m above sea level is indicated by map contour lines and SRTM (Shuttle Radar Topography Mission) measurements. In the shore-displacement curve (fig. 8) 4 m above sea level is used as the highest Ancylus transgression level; it is possible that the maximum was a few metres lower.

The Ancylus Lake did not stay long at its high stand – soon a quite fast regression down to the ocean level begun. The nearby (12 km to the east) former Lake Vesan, with a threshold around, or maybe a few metres below, the present-day sea level, was isolated from the Ancylus Lake c. 7900 BC (Persson 1995). Sundelin (1922) confidently states, based on the investigation of several fens in the Kristianstad area, that the regression reached down to 4 m below present sea level or slightly lower.

The first indication of the rising sea during the Mastogloia/early Littorina is found in the former Lake Vesan, where Persson (1995) dates the ingression and first occurrence of diatoms indicating slight brackish water to somewhat later than c. 6700 BC. At nearby Nymölla, a peat layer at 3 m above present sea level (Ringberg 1991b) buried below 4–5 m of beach sand dates the transgression to somewhat after c. 6300 BC. At Listerlandet, in westernmost Blekinge, peat layers have frequently been found below sand and gravel deposited by the transgressing Littorina Sea. Persson (1995) has dated some of these deposits, but, unfortunately, the three sites with dates possibly indicative of shore displacement show signs of erosion of the

uppermost peat layer, contamination of rootlets or unusually high ^{14}C uncertainty. These data have thus only been used to confirm that the Littorina transgression reached above 4.65 m above present sea level in the mid-Holocene.

At the Årup site, a thin clay layer on top of fen peat originates from the Littorina transgression. The clay, deposited in the former outlet area of the River Skräbeån, is observed up to 5.5 m above present sea level (fig. 21c). It shows that the sea must have reached above this level and, since the clay has been deposited at some depth, it indicates a Littorina maximum sea level of approximately 7 m above sea level.

The transgression shoreline of the Littorina Sea is well developed at nearby Listerlandet. In the 1970s, Kerstin Bengtsson (in a mimeographed paper at Lund University, Department of Geography) studied the post-glacial shorelines at Listerlandet and on the island of Hanö. The Littorina shoreline is mostly a boulder or gravel ridge with its crest at 7–9 m above sea level, and is interpreted as corresponding to a mean sea level of 7.0–7.5 m above the present.

Lake Färsksjön, situated about 40 km ENE of Årup, has been investigated by both Liljegren (1982) and Yu (2004). Liljegren states the lake to have a threshold at 5.9 m above sea level, and it was reached by the Littorina transgression c. 5700 BC and isolated at 3700 BC. Liljegren also notes that the stratigraphy shows no traces of the Ancylus transgression reaching the basin. Yu states a threshold elevation of 7.2 m and dates the ingression to c. 5600 BC and the isolation to c. 3600 BC. In the shore displacement curve presented here a mean of this information is used and corrected for differential isostasy (fig. 9) with -1.2 and -0.8 m for the ingression and isolation respectively.

Investigations of the Neolithic dwelling place and the fen at Siretorp, in western Blekinge just 9 km ESE of Årup, have resulted in several quite similar shore displacement curves for mid-Holocene. The first shore displacement curve for the site was presented by Sandegren (1939), and renewed studies by Berglund (1971) and Berglund and Welinder (1972) resulted in a radiocarbon-dated shore displacement curve which has partly been used for the Årup curve.

A Neolithic dwelling place at Nymölla (Wyszomirska 1986) is situated on a gentle slope towards the former estuary of the Skräbeån. The mean elevation of the settlement layer is 5 m above sea level, and the eastern edge of the cultural layer reaches down to 3 m above sea level. A series of four dates shows that the site was inhabited from 3200 BC until 2200 BC. After this time a gravel/sand layer was deposited above the settlement layer by the sea during a transgressive Baltic episode (Wyszomirska 1986).

The transgression burying the Nymölla site with beach gravel after *c.* 2200 BC correlates well with the youngest transgression VI at Siretorp (Berglund & Welinder 1972), and with the last transgression observed in the Ryssjön sediment at 2450–2050 BC (Yu 2004). The transgressive phase Siretorp V, which culminated at *c.* 3000 BC according to Berglund and Welinder, was not seen in the simultaneously deposited cultural layer at Nymölla I. This event may have taken place at elevations lower than 3 m above sea level. Another alternative would be to reject the oldest date of the Nymölla settlement, and then the Siretorp V transgression would pre-date the settlement.

One of the few shoreline studies in southern Scandinavia covering the Neolithic period is the study from Spodsberg at Langeland, Denmark, by Christensen (1998). This curve shows a long period of low sea level during the Middle Neolithic and a Late Neolithic transgression which conforms well with the dated stratigraphy at the Nymölla site.

Methods

FOR REGIONAL PALAEOGEOGRAPHIC RECONSTRUCTION

As the regional reconstructions cover quite large areas, it is important to consider the effects of differential land uplift, i.e. that the land uplift has increased towards the former glaciation centre. This effect is larger for the older periods, thus the elevation of the highest coastline (fig. 10a) is most tilted and almost 20 m higher in the northernmost part of the map than at the southern edge. For the youngest reconstructed stage, the highest Littorina shoreline (fig. 10e), this difference is just 4 m.

For each reconstructed period, a data set of dated sea-level observations was compiled for Sweden and surrounding areas from a large shoreline database compiled by Nils-Olof Svensson. A surface was then fitted to the observations with the kriging method and saved as a grid. This surface is shown in figure 9 as isolines for each period.

The second data set is a 50 m resolution digital elevation model from the Swedish Ordnance Survey (LMV) which was compiled into a grid similar to that for the shoreline information. By subtracting shoreline elevation for each grid point from present-day land surface elevation, a resulting elevation model shows the ancient terrain elevation. More details on the procedure are given by Svensson (1999).

The elevation data from LMV in the region normally seem to be derived from the 5 m contours on the Cadastral Index Map and are of very poor quality between widely spaced contours. Attempts have been made to replace such inferior data with data from the US SRTM data set of 90 m resolution. In addition, depths from the Baltic and some lakes were digitised and added to the elevation model. An important source of error in the reconstructions is the use of a present-day elevation model, which incorporates topography of younger landscape elements, such as sand dunes, river valley infills and beach deposits.

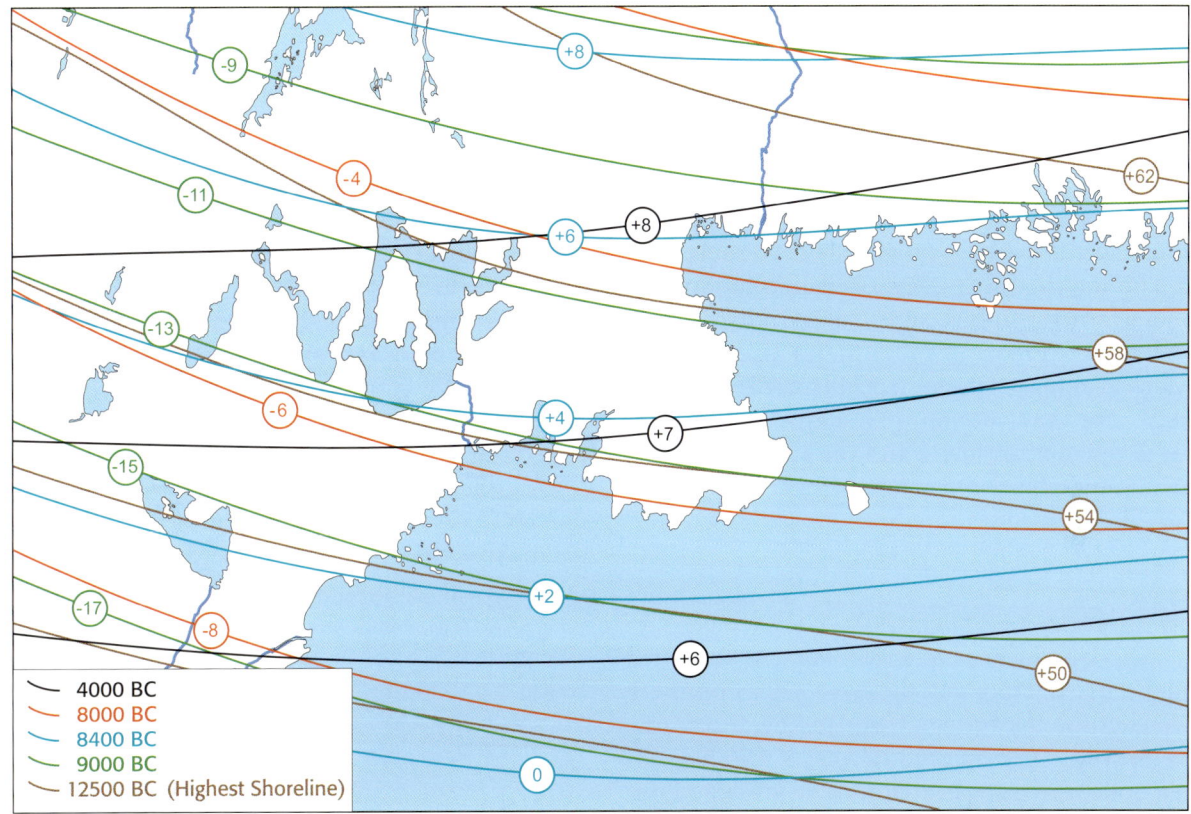

Figure 9. Map showing the shoreline isobases that were used as calculation bases for the reconstructions in figures 10a–f. Since the depression of land by the heavy ice sheet during the Ice Age was greater towards the north (i.e. closer to the glaciation centre) than to the south, the subsequent land uplift after the deglaciation has also been greater to the north than to the south. This differential land uplift has resulted in the tilting of ancient shorelines, so that a shoreline of any specific age today is to be found at higher elevations in the northern part of the investigation area than to the south. The isobases on the map reflect this tilting for some selected time slices. The black lines, for example, show that the shorelines of 4000 BC are to be found at an elevation of 6 m above present sea level in the southern part of the area, at 7 m in the middle part and at 8 m and more in the northern part. The isobases on the map also show that older shorelines are more tilted than later ones, which is because the land uplift was fast soon after the deglaciation and then gradually slowed down.

CONCLUDING COMMENTS ON THE NEW CURVE

Comparing the reconstructed shore displacement at Årup (fig. 8) with other studies gives occasion for a few remarks: (1) As indicated by beach ridge sequences, the onset of the Baltic Ice Lake drainage, at 17 m above sea level, is significantly lower than found in Blekinge (Björck 1979, 1981, 1995) by dating isolation sequences from lakes. (2) The extent of the regression during the Yoldia stage is less than normally assumed for the region, only about 8 m, still rather low levels are reached due to the lower elevation of onset/end of the Baltic Ice Lake drainage. The estimated lowest level reached by the Yoldia regression, approximately 13 to 16 m below present day sea-level, is rather moderate; much lower levels have previously been suggested. (3) The maximum level reached by the Ancylus and Littorina transgressions seems not to differ much between Årup and the studies in central and eastern Blekinge (Berglund 1964, 1971; Liljegren 1982). The Ancylus transgression may have reached a few metres lower and the Littorina transgression possibly 0.5–1 m lower at Årup.

Regional reconstructions

In this section and in figure 10a–f, the regional reconstructions of ancient shorelines are presented and discussed. Note that these reconstructions are corrected for the tilting effect (see fig. 9 and the box on page 28). In studies where this has not been done, the reconstructions may give good impressions of the magnitude of sea-level changes, but they do not show real shoreline situations (e.g. Andersson et al. 1988; Åkerlund 1996).

The highest shoreline of the Baltic Ice Lake (c. 12,500 BC)

Due to isostatic depression of the Earth's crust by the heavy ice-sheet, the highest shoreline in the area was formed soon after the deglaciation, approximately 12,500 BC. It was situated at an elevation of about 53 m above present level. As is evident from the map, most of the area was under water at this time, and dry ground was confined to the peaks of Fjälkinge Backe, Mount Ryssberget, etc. This stage of the Baltic is called the Baltic Ice Lake and it was characterised by cold glacial meltwater with a high sediment load.

The Baltic Ice Lake was dammed by the ice, and in the course of the deglaciation it was lowered in a series of drainage events. The most abruptly one has been dated to *c.* 9600 BC. Due to a new outlet between the retreating ice front and the northern part of Mount Billingen (in the province of Västergötland, central Sweden), the level of the lake was lowered by 25 m more or less instantaneously. The geography of the investigation area, as well as of other low-lying areas along the Baltic coast, was changed dramatically when large areas of new land emerged due to the rapid regression. Possible coastal settlement sites would suddenly have been situated as much as 30 km inland.

Another consequence of the drainage was that the level of the Baltic reached sea level, which means that the eustasy of the oceans from now on influenced the Baltic. After some time, marine waters started to enter the basin, resulting in gradually increased salinity. This brackish stage of the Baltic is called the Yoldia Sea.

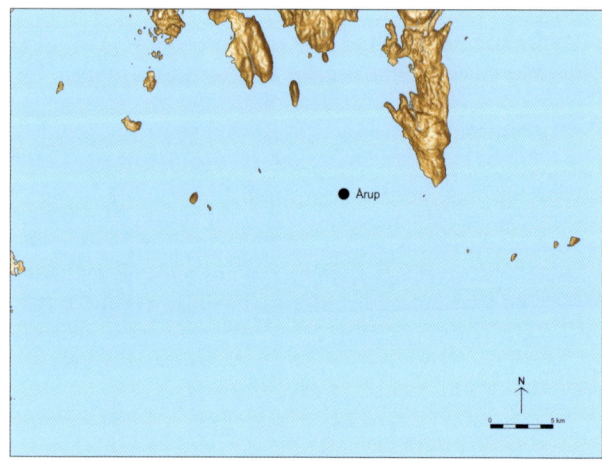

Figure 10a. The highest shoreline of the Baltic Ice Lake, c. 12,500 BC.

The Yoldia regression (c. 9000 BC)

Regression continued after 9600 BC, but at a much slower rate. The climatic amelioration and the melting of ice-caps resulted in a rapid rise in eustatic sea levels of two centimetres per year, but the isostatic uplift in the investigation area was even more rapid, resulting in regression. The lowest level, i.e. the Yoldia regression maximum, was reached about 9000 BC and has been estimated at approximately 15 m below present level.

During the Yoldia stage, the large areas of new land that had resulted from both the drainage of the Baltic Ice Lake and the succeeding Yoldia regression were slowly occupied by vegetation. Pine (*Pinus sylvestris*) obviously thrived on these virgin soils, since pine stumps from this time have frequently been found far out in the Hanöbukten Bay. According to a compilation by Hansen (1987) stumps have been found at depths down to -52 m. It must be noted that the finds are rarely proved to be in growth position.

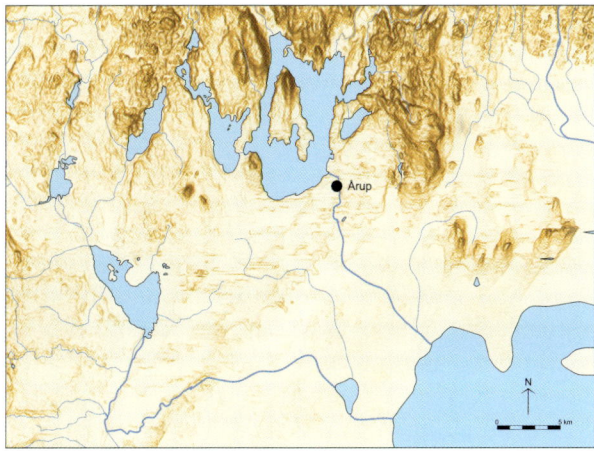

Figure 10b. The Yoldia regression, c. 9000 BC.

The Ancylus transgression (c. 8400 BC)

The contact between the Baltic and the ocean that characterised the Yoldia stage was relatively short-lasting. Due to the rapid land uplift, the Baltic was once again isolated, which marks the beginning of the phase called the Ancylus Lake. The isolation and damming resulted in rapid transgression. Lake level rose approximately 20 m – from 15 m below the present level to 4 m above – in only 600 years, with the transgression maximum fixed at *c.* 8400 BC.

In the flat and low-lying parts of the investigation area, the shoreline moved rather quickly during the transgression – in the River Skräbeån area as much as 15 km in 600 years (fig. 11). It was also during this transgression that the pine forests of the Hanöbukten Bay were flooded.

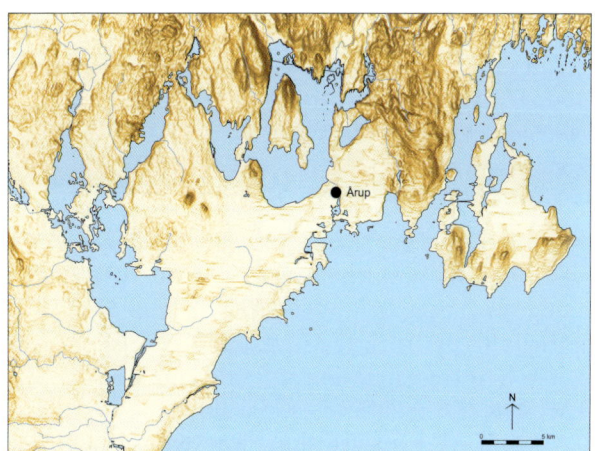

Figure 10c. The Ancylus transgression, c. 8400 BC.

The Ancylus regression (c. 8000 BC)

Rapid land uplift in the north tilted the Ancylus Lake to the south, and, eventually, a new outlet was formed in the Great Belt area of Denmark. The threshold of the outlet was quickly eroded, resulting in rapid regression. In the investigation area, a regression maximum of 3 m below present level was reached at approximately 8000 BC.

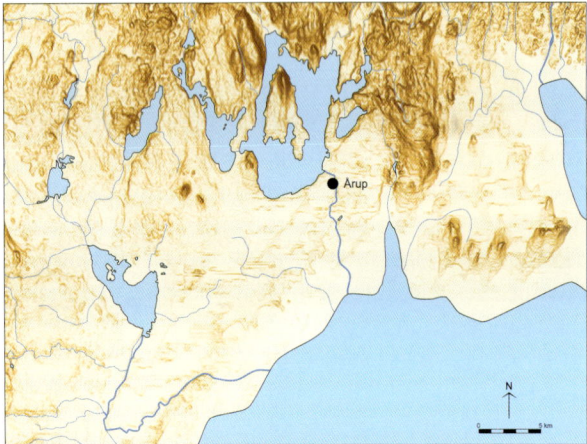

Figure 10d. The Ancylus regression, c. 8000 BC.

The Littorina transgression (c. 4000 BC)

After the Ancylus regression, the Baltic was once again in level with the ocean. The ocean was still rising, and together with a now rather slow isostatic land uplift in the investigation area this resulted in a transgression starting about 8000 BC. This was the beginning of the slow and long-lasting Littorina transgression. The transition from the Ancylus Lake to the Littorina Sea, however, has been set at *c.* 6900 BC – a time when the salinity of the southern Baltic started to increase more significantly due to inflowing marine water.

The Littorina transgression maximum in the investigation area reached approximately 7 m above present level and has been dated to *c.* 4000 BC. Detailed studies of the transgression have identified a series of transgression peaks that may

reflect global climatic cycles (Yu 2003; Berglund et al. 2005), but these small-scale sea level fluctuations had no major effect on the shoreline. On a broader scale, the Littorina transgression maximum may be dated to 6000–3500 BC, during which period the level was situated more than 5 m above present level. In course of the transgression, the salinity of the Baltic also increased, which had an impact on the fauna.

Figure 10e. The Littorina transgression, c. 4000 BC.

Present shoreline (c. AD 2000)

Since the end of the Littorina transgression maximum, the general trend has been a regression to present level. However, the dramatic (and probably anthropogenic) rise of global temperatures during the last few decades, which result in increased melting of ice-sheets in Greenland and Antarctica, leads to eustatic sea level rise in the oceans (Lambeck et al. 1998; Milne et al. 2001). Since the isostatic land uplift of the investigation area for the last 100 years has approximately equalled the rate of eustatic sea level rise (Ekman 1996), an increase in eustatic rise will result in a local transgression.

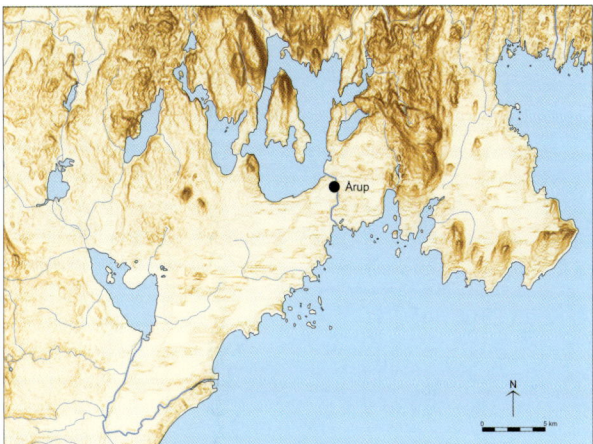

Figure 10f. Present shoreline, c. AD 2000.

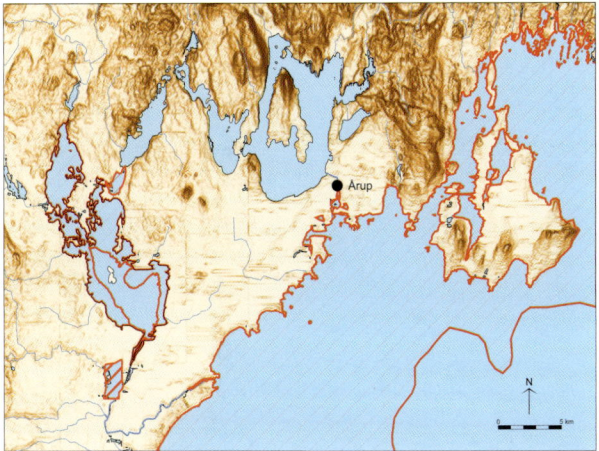

Figure 11. Red hatching indicates areas flooded by the Ancylus transgression, c. 9000–8400 BC.

After the regional shoreline reconstructions in the previous section, the focus will now be on the close vicinity of the Årup site. The aim is to show how past fluctuations of the Baltic influenced the local environment, which may help in understanding when and why Stone Age people settled at the site. The same time slices as for the regional reconstructions are used to enable comparison. Also, the same background data on shore displacement are used, but a different and more detailed elevation database. Each local reconstruction is presented in the form of a three-dimensional landscape, observed in a bird's-eye view from the north-east. Since only a rather small area was covered by the detailed elevation database that we used, the reconstructed landscapes do not reach the horizon (fig. 13a).

The reconstruction area is characterised by the River Skräbeån, which today is a 5 km long and relatively fast-flowing river, which drains Lake Ivösjön in the north into the Hanöbukten Bay of the Baltic in the south. The river forms a distinct geographical boundary in the landscape. The western side is characterised by the gentle slopes of the Gualövsåsen Ridge, which is dominated by glaciofluvial sand. Årup as a site may be characterised as situated on the north-eastern extension of the Gualövsåsen Ridge facing the River Skräbeån. The eastern side of the river is dominated by till and has a relatively high frequency of stones and boulders (Ringberg 1991b). The present elevation of the reconstruction area ranges between 2 and 15 m above mean sea level, with the highest elevation on the eastern side.

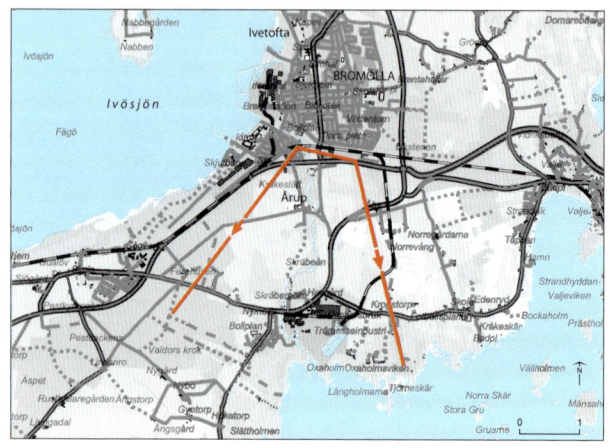

Figure 12. The agriculture plain of Kristianstadslätten. In this flat landscape, the sea-level changes of the Baltic had a great impact on shorelines and the overall geography. During the stage of the Baltic Ice Lake, the entire plain was under water, and the hill Fjälkinge Backe (visible in the back-ground) was an isolated island. Photo by Thomas Hansson.

Figure 13a. Map showing the view direction and the area covered by the local reconstructions. 13b–g. A series of three-dimensional reconstructions showing the local to-pography and shorelines of the Årup area at different time slices seen in a bird's-eye view. The investigation area is indicated in the reconstructions.

Local reconstructions

The highest shoreline of the Baltic Ice Lake (c. 12,500 BC)

After the deglaciation, the whole area covered by the local reconstructions was under water, with depths ranging roughly between 40 and 50 m.

Figure 13b. The highest shoreline of the Baltic Ice Lake, c. 12,500 BC.

The Yoldia regression (c. 9000 BC)

Dry land appeared for the first time around 9600 BC as a result of the last and major draining of the Baltic Ice Lake. The succeeding regression during the Yoldia stage resulted in very low water levels, and the area turned into an inland environment. The shortest distance between the Årup investigation site and the coast during the regression maximum was about 15 km (the present distance is 3 km).

Figure 13c. The Yoldia regression, c. 9000 BC.

The Ancylus transgression (c. 8400 BC)

Land was rapidly flooded during the Ancylus transgression, and, as consequence, the area a few hundred metres downstream of Årup turned into a lagoon. It reached a maximum size of about 50 hectares (500,000 m²) and a water depth of 2 m.

Figure 13d. The Ancylus transgression, c. 8400 BC.

The Ancylus regression (c. 8000 BC)

The lagoon dried up when the Ancylus transgression was succeeded by regression. At the regression maximum, the distance between the Årup site and the coast was approximately 8 km.

Figure 13e. The Ancylus regression, c. 8000 BC.

The Littorina transgression (c. 4000 BC)

A lagoon started to form once again around 6700 BC during the Littorina transgression. It grew gradually and reached a much larger size than during the Ancylus transgression. At 4000 BC, when the maximum size was reached, it covered approximately 240 hectares and partly flooded the investigation site of Årup. The maximum water depth of the lagoon reached 5 m.

Figure 13f. The Littorina transgression, c. 4000 BC.

Present shoreline (c. AD 2000)

After 4000 BC, the lagoon became gradually smaller due to regression, and by approximately 500 BC it was gone. Regression continued until the present day, and now the distance between the Årup site and the coast is 3 km.

Figure 13g. Present shoreline, c. AD 2000.

FOR LOCAL RECONSTRUCTION

The elevation database used for the reconstructions consisted of contour lines (polylines with annotation) with a 1-metre equidistance and 0.3 m vertical standard error. Lines connected to roads, bridges, and settlement were erased to avoid the most obvious modern alterations of the topography. The annotations that hold the elevation values were first transformed to points and then spatially joined with the polylines. Values of the contour lines were then manually evaluated with the annotation points and transformed into a triangulated irregular network (TIN). The computer program used was ESRI ArcView with the extensions Spatial Analyst and 3D Analyst.

In the database, the River Skräbeån lacked detailed elevation values. To solve this problem, height values were assigned to a simplified rendering of the Skräbeån by spatial joining with the TIN, and, after that, the river was lowered 0.5 m to create a river channel. Furthermore, in the three-dimensional reconstructions the z-values (i.e. the elevation) were exaggerated by a factor of ×1.5, in order to give a more realistic impression of the topography.

Vegetation development and on-site stratigraphy

During the archaeological excavation a sequence of sand-covered organogenic deposits was discovered in the eastern part of the investigation area, i.e. in the lower part of the slope facing the River Skräbeån. These deposits were documented and sampled for different kinds of palaeoecological analyses (pollen, plant macrofossils, charcoal, diatoms, phytoliths) and for radiocarbon dating.

In this section the results of these different analyses are presented first independently, and then together in a concluding interpretation. The aim is to interpret the local vegetation development as well as the environmental processes behind the documented stratigraphy.

Methods

FOR PALAEOECOLOGICAL ANALYSIS

Sample sizes were approximately 5 ml for pollen analysis and diatom/phytolith analysis, and approximately 500 ml for combined plant macrofossil and charcoal analysis. Positions of the samples are shown in figure 14. In addition, several archaeological features (postholes, hearths, etc.) on the site were sampled for plant macrofossil analysis, but turned out to contain only charcoal.

Chemical preparation of the pollen samples followed standard procedures (Berglund 1986; Moore et al. 1991), and included sieving (mesh: 250 µm), treatment with 10% HCl, 10% NaOH, and 40% HF, acetolysis with 1 part H_2SO_4 to 9 parts $C_4H_6O_3$ and final mounting in glycerine. Pollen identification and counting were carried out at magnifications of ×400 and ×1000/phase contrast, using standard identification keys and a reference pollen collection. Pollen types, taxonomy, and nomenclature follow Moore et al. (1991). Calculations of pollen and spore percentages are based on the sum of terrestrial pollen in each sample.

The analysis of siliceous microfossils (diatoms, phytoliths, etc.) was conducted on the same samples as the pollen analysis, as well as on two additional samples from the superimposed sand layer. The chemical preparation followed standard procedures for diatom analysis (Battarbee 1986), including treatment with 17% HCl, H_2O_2, and NH_3, and final mounting in Naphrax. Identification and counting were carried out at a magnification of ×1000, using reference literature (Krammer & Lange-Bertalot 1986, 1988, 1991a, b). The same literature was used for information on the ecological and environmental preferences of diatoms.

Samples for macrofossil analysis were treated with 10% NaOH and sieved (mesh: 0.4 mm). The analysis was carried out using a microscope with reflected light and a magnification of up to ×80, and access to a reference collection and standard literature (Berggren 1981; Jacomet 1987; Körber-Grohne 1991; Anderberg & Berggren 1994).

Charcoal found during the plant macrofossil analysis was identified to tree species or genera. The analysis, which is based on cell structure, followed standard procedures (Schweingruber 1976, 1978; Bartholin et al. 1981; Bartholin & Berglund 1992), using a microscope with reflected light and a magnification of ×30–300. A reference collection of modern wood and charcoal was used. Most of the identified charcoal pieces were only a few millimetres in size.

A relatively large number of radiocarbon datings were carried out, but only those that are relevant for the palaeoenvironmental study are presented here. From the sand-covered organogenic sequence four samples were radiocarbon-dated. The dated material consisted of plant macrofossils and charcoal (table 1). Apart from the organogenic sequence, charcoal from several different archaeological contexts was radiocarbon-dated. All radiocarbon dating was carried out using accelerator mass spectrometry (AMS) technique.

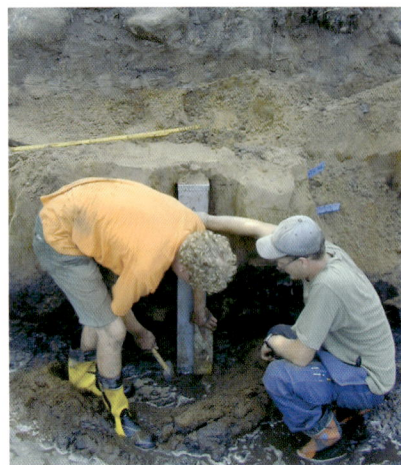

Figure 14. The sequence of sand-covered organogenic deposits from Årup that was subject to palaeoecological analyses. Sample levels for different analyses are indicated. The picture above shows sampling in the field. Photo by Conleth Hanlon.

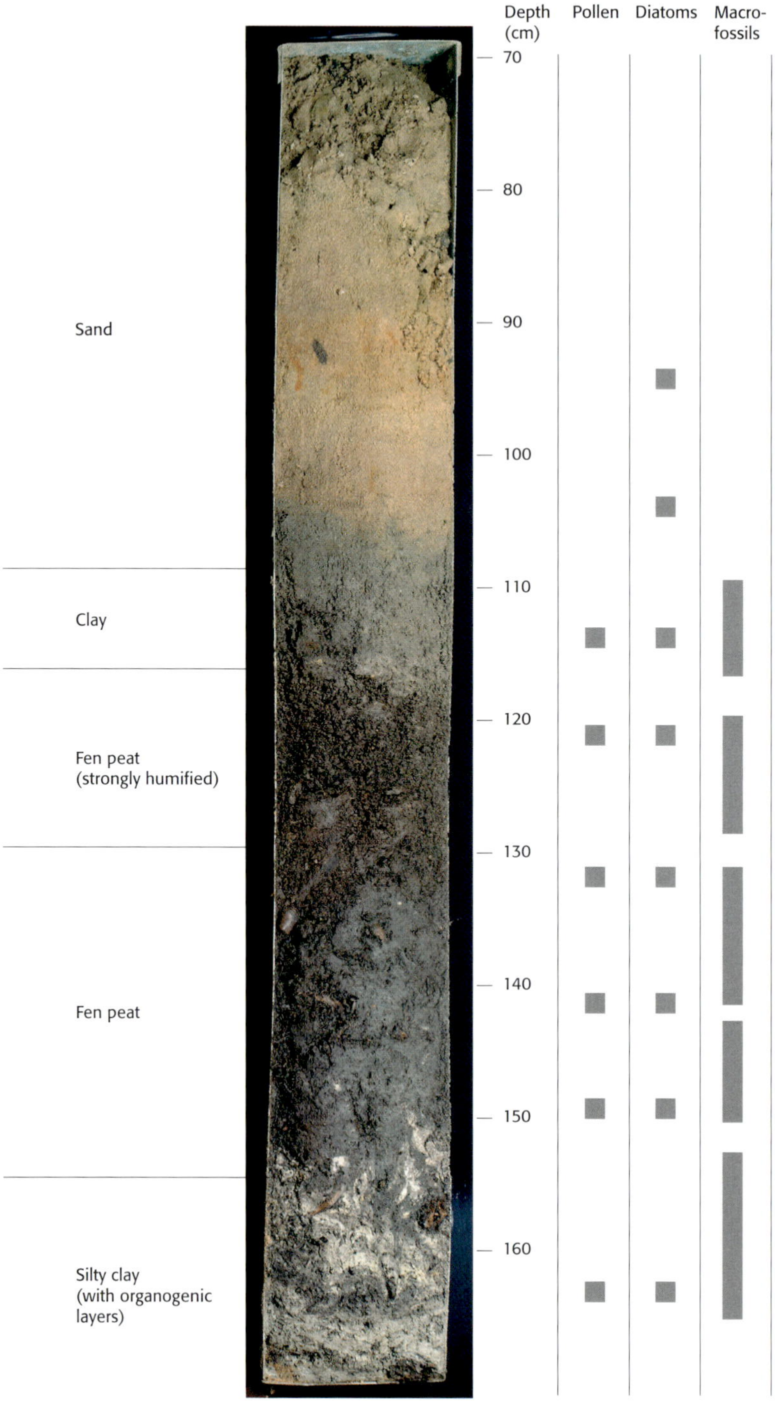

Depth (cm)
Pollen
Diatoms
Macro-fossils
70
80
90
100
110
120
130
140
150
160
Sand
Clay
Fen peat (strongly humified)
Fen peat
Silty clay (with organogenic layers)

Table 1. Radiocarbon dates from the analysed peat sequence.

Lab.no	Dated material	^{14}C-years BP ± 1 sigma	Cal. interval 2 sigma
Beta-186155	Charcoal of *Alnus* sp.	3250 ± 40	1620–1430 BC
Beta-186156	Charcoal of *Alnus* sp.	6960 ± 50	5970–5730 BC
Ua-26447	Fruits and scales of *Betula* sp.	7055 ± 165	6250–5600 BC
Ua-26448	Fruits and scales of *Betula* sp.	9465 ± 105	9250–8450 BC

RESULTS OF THE DIFFERENT ANALYSES

POLLEN AND CHRONOLOGY

Results of the pollen analysis are presented in the diagram in figure 15. Based on the pollen frequencies three local pollen assemblage zones (Hedberg 1976; Berglund & Ralska-Jasiewiczowa 1986) may be distinguished: P1, P2, and P3. These local pollen assemblage zones (LPAZ) may be correlated to the regional pollen assemblage zones (RPAZ) as defined for southern Sweden (Nilsson 1935, 1964).

P1 is the bottommost zone in the diagram and consists of one sample only (164 cm). It is characterised by high percentages of *Pinus* and *Salix*, and relatively high percentages of *Hippophae rhamnoides*, Cyperaceae, and *Betula*. It reflects an open vegetation dominated by herbs [e.g. sedges (Cyperaceae), mugwort (*Artemisia* sp.), dropwort/meadowsweet (*Filipendula*), sorrel (*Rumex acetosa/acetosella*), and grasses (Poaceae)] and shrubs [e.g. willow (*Salix* sp.), sea-buckthorn (*Hippophae rhamnoides*), juniper (*Juniperus communis*), and hazel (*Corylus avellana*)]. There were also some scattered trees [pines (*Pinus sylvestris*) and birches (*Betula* sp.)] in the area, but no dense woodlands.

The pollen composition of P1 corresponds well to the regional Preboreal pollen zone (PB), which has been described for Scania, for example, by Nilsson (1964) and for Blekinge by Berglund (1966). According to these authors the Preboreal pollen zone lasted from 9500 BC to 9000 BC (10,000–9600 ^{14}C-years BP). However, recent

studies have shown that these dates are too old, probably due the so-called reservoir effect (Olsson 1986; Olsson & Possnert 1992; Lagerås 1996), and according to a revised chronology the end of the Preboreal pollen zone is dated to approximately 8400 BC (9000 ^{14}C-years BP) (Gaillard et al. 1996). In Årup a sample from P1 was radiocarbon dated to c. 8800 BC (9465±105 BP; 9250–8450 cal. BC with 2 sigma).

P2 constitutes of three pollen samples (150, 142, 132 cm), and is characterised by high percentages of *Pinus* and relatively high percentages of *Corylus* and *Alnus*. Herbs and shrubs (except hazel) are not as strongly represented as in the previous pollen zone, which reflects a more closed vegetation than before. The woodlands were however still rather light, at least on dry ground where they were dominated by pine (*Pinus sylvestris*) and hazel (*Corylus avellana*). Some trees of elm (*Ulmus* sp.) and oak (*Quercus* sp.), and possibly lime (*Tilia* sp.) and ash (*Fraxinus excelsior*), were also present but in small numbers. Damper soils were occupied by alder (*Alnus* sp.).

The composition corresponds to the later part of the regional Boreal pollen zone (BO2). The early part of the Boreal zone (BO1), which is defined by high *Corylus* percentages but very low *Alnus* percentages, is missing in the Årup diagram. BO2 lasted from 7500 BC to 6900 BC (8500–7950 ^{14}C-years BP) according to the traditional chronology (Nilsson 1964), and from approximately 6400 BC to 5700 BC (7600–6800 ^{14}C-years BP) according

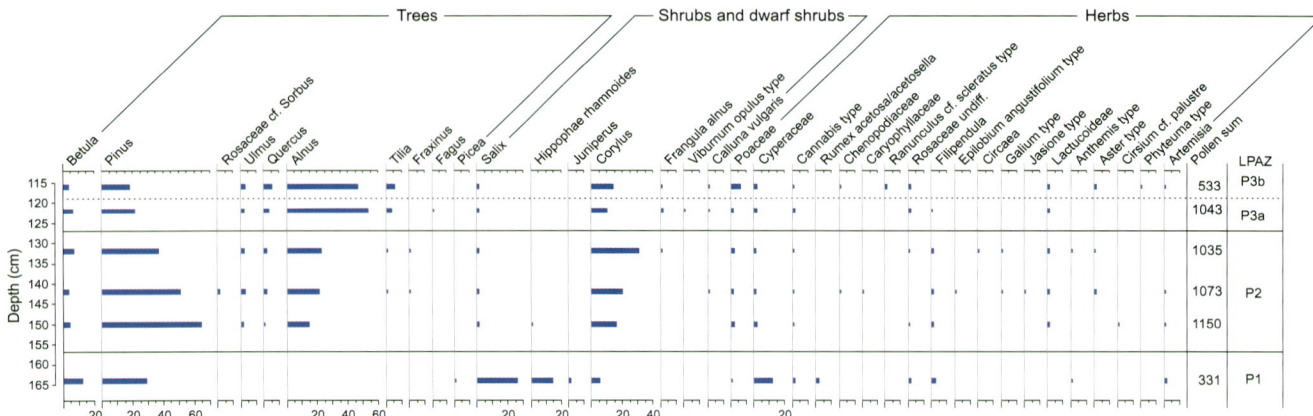

Figure 15. Result of the pollen analysis of the organogenic sequence presented as a percentage diagram. Spore taxa are excluded. The pollen zones (LPAZ) are described in the text. Analysis by Björn Gedda.

to the revised one (Gaillard et al. 1996). In Årup a sample from P2 was radiocarbon dated to *c.* 5900 BC (7055±165 BP; 6250–5600 cal. BC with 2 sigma), which fits well with the revised chronology.

P3 is the uppermost pollen zone in Årup and it consists of two samples (122, 116 cm). It is characterised by high percentages of *Alnus* and relatively high percentages of *Pinus*, *Corylus*, *Betula*, *Tilia*, and *Quercus*. The pollen zone is interpreted as reflecting alder (*Alnus* sp.) woodlands on damp soil (certainly over-represented in the pollen diagram because it grew on the sampled peatland), and a mixed-deciduous forest on dry ground with for example lime (*Tilia* sp.), oak (*Quercus* sp.), elm (*Ulmus* sp.), hazel (*Corylus avellana*), and probably also some pine (*Pinus sylvestris*) and birch (*Betula*). Lime tree (*Tilia* sp.), which is an insect-pollinated (enthomopholous) tree that produces and disperses only small amounts of pollen, may have been dominant in climax woodlands. It is a shade-tolerant tree which created a denser forest than before.

Figure 16. The Preboreal vegetation was open with some scattered stands of pine and birch. Photo by Per Lagerås.

In addition to the general character of the zone, there are differences in the Poaceae percentages, which are much higher in the uppermost sample. The two samples are therefore separated as two sub-zones (P3a and P3b).

The transition from P2 to P3a represents the beginning of the regional Atlantic pollen zone (AT), characterised by a marked increase in *Tilia*. The Atlantic zone lasted from 6900 BC to 4000 BC (7950–5100 ^{14}C-years BP) according the traditional chronology (Nilsson 1964), while Gaillard et al. (1996) dated the beginning of the zone to *c*. 5700 BC (6800 ^{14}C-years BP). In the Årup diagram a sample from sub-zone P3a was radiocarbon dated to *c*. 5800 BC (6960±50 BP; 5970–5730 cal. BC with 2 sigma). This date is a bit old in comparison with the revised regional chronology, which may be due to the fact that in this case charcoal was used for dating (Table 1).

In Årup a sample from sub-zone P3b was also radiocarbon-dated. The result was *c*. 1500 BC (3250±40 BP; 1620–1430 cal. BC with 2 sigma) – a surprisingly late date, which shows that there must be a *hiatus* between P3a and P3b (read more about the interpretation of the stratigraphy in the section *Concluding interpretation of the stratigraphy* below). The sub-zone is difficult to date by pollen correlation, but there is no reason not to believe in the radiocarbon date. The date corresponds to the Bronze Age and it is likely that the relatively high Poaceae percentages reflect grazed pastures in a cultural landscape.

Diatoms and other siliceous microfossils

The results of the analysis of siliceous microfossils are presented in figure 17. In this section results are presented in stratigraphical order from bottom to top.

The lowermost sample (165 cm), which corresponds to local pollen zone P1, contained no siliceous microfossils.

The next four samples (150, 142, 132, and 122 cm), which correspond to local pollen zones P2 and P3a, contained some phytoliths, but very few diatoms and chrysophyte cysts. Sponge spiculae were relatively common in one sample (122 cm). The diatom flora was represented by some fragments of lacustrine taxa, e.g. *Gomphonema angustatum*, *Pinnularia* sp., *Cymbella* sp., but also of single finds of *Melosira westii* and *Diploneis interrupta* which live in brackish water. The small numbers of diatoms in relation to phytoliths indicate terrestrial conditions, and the few diatom fragments may have been wind-transported to the site. The sample at 122 cm, however, with its high content of sponge spiculae, indicates an increasing lacustrine influence.

A sample from the thin clay layer on top of the peat (115 cm), representing local pollen zone P3b, differs from the other samples in its much higher concentration of siliceous microfossils in general, and of diatoms and chrysophyte cysts in particular. The diatoms are strongly dominated by lacustrine taxa, e.g. the planctonic species *Aulacoseira distans*, *A. ambigua*, *Cyclotella radiosa*, and *C. ocellata*, and the bentic species *Gomphonema angustatum* and *Meridion circulare*. The latter two indicate fluvial conditions. A brackish influence, however weak, is indicated by the presence of *Diplonesis interrupta* and *Melosira westii*.

Finally, two samples from the superimposed sand layer were also analysed (105 and 95 cm). They were dominated by phytoliths but were also relatively rich in diatoms. Lacustrine species dominate, the most common being *Gomphonema angustatum* which indicates fluvial conditions.

Plant macrofossils

The result of the plant macrofossil analysis of the organogenic sequence is presented in figure 18, where identified charcoal from the same samples are also included. In this section the results of the

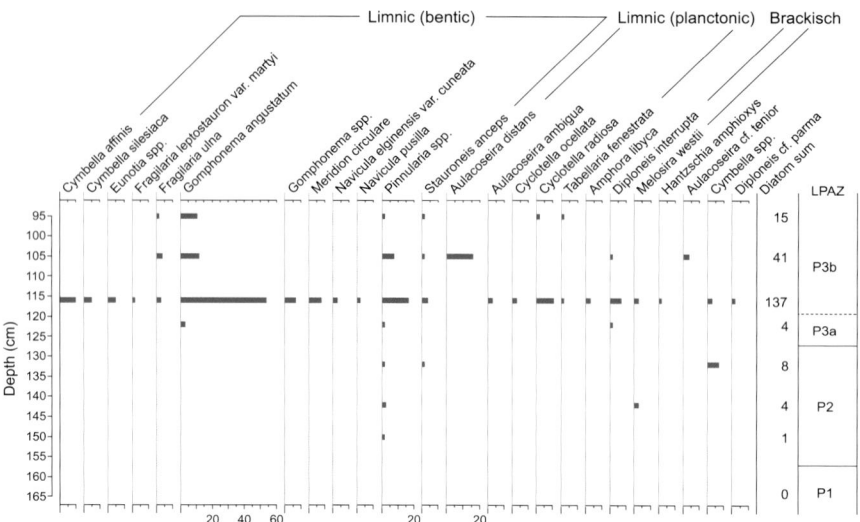

Figure 17. Result of diatom analysis of the organogenic sequence. Due to the low diatom sums, results are presented as numbers and not as percentages. Pollen zones (LPAZ) are indicated to enable comparison. Analysis by Jan Risberg.

five analysed samples are presented and interpreted in stratigraphical order from bottom to top.

The bottommost sample (166–154 cm) corresponds stratigraphically to the local pollen zone P1, and was radiocarbon dated to 9465 ^{14}C-years BP. Its macrofossil content was dominated by fruits and scales of birch (*Betula* sp.) and fruits of bottle sedge/bladder-sedge (*Carex rostrata/vesicaria*). Represented in smaller numbers were seeds of orache (*Atriplex* sp.), meadowsweet (*Filipendula ulmaria*), and skullcap (*Scrophularia galericulata*), and wood and needle bases of pine (*Pinus sylvestris*). The sampled material was a silty clay with thin organogenic layers and lenses.

The next two samples (152–144, 142–132 cm) are presented together, since they come from the same layer of fen peat and have a similar macrofossil content. They correspond to the local pollen zone P2, and the lowermost one was radiocarbon-dated

to 7055 ^{14}C-years BP. The macrofossil content was relatively rich and dominated by fruits of birch (*Betula* sp.), alder (*Alnus* sp.), and bottle sedge/bladder-sedge (*Carex rostrata/vesicaria*), stones of raspberry (*Rubus* cf. *idaeus*) and blackberry (*Rubus* cf. *fruticosus*), and seeds of gipsywort (*Lycopus europaeus*). Represented in smaller numbers were seeds of e.g. common water-plantain (*Alisma plantago-aquatica*), pale persicaria (*Persicaria lapathifolia*), buttercups (*Ranunculus* sp.), and wild strawberry (*Fragaria* sp.). Apart from birch and alder, other represented tree taxa are pine (*Pinus sylvestris*), hazel (*Corylus avellana*), bird cherry (*Prunus* cf. *padus*), and lime (*Tilia* sp.). The sampled material was a dark-brown strongly humified fen peat.

The uppermost two samples (128–120, 118–112 cm) both correspond to the local pollen zone P3, but represent two different layers. The lower one of these layers was a rather dried-out strongly

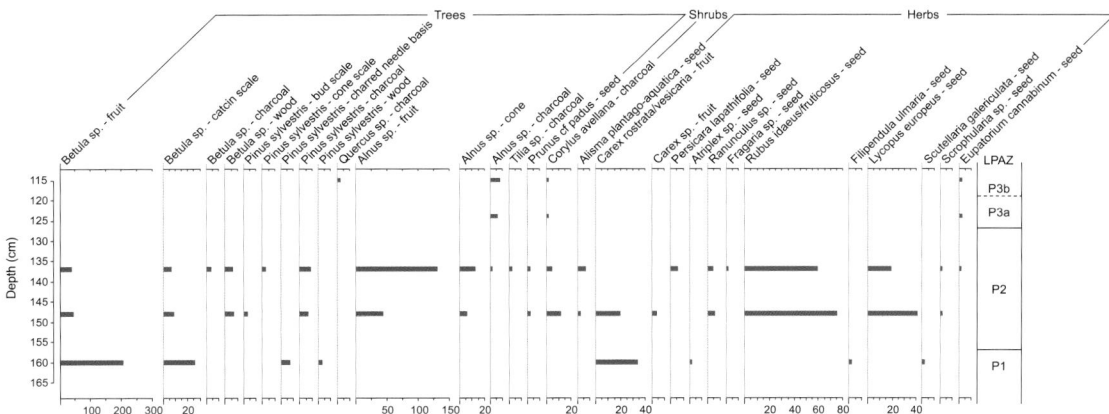

Figure 18. Result of plant macrofossil analysis of the organogenic sequence. The diagram shows absolute numbers and not percentages. Note also that scale on the x-axes differs between different taxa. Pollen zones (LPAZ) are indicated to enable comparison. Analysis by Annine S. A. Moltsen, Björn Gedda, and Thomas Bartholin.

humified fen peat with some silt (radiocarbon-dated to 6960 ^{14}C-years BP), while the upper one was a grey clay with some humic content (dated to 3250 BP). They were both very poor in plant macrofossils, the only identifiable ones being some charcoal fragments of hazel (*Corylus avellana*) and alder (*Alnus* sp.), and some seeds of hemp-agrimony (*Eupatorium cannabinum*). The poor preservation is probably due to drying-out of this upper part of the stratigraphic sequence.

CHARCOAL

Identified and dated charcoal from the stratigraphic sequence and from archaeological features on the site is summarised in figure 19. This bar chart shows high-quality data since it is based on directly radiocarbon-dated charcoal only. Two phases may be distinguished: one phase before 5000 BC with only pine charcoal (*Pinus* sp.), and one phase

after 5000 BC with no charcoal from pine but from several different deciduous taxa.

Charcoal data reflect tree and shrub vegetation that has not only been present but also have burnt. In a complex way such data may reflect vegetation history, natural forest fires, anthropogenic forest fires, domestic fires, etc. Forest fires are very rare in the deciduous forests of temperate northern Europe (Rackham 1994), and a reasonable interpretation of the deciduous charcoal from Årup is that it reflects human activity in one way or the other. The pine charcoal, however, is more difficult to interpret since pine woodlands are susceptible to fire. We know from pollen data that pine woodlands were common in southern Sweden during the early Holocene, and palaeoclimatic data indicate a rather warm and dry climate (Digerfeldt 1988). These were optimal conditions for forest fires. The very existence of forest fires – natural or

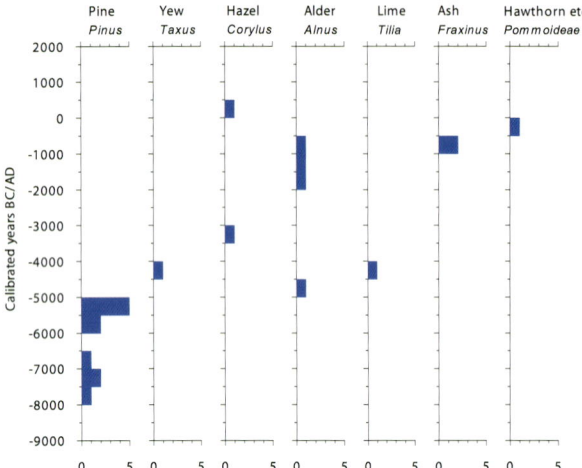

| | Pine
Pinus | Yew
Taxus | Hazel
Corylus | Alder
Alnus | Lime
Tilia | Ash
Fraxinus | Hawthorn etc.
Pommoideae |

Figure 19. Summary of all identified and radiocarbon-dated macroscopic charcoal from Årup. Bars show the number of charcoal pieces of each taxa that were dated to the corresponding 500-year interval (mid-points of one-sigma intervals were used). Analysis by Thomas Bartholin.

anthropogenic – during the early Holocene is also indicated by the frequent occurrence of pine charcoal in soil profiles all over southern Sweden (Lagerås 2002; Lagerås & Bartholin 2003).

Whatever the origin of the pine charcoal at Årup, the change in charcoal composition around 7000 ^{14}C-years BP certainly reflects a vegetational change. This date fits with the border between the Boreal and the Atlantic pollen zones, dated to *c.* 6800 ^{14}C-years BP by Gaillard et al. (1996) (see discussion in the pollen section above).

CONCLUDING INTERPRETATION
OF THE STRATIGRAPHY

In this section, the analytical results presented above are put together into an interpretation of the local environmental development, and of the depositional processes reflected in the on-site stratigraphy. The interpretation is linked to background data on the history of the Baltic Sea, which were presented above in the section *Shore displacement: regional perspective*. The discussion and interpretations follow the stratigraphic sequence from bottom to top, which corresponds to the approximate time interval 9500–1000 BC (fig. 20).

PREBOREAL TOPSOIL

Apart from till and glaciofluvial sand – which were deposited in close connection with the Weichselian ice-sheet during the deglaciation – the oldest deposit on the site was a silty clay with a bluish grey colour, containing thin layers and lenses of sand and brownish organogenic material. The deposit has been radiocarbon-dated to about 8800 BC, which fits well with its typical Preboreal pollen content. The clayey character of the deposit may suggest a sub-aquatic origin. However, at this time (soon after the Yoldia regression maximum), the level of the Baltic was low, approximately 10 m below present sea level, and the site was situated several kilometres inland. This speaks for a terrestrial deposition – an interpretation that is further supported by the total lack of diatoms.

The most plausible interpretation is that this heterogeneous silty clay, with lenses of sand and organogenic material, is the result of solifluction or soil erosion. These processes – which mean that silt, clay, and other fine-grained material move down-slope to deposit in topographical hollows – may be expected in a Preboreal landscape with virgin soils and sparse vegetation cover. True solifluction occurs pre-dominantly in periglacial environments, where seasonal thawing leads to water saturation and instability of the topsoil, while soil erosion occurs on all kinds of barren ground.

At the time of deposition, the local environment was characterised by open vegetation with scattered trees and shrubs. Pollen data show that the local vegetation around 8800 BC included grasses (Poaceae), sedges (Cyperaceae) and several different herbs, e.g. mugwort (*Artemisia* sp.), dropwort/meadowsweet (*Filipendula* sp.), and sorrel (*Rumex acetosa/acetosella*). Trees were represented by pine (*Pinus sylvestris*) and birch (*Betula* sp.), while typical shrubs were willow (*Salix* sp.), sea-buckthorn (*Hippophae rhamnoides*), and juniper (*Juniperus communis*). Pollen data from such an open landscape may be difficult to interpret due to long transportation. In particular pine pollen may be problematic, because of their efficient wind-dispersal. However, that pine was locally present is evident from the macroscopic charcoal record from the site. In the same way, macroscopic remains prove the local presence of birch.

PREBOREAL–EARLY BOREAL GROUND SURFACE AND THE ANCYLUS TRANSGRESSION

After the period of solifluction, there was no deposition on the site until peat accumulation started around 6000 BC (see below). In the meantime, the Preboreal topsoil constituted the ground surface, but, for a short time, it was also the bottom bed of a shallow bay.

The level of the Baltic (i.e. the Ancylus Lake) was generally low during this period, but with one important exception: the dramatic but short-lasting Ancylus transgression. During its maximum phase – dated to about 8400 BC – the transgression reached four metres above present sea level. Since levels from the same time in the analysed sequence are situated at about four metres, these lower parts of the site may have been flooded during the transgression maximum. However, the short-lasting sub-aquatic phase did not result in any local sedimentation. The very sheltered setting in a lagoon (see section *Shore displacement: local perspective* above) may be the reason why no sand was deposited, while the lack of more fine-grained and organogenic sediments may be explained by

the shallow water-depth, and, above all, by the very short duration of this phase.

Apart from some pine charcoal, we do not have any proxy data on local vegetation from the period *c.* 8400–5900 BC, i.e. the time corresponding to the regional early Boreal pollen zone. Based on pollen data from other sites in southern Sweden, we may, however, expect still rather open vegetation, similar to that in the Preboreal, but now also with a lot of hazel (*Corylus avellana*).

LATE BOREAL–EARLY ATLANTIC FEN PEAT

After a long dry period, the site became gradually wetter starting shortly before 6000 BC – an environmental change reflected on the site in a thick layer of dark-brown fen peat. This change to wetter conditions was due to the slow and gradual Littorina transgression, which at this time was approaching the maximum level of the earlier Ancylus transgression. The peat layer was radiocarbon-dated to *c.* 5900 BC in its lower part and to *c.* 5800 in its upper, and the dated levels were at 4.1 and 4.3 m above present sea level respectively. The Baltic (now the Littorina Sea) would at this time have reached approximately 5 m above present sea level, thus flooding the levels of the peat layer. Direct contact with the Littorina Sea is, however, not supported by the content of siliceous microfossils: the very few diatoms in relation to phytoliths rather suggest a terrestrial environment. Hence, the relationship between transgression and peat accumulation must have been of a more indirect nature. A plausible interpretation is that the transgression caused a rise in the groundwater table in coastal areas, which in turn resulted in peat formation. The peat sequence preserved on the site thus reflects a fen, isolated from the Littorina Sea but still situated very close to the coast. Eventually, the fen was flooded by the transgression, but this phase is discussed later in connection with the superimposed clay.

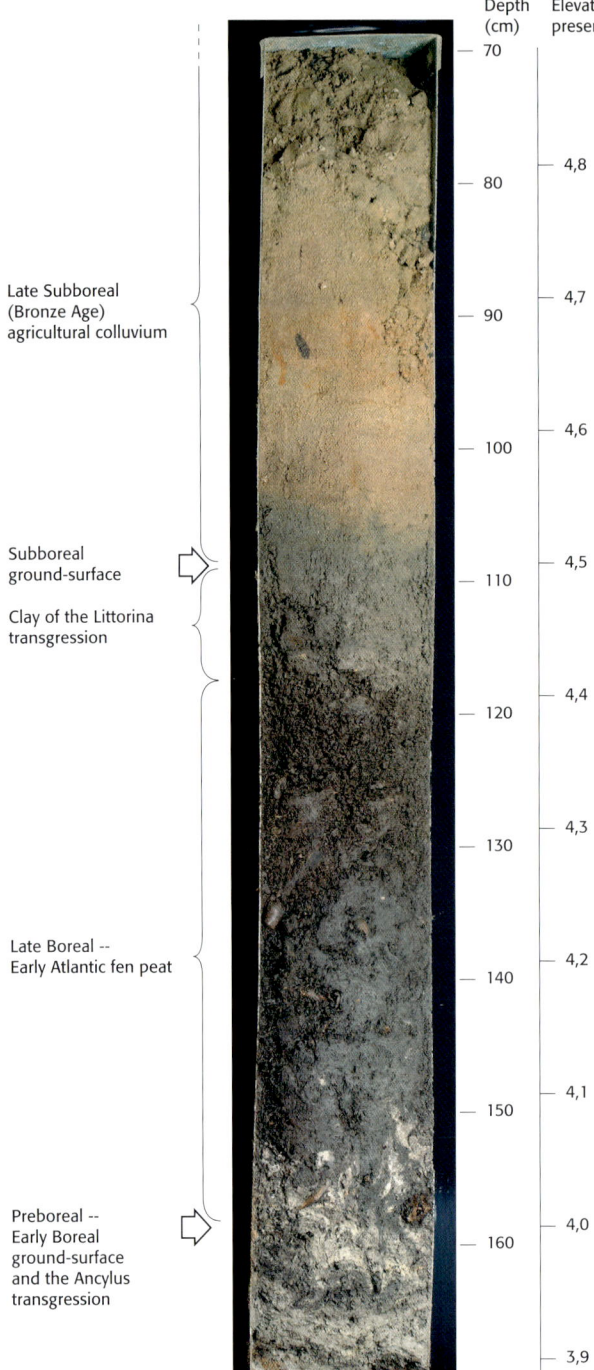

Depth (cm)

Elevation above present sea level (m)

— 70

— 80 — 4,8

Late Subboreal
(Bronze Age)
agricultural colluvium — 90 — 4,7

— 100 — 4,6

Subboreal
ground-surface — 110 — 4,5

Clay of the Littorina
transgression

— 120 — 4,4

— 130 — 4,3

Late Boreal --
Early Atlantic fen peat — 140 — 4,2

— 150 — 4,1

Preboreal --
Early Boreal
ground-surface
and the Ancylus
transgression — 160 — 4,0

— 3,9

Figure 20. Interpretation of the sand-covered organogenic sequence.

The peat contained well-preserved pollen and plant macrofossils, which give us a relatively detailed picture of the local vegetation. Pine (*Pinus sylvestris*) and hazel (*Corylus avellana*) were common on dry ground, while alder (*Alnus* sp.) occupied fens and lake shores. The immigration of alder into southern Sweden was a quick process, dated to approximately 6400 BC (Gaillard et al. 1996), resulting in a transformation of open fen meadows to alder swamp forests. Since fen meadows served as natural grazing grounds for aurochs (*Bos primigenius*) and other large herbivores (Ekström 1993), the alder expansion probably had effects on the fauna. On dry ground, pine and hazel were most common, but several deciduous tree species were now spreading in the landscape, for example oak (*Quercus* sp.), elm (*Ulmus* sp.), and ash (*Fraxinus excelsior*). In comparison to the Preboreal vegetation, tree cover was now more widespread and the woodlands were gradually closing in. However, more dense and dark woodlands, with sparse undercover, were established later in connection with the immigration and expansion of lime (*Tilia* sp.). Increasing frequencies of lime pollen are noted in the upper part of the peat sequence. This event marks the beginning of the Atlantic regional pollen zone and has tentatively been dated to *c.* 5700 BC (Gaillard et al. 1996). Lime is a very shade-tolerant tree and it has a dense canopy resulting in a dark forest floor with only sparse vegetation.

The local vegetation on the fen and in its close surroundings is reflected in the plant macrofossil record. The fen had a tree cover of alder, and a ground vegetation of, among other species, sedges (*Carex rostrata/vesicaria*), gipsywort (*Lycopus europaeus*), and common water-plantain (*Alisma plantago-aquatica*). Close to the fen grew pale persicaria (*Persicaria lapathifolia*), raspberry/blackberry (*Rubus idaeus/fruticosus*), and wild strawberry (*Fragaria* sp.).

Raspberry, blackberry, and wild strawberry are all edible plants. They do not usually grow on peat, but due to the very small size of the sampled fen, the presence of nutlets from these species in the peat samples may very well be natural. The possibility that they reflect human activity cannot, however, be completely ruled out. Since settlement remains are documented very close to the fen, the nutlets of raspberry/blackberry in particular may be waste from food processing on the site.

As mentioned above, dry ground vegetation was characterised by pine and hazel, but also by birch and bird cherry (*Prunus* cf. *padus*), and eventually some lime. Even if it is difficult to quantify the degree of openness, the local vegetation before the lime expansion may be characterised as semi-open or light woodland.

Late Atlantic–early Subboreal clay of the Littorina transgression

Eventually, the gradual Littorina transgression flooded the fen. In a wide sense, the transgression maximum lasted approximately 6200–2200 BC, during which period the sea level was more than 5 m above the present level. The maximum peak of about 7 m above present sea level was reached *c.* 4000 BC. In the local stratigraphy, the transgression is reflected only in a thin clay layer on top of the peat. As during the Ancylus transgression, the reason why no sand was deposited is that the local environment also during the Littorina transgression was a sheltered lagoon.

The clay was relatively rich in diatoms and chrysophyte cysts reflecting a sub-aquatic deposition. Some brackish diatom species were found but the diatom record was strongly dominated by lacustrine taxa, both planctonic and bentic. Some of the taxa also indicate fluvial conditions. A plausible interpretation is that the water of the lagoon had a lower salinity than the sea outside, mainly due to the River Skräbeån which transported large water masses from Lake Ivösjön to the lagoon and further out into the sea.

Subboreal post-transgression ground surface

After the Littorina transgression followed regression. The withdrawal of the sea resulted in desiccation of the clay layer and also of the underlying peat. The upper part of the peat was strongly humified and compacted due to this secondary drying-out, with only charred macrofossils preserved. Also the clay layer showed the same poor preservation.

Charcoal from the clay layer was radiocarbon-dated to *c.* 1500 BC. At this time, the site was some distance inland from the coast and it is certainly not the clay sedimentation that is dated. After the transgression, the clay layer deposited by the Littorina Sea constituted ground surface and topsoil for some millennia, and it is likely that the dated charcoal originates from down-mixing by worms etc. and thus reflects terrestrial conditions. Also, the composition of the pollen content of this layer is mainly the result of secondary down-mixing.

Late Subboreal (Bronze Age) agricultural colluvium

On top of the clay was a layer of sand, which in the lower part of the slope reached a thickness of approximately one metre. In the field, this layer was tentatively interpreted as reflecting the Littorina transgression. The interpretation was based primarily on the altitudinal distribution of the sand – approximately 4.5–5.5 m above present sea level – which seemed to fit well with a deposition in shallow water during the transgression maximum. However, since charcoal from the clay layer, i.e.

from under the sand, was radiocarbon-dated to well after the transgression maximum, the preliminary interpretation turned out to be wrong.

Based on the radiocarbon dating from the clay layer together with a radiocarbon dating from a hearth on top of the sand layer, it can be concluded that the sand was deposited sometime between 1500 BC and the Birth of Christ. From this time interval, which corresponds to the Bronze Age and the Pre-Roman Iron Age, a long-house and other settlement remains have been documented on the site. Since the sandy slope has been very susceptible to erosion, we may expect down-slope sand movement due to wind erosion or surface run-off in combination with trampling, over-grazing, and cultivation. Thus, the most plausible interpretation is that the sand originates from anthropogenic erosion, possibly in the habitation area itself or in grasslands, but more probably in fields or plots used for cultivation.

The sand layer has not been analysed for pollen, but the clay layer immediately beneath the sand shows relatively high frequencies of grass pollen (Poaceae undiff.) in comparison to older samples. It reflects deforestation and grazing sometime before the sand deposition, probably during the Late Neolithic or the Early Bronze Age.

MICRO-TOPOGRAPHY
OF THE SETTLEMENT SITE

The interesting and rather complex stratigraphy on the site was presented and interpreted above. In this section, the aim is to add a three-dimensional view of the stratigraphy in order to enable a realistic reconstruction, and to give a better understanding of the distribution and setting of archaeological structures and artefacts.

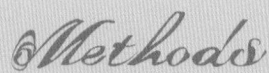

Methods
FOR MICRO-TOPOGRAPHY RECONSTRUCTION

During excavation, the different stratigraphical units were documented and given id-numbers. Using a total station with a minimal level of precision of 0.05 m, the surface of each stratigraphical unit was measured and digitally stored as a multi-point layer, while limitations were stored as lines or polygons. The measured input points were rather evenly dispersed over the surfaces, with a mean density of one point per two square metres, but more concentrated in areas with strong relief.

After completed excavation, the descriptions and measurements were evaluated and the units that were most suitable for reconstruction were chosen. Raw data were added to an ESRI ArcView project, and terrain models for each unit were generated using spline interpolation. For a smoother surface, all the deposits were transformed to contour lines and then to a triangulated irregular network (TIN). The three-dimensional reconstructions (fig. 21a–d), were generated in ArcView, with the extensions Spatial Analyst and 3D Analyst, and given a final touch in Adobe Illustrator.

The three-dimensional approach may also favour the identification of similar site locations in the region and aid predictive modelling.

The reconstruction area is the eastern part of the excavation area, and covers a sandy slope down to the bank of River Skräbeån. Late Palaeolithic and Mesolithic remains were found on the slope, while Bronze Age and Iron Age remains were documented at slightly higher elevations immediately to the west of the reconstruction area. The Stone Age remains were buried under a thick layer of sand and peat, and it was realised right from the start of the excavation that a careful documentation of the stratigraphy was important for the scientific outcome.

During the excavation, the soil and other deposits were removed layer by layer, and a total station carefully measured the upper surface of each layer. The measured surfaces were digitally stored and later used for interpretations and reconstruction.

The easternmost part of the reconstruction area was partly destroyed by a millpond. The present ground surface of the area was also affected by an old road, a stone wall, some shallow ditches, and by roots and stumps of numerous large trees, but the Stone Age remains were protected from these disturbances by the sand cover.

LAYERS OF RECONSTRUCTION

The three-dimensional distribution of the different layers, as documented on the excavation site, is presented in figures 21a–d. In the following text, the different layers are described and interpreted as a complement to the figures. The layers are presented from top to bottom, i.e. in the order of deposition.

PREBOREAL GROUND – THE BASIS

The oldest reconstructed surface shows the topography of glaciofluvially deposited sand and, in the lower part of the slope, also some clay. The clay seemed to fill up a glaciofluvial water channel. Beneath the sand, which had a maximum thickness of 1.5 m, there was till. Some large stones and boulders, probably originating from till washed and eroded by glaciofluvial water, were also present. The elevation of the surface of sand and clay ranged between 3.6 and 7.3 m above present sea level within the reconstructed area.

The reconstructed topography constituted the ground during Preboreal time. The archaeological remains that could be connected to this ground surface were a flint concentration from the Ahrensburg culture, believed to be older than c. 9200 BC (Context 1; see chapter by Nilsson and Hanlon), and a windbreak, flint, etc. from the early part of the Maglemose culture, tentatively dated to c. 9000 BC (Context 2) and c. 8000 BC (Context 3).

Figure 21a. Late-glacial sand and clay – the Preboreal ground.

ADDING FEN PEAT FROM THE LATE BOREAL AND EARLY ATLANTIC

In connection to the onset of the Littorina transgression and a rise in groundwater table c. 6000 BC, clay and sand in the lower part of the slope were covered by fen peat. The preserved thickness of this peat was 0.45 m in the south-eastern corner, but it decreased further up the slope where it reached a maximum elevation of 6.4 m above present sea level. Peat at elevations above 4.5 m was decomposed and poorly preserved due to secondary drying-out. The elevation of the present peat surface ranged between 4.2 and 6.4 m, but, due to the secondary decomposition, this was certainly not the originally elevation. In the north-eastern part, the maximum elevation of the peat is lower than 6.4 m, which may be due to erosion in connection with Bronze Age cultivation.

Flint artefacts and charcoal were found in and on top of the thin, decomposed peat, but the stratigraphical and chronological relationship was difficult to sort out. More obvious, however, was that the two archaeological contexts that were mentioned above – the Ahrensburg flint and the Maglemose windbreak and flint – were covered by undisturbed peat.

Some other find contexts are also of major interest here. At higher elevations – at about 6.5 m above present sea level – two contexts with flint and hut remains were found (Contexts 5 and 6). These were situated outside the range of the peat, and, hence, there is no stratigraphical relationship. They have, however, been dated to approximately 6000 BC and are interpreted as being contemporary with the fen. On a small island surrounded by peat, a feature interpreted as a posthole from a totem pole was dated to approximately the same time (Context 7).

Figure 21c. Adding clay from the Littorina transgression.

ADDING AGRICULTURAL COLLUVIUM FROM THE BRONZE AGE – CLOSING THE SITE

The fen peat and the clay layer together gradually filled up the south-eastern and eastern lower parts of the slope. A more drastic change of the topography, however, happened later, during the Bronze Age, when a layer of sand up to 1.0 m thick was deposited. This colluvium is interpreted as a result of soil erosion in arable fields connected to the Bronze Age settlement that was documented on the crest of the ridge. The sand filled up several depressions, smoothed out the earlier topography, decreased the gradient, and effectively buried the Stone Age remains. The elevation of the present surface range from 5.0 to 8.0 m above mean sea level and should be compared to the original Preboreal range of 3.6 to 7.3 m.

Figure 21b. Adding fen peat from the Late Boreal and the Early Atlantic.

ADDING CLAY FROM THE LITTORINA TRANSGRESSION

On top of the peat, a thin clay layer was deposited during the Littorina transgression. It had a maximum thickness of 0.3 m in the south-eastern part, and its surface ranged from elevations of 3.3 to 5.5 m above present sea level. Hence, the Littorina transgression reached at least 5.5 m, but probably higher since the sediment limit rarely reaches the water surface.

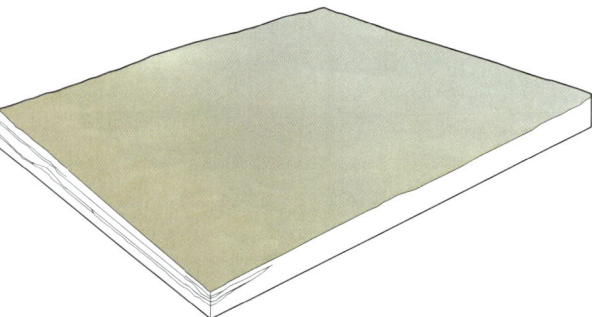

Figure 21d. Adding agricultural colluvium from the Bronze Age.

Three Stone Age environmental reconstructions

By combining archaeological and palaeoecological data from Årup with background information on shore displacement, fauna history, and climate, we are able to reconstruct some possible sceneries from the Stone Age (fig. 22–24). The aim is to provide an environmental setting for the archaeological features and interpretations that are presented in more detail in the next chapter. The aim is also to visualise the greatness of Stone Age landscapes and to give an impression of the beauty that is so easily lost in palaeoecological data, tables, and diagrams.

The selected time slices – 9500 BC, 8000 BC, and 6300 BC – are distinctly represented in the archaeological material on the site, and also represent three different environmental periods. Together they capture the gradual but decisive transition from late-glacial open landscapes to post-glacial woodlands.

9500 BC

A warm but windy evening in May 11,500 years ago, a small group of hunters stopped on the western side of the River Skräbeån. They had managed to kill a full-grown reindeer when it was trying to cross the river. Satisfied after the successful hunt, but also tired and hungry, the hunters now started butchering. Meat and skin had to be prepared so that it could be carried back to the settlement. In the distant, they could still see the group of reindeer they had been following all day.

The earliest traces of humans at Årup are some flints, which have been interpreted as the remains of a temporary butchering site (Context 1). They belong to the Ahrensburgian Culture, tentatively dated to 9500 BC, which corresponds to the transition between the Younger Dryas and the Preboreal or, in other words, between the late-glacial and the Holocene.

The onset of the Younger Dryas was characterised by a dramatic cooling, in particular in land areas around the North Atlantic. The cause of this climatic change has been debated, but most authors seem to agree that it was triggered by an outlet of cold meltwater from dammed ice-lakes in North America, which in a complex way led to a southward shift of the Gulf Stream (Broecker et al. 1989). Temperatures all over Europe fell by several degrees, and the Weichselian Ice Sheet, which covered northern and central Sweden, started to expand again. In the deglaciated parts of southern Sweden, permafrost conditions expanded and vegetation changed to a more open, treeless tundra.

These severe climatic conditions lasted for about one thousand years. At 9500 BC – the time of the reconstruction – the cool period ended rather abruptly (e.g. Björck et al. 1996b). Mean temperatures rose several degrees within a few decades and reached almost the same levels as today. In spite of improved climatic conditions, the vegetation was still tundra-like, or rather steppe-like. The reason for this lag between climate and vegetation is that temperature-dependent species had been pushed far back into southern Europe during the Younger Dryas cooling, and they simply needed some more time on their northward expansion to reach Sweden. Not only vegetation, but also the ice sheet, reacted rather slowly to the rapid rise in temperature, and, at the time of reconstruction, the ice front was situated only 300 km to the north.

The landscape around Årup was dominated by a wide horizon, since the only trees present were some scattered stands of birch. There were also some shrubs, such as willow, dwarf birch, and juniper, but mostly low vegetation such as grasses,

Figure 22. Environmental reconstruction for the Årup area at 9500 BC. Water-colour by Per Lagerås.

sedges, mugwort, goosefoot, etc. In this virgin landscape, there were probably also patches of barren soil, not yet colonised by vegetation, since the entire area had been under water only a few hundred years earlier.

Not only humans inhabited this open landscape, but also, of course, the herbivores that they were hunting. Reindeer was the most common species, which is evident from a large number of antlers found all over Scania (Liljegren & Lagerås 1993). During this time there was a land bridge between Sweden and Continental Europe, due to the very low water levels of the Yoldia Sea, and

reindeers may have used it for seasonal migration between summer and winter pastures. Another possibility is that southern Sweden was used for winter pasture and that summers were spent further north, close to the ice front (Björck et al. 1996a; Liljegren & Ekström 1996).

Reindeer was certainly the most important prey at the time and the butchering site at Årup is therefore interpreted as a reflection of a successful hunt of this species. Hunters probably followed the migrating reindeer or at least located their settlements along migratory routes. However, other mammals may also have been hunted, for example elk and wild horse. On the whole, we can be pretty sure that the economy around 9500 BC was based on mammalian hunting, since other food resources were scarce. The technique of hunting large herbivores in open terrain was based on a very long tradition – a way of life rooted in the mammoth steppe of the Ice Age.

8000 BC

Two hunters came paddling down the river on a hot summer afternoon 10,000 years ago. They had left their settlement at Lake Ivösjön already at sunrise, and they now needed a rest to stretch their legs and have some food. The riverbank was easy to enter on this spot, and they had stopped here many times before on their hunting and fishing expeditions to the coast. The windbreak from last year was still standing and only needed some minor restoration. Soon, smoke rose to the sky and they could relax by the fire, eat, and have a chat.

Some flints and the remains of a fireplace and a windbreak at Årup were dated to approximately 8000 BC (Context 3), which falls within the early part of the Boreal in early post-glacial time. From a palaeoenvironmental point of view, this was an interesting time – a transition period when the open landscape of the late-glacial gradually was replaced by forest.

Climate during the early part of the Boreal was rather warm, but due to the slowness of tree immigration and soil formation, the woodlands were still open and patchy with a rich under-storey. The closing in of woodlands may also have been delayed by the dry conditions that prevailed during this time. Studies of lake-level fluctuations in Scania have shown that the late Preboreal and the early Boreal was one of the driest periods of the

entire Holocene (Digerfeldt 1988). The tree species composition in the Årup area during the early Boreal was dominated by birch, pine, and hazel, and in smaller numbers elm, aspen and others. In these open woodlands, there was also a rich bush and herb vegetation with willows, heather, grasses, sedges, etc. Due to the dry climate and the large amounts of pine, these woodlands were susceptible to fire, and natural forest fires may have been an important factor affecting the vegetation structure.

As mentioned above, this was a transition period and the vegetation may be defined as a long-term succession from open land to forest. A warm climate and open woodlands provided good conditions for large herbivores, and there was plenty of game for the hunters. Most important were probably aurochs and bison, which both reached their peak in population at this time (Ekström 1993). Elk was also numerous and was certainly an important prey. Carnivores competing with humans were, for example, brown bear and wolf (Liljegren & Lagerås 1993).

Aurochs, bison, and elk were large animals and – from a human point of view – great meat suppliers. They probably provided the economic basis for the settlers at Årup as well as in other parts of southern Sweden at this time. In the relatively open vegetation, hunting could still be practised according to old traditions, but, eventually, the gradual closing in of woodlands must have led to changes in hunting strategies and food gathering. In this sense, the early Boreal was the last phase of a 100,000-year-long tradition of open-land big game hunting.

The expansion of woodlands was the main factor behind changes in economic strategies at this time, since it led to declining populations of large herbivores. Another contributing factor, however, was the large-scale establishment of hazel. The hazelnuts were very rich in energy, highly accessible,

Figure 23. Environmental reconstruction of the Årup area at 8000 BC. Water-colour by Per Lagerås.

and easy to store, and, therefore, they played an important role in hunter-gatherer economies from this time ever on (Regnell 1998; Karsten & Knarr-ström 2003).

Also the fauna of the Ancylus Lake, which was a limnic stage of the Baltic, may have contributed to the menu. In particular ringed seal and grey seal must have been appreciated prey, and perhaps also some fishing was practised. Due to the low levels of the Ancylus Lake at this time (some metres lower than today), the Årup site was rather distant from the coast. With the use of log boats, however, the shores and coastlines of both Lake Ivösjön in the north and the Ancylus Lake in the south were

easily within reach. The river itself may also have been a fishing ground, in particular for salmon.

6300 BC

It was a still day 8300 years ago and summer was turning into autumn. A young settler at Årup looked up at the September sky, took a deep breath and filled her lungs with fresh air. It smelled of damp forest soil mixed with the distinct smell of rotten seaweed brought by a coastal breeze. This time of the day, members of the group were engaged in different everyday activities, such

Figure 24. Environmental reconstruction of the Årup area at 6300 BC. Water-colour by Per Lagerås.

as foraging, flint knapping, and hunting in the lagoon. There was also cooking going on. Some of her friends, who had been away visiting another settlement, were expected to be home by dinner.

The remains of two huts or tents, workshops, fireplaces, and a lot of flint (Context 5–6), show that Årup was used rather intensively around 6300 BC. The approximate size of the group was ten to fifteen people. The dating of this settlement phase falls around the transition from Boreal to Atlantic Time, when deciduous forest for the first time covered almost the entire landscape.

By late Boreal time, most tree species had reached Sweden on their late-glacial and early Holocene migration from Ice Age refuges in southern Europe. Characteristic species were elm, oak, hazel, birch, and alder. The latter was a new immigrant during the late Boreal, and it quickly colonised fens, lakeshores, and riverbanks. By and large, it was deciduous woodland, but pine stands still prevailed on sandy soils, for example on the glaciofluvial deposits west of Årup. One tree species that slowly started to expand at this time was lime. It was typical of the Atlantic when dense lime-tree canopies resulted in dark forest floors with little ground vegetation (Iversen 1973). In the absence of larger lime stands, the woodlands of the late Boreal were still rather light, and grass, willows, and hazel still provided relatively good conditions for grazing and browsing herbivores. Climate was warm and more humid than before, which favoured, for example, ivy, mistletoe, and water chestnut.

By the time of reconstruction, bison was already extinct in Sweden. Aurochs was still around, but the population was declining as a result of the closing in of forests. It finally came to extinction in the Atlantic, as a result of the combined effect of environmental change and human hunting. Also elk, which today is highly associated with forests, was probably disfavoured by the expanding forests. It survived, however, but in smaller numbers than in the open landscapes of late-glacial and early Holocene times. When the old species became rare, new ones grew more important. In pace with expanding woodlands, species like roe deer, red deer and wild boar were getting more and more common, and, eventually, became the basis for the hunting society. Another animal of this time that is worth mentioning – although not of any economic importance – is the pond tortoise (Persson 1992). It is a species that is dependent on warm summer temperatures and its former occur-

rence in Sweden is a good indicator of the Holocene climatic optimum.

In the Årup area, not only changes in tree cover and fauna had an impact on the life of settlers, but also the lake-level changes of the Baltic. This was during an early phase of the Littorina transgression, when the rising water level had reached about four metres above present level, and salinity was gradually increasing. As a result of the transgression, the area around the river outlet was turned into a lagoon, which offered excellent conditions for hunting and fishing. The lagoon was situated only a few hundred metres downstream from the Årup site, and the settlers certainly visited it regularly for fishing and fowling. On the other side of the lagoon was the open coast of the Littorina Sea, with a rich fauna not only of fish and birds but also of harbour porpoise and several species of seal (Liljegren & Lagerås 1993). The open coast as well as the lagoon area could easily be reached on a one-day trip.

In conclusion, the combination of a rich and varied environment and declining populations of aurochs and other large herbivores, led to a more complex economy around 6300 BC than at the two older reconstructed time slices.

*Life and work
during 5,000 years*

By Björn Nilsson & Conleth Hanlon

The contexts

DWELLINGS AND ACTIVITY AREAS

Årup was repeatedly inhabited from the Late Palaeolithic to the Late Mesolithic, a period spanning roughly 5,000 years, encompassing the Younger Dryas, the Preboreal, the Boreal and the Atlantic chronozones. In cultural terms, we are primarily dealing with the Ahrensburgian, Maglemosian and Kongemosian traditions although some conspicuous deviations from the archaeological cultural norm have been noted.

As mentioned in the previous chapter, the River Skräbeån constitutes a clearly defined geographical dividing-line between an area of sand and gravel to the west and an area of till to the east, in places with a marked element of boulders. When choosing a suitable campsite, well-drained grounds beside good supplies of water and firewood are prerequisites that have to be met. Slightly sloping sandy, gravelly, or stony soils with a thin vegetation cover are most often the best places. Besides the permeable nature of such soils, they also store the warmth of the sun during the daytime. In these respects, the western shore of the River Skräbeån has been most suitable for human habitation.

The Late Palaeolithic site and the Early Mesolithic hut structures were situated in the eastern part of the investigation area, close by River Skräbeån on an elevation of approximately 5 m above present sea level. The late Early Mesolithic and Middle Mesolithic dwellings and activity areas were situated on somewhat higher terrain on an elevation of approximately 6–7 m above present sea level (fig. 25).

LET THE STORY BEGIN...

Once upon a time, two and a half millennia before the birth of the Barum woman, in about 9500 BC, a small group of hunters temporarily camped on a sandy beach near the River Skräbeån. They had been hunting reindeer on the open grass plain. They sat down and made some stone tools with blanks they had brought along with them. They butchered their quarry and filled their stomachs with fresh meat. They were modern humans, pioneers in north-eastern Scania. They were the earliest visitors.

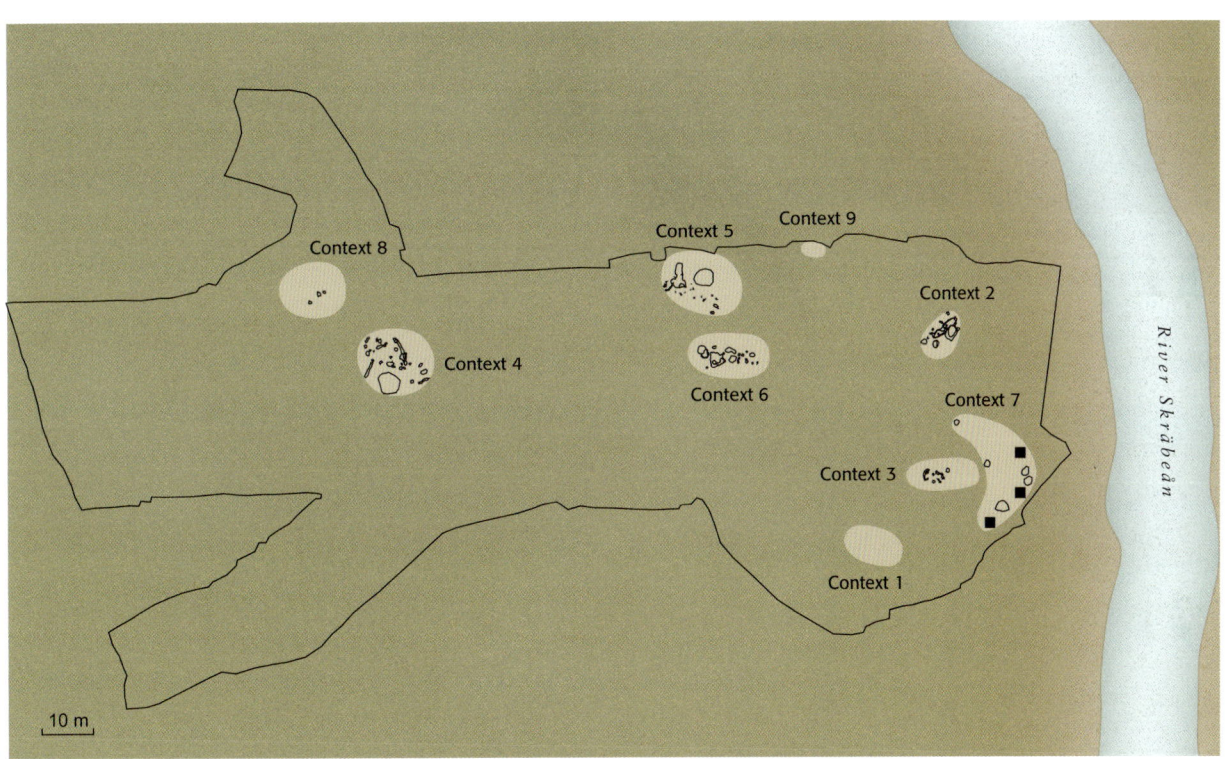

Figure 25. Plan of the area of investigation showing the huts and activity areas.

Context 8

Context 5

Context 9

Context 2

Context 4

Context 6

Context 7

Context 3

Context 1

River Skräbeån

10 m

59

Figure 26. Late Palaeolithic flints exposed at the very bottom of the trench. Photo by Björn Nilsson.

Figure 27. Close-up of some of the flints at the bottom of the trench. Photo by Tony Björk.

THE EARLIEST VISITORS

Layer by layer had been removed, remarkable discoveries and sensational finds had been made, and traces bearing witness to the site being attractive for many generations during the Early and Middle Mesolithic had been found. As the excavation proceeded, there were also growing hopes that the layers underneath the Early Mesolithic level would contain even older remains, but occasional deep trenches on the gentle slope gave no such indications.

However, at the end of the excavation period, in the south-eastern part of the investigation area, a final deep trench was dug, with the sole intention of documenting the layer sequences and their formation. Nothing was found in this trench either. Then, when a section was being cleaned in preparation for documenting the stratigraphy and taking samples, a finely worked platform core and a few flakes fell out of the sand wall. The surprising thing was not the finds themselves, but the fact

OF CONTEXT 1

In total 2,118 pieces or 4,120 g of flint are associated with the context. Of these, 41 pieces or 73 g are burnt. The assemblage is dominated by 1,851 pieces or 3,839 g of Kristianstad flint, while 267 pieces or 281 g are of Senonian flint. Two pieces or 301 g of stone were found. Divided into categories, the assemblage comprises 1,030 flakes, 880 splinters, 116 blades and blade fragments, 10 microblades, 10 cores, 6 rejuvenation flakes, 10 formal scrapers, 3 formal knives, 3 formal burins, 3 burin spalls, 6 awls, 25 microliths, 1 transverse arrowhead, 10 microburins, 6 other flints, 1 hammerstone, and 1 stone with wearing surface.

that they came from a layer more than 1.5 m beneath the ground level. At this stage it was realised that the material must be of considerable age, at least of earlier date than the Early Mesolithic remains higher up in the layers. We decided to move fast and concentrate the resources to make it possible to excavate the total area. After 14 days of digging it was possible to determine the limits of the whole activity area, which proved to cover an area of approximately 33 m², located on an elevation of 5.2–5.5 m above present sea level.

The stratigraphy observed in the trench (fig. 28) was comparable to the southern section described by Lagerås et al., in the previous chapter, though with a more distinct stratigraphy in the western part, where three different organogenic layers were identified. A charcoal sample retrieved from the bottommost layer overlying the assemblage was identified as being of pine (*Pinus silvestris*). The sample was dated to 9390 ± 65 BP, in the interval 9150–8450 cal. BC with 2 sigma, which correlates with the bottommost zone (P1) in the southern section.

The find assemblage was concentrated in a layer of fine flame-coloured sand, at a level on average 0.1 m beneath the dated layer. Unfortunately, no datable material was found in this part, but the stratigraphy provides the find material with a *terminus ante quem,* telling us that the assemblage is undeniably older than the dated layer which locks the context upward in time, no later than the early to middle Preboreal chronozone. The date itself indicates that the layer is associated with the Ancylus transgression, which was initiated at *c.* 8800 BC thus showing that the assemblage was already in place at this event. Our immediate standing point was that we were dealing with very old remains, probably a Late Palaeolithic assemblage, dating back to the Ahrensburg culture.

The material is very well preserved and except for some colour patination caused by the ferric oxide, no signs of altered surfaces such as wind polishing and water rolling are present. This suggested that the assemblage was covered in a short time and that the material was in fact *in situ*. All in all, the lithic material was well suited for a combined use-wear and refitting analysis.

Kristianstad flint totally dominates the flint assemblage. This is of quite good quality, probably collected in the vicinity. Present evidence shows that late-glacial hunters primarily exploited the local flint, collected in streams and ravines in the moraines or from washed-out chalk clays with a high density of flint nodules (Madsen 1992:96, 1996:62). The different types of cortex remains on the flakes and blades from Context 1 support this assumption. However, it cannot be ruled out that fresh nodules were taken from exposed calcareous layers in the neighbourhood of Kristianstad. The assumption that Late Palaeolithic groups actively searched out good raw material deposits is supported by the Late Palaeolithic pit in the cretaceous layers at Ängdala, outside Malmö in south-western Scania (Gaillard & Lemdahl 1993; Andersson & Knarrström 1999:92ff; Knarrström 2004:48). Moreover, the fact that several of the Late Palaeolithic Kristianstad flints found further north at Lake Finjasjön also are of very high quality further strengthens this assumption (Larsson 1994a, 1994b, 1996). A few artefacts are of Senonian flint, perhaps deriving from only one or two single nodules. Senonian flint, naturally occurring only in primary and secondary deposits in the south-western part of Scania and Zealand (Knarrström 2000a:26, 2001: 20ff), must have been exported to the north-east.

Flakes, blades, and splinters of all sizes dominate the excavated material, which suggests that serious manufacture of diverse objects was practised on the site. A technological attribute analysis of the blades and flakes may add a great deal of information regarding the flint knapper's choice of method, intentions, and final results (cf. Knarrström

1 m

Figure 28. Part of the section in the deep trench with approximately 0.5 m overlying sand removed. Chemical processes have resulted in a clearly visible edge of ferric oxide breaking through the section. The three different organogenic layers are marked with blue plastic markers. The averaged level of the find assemblage is marked with red lines. Photo by Helén af Geijerstam.

Figure 29. Context 1 during excavation. Photo by Sven Waldemarsson.

Figure 30. The excavation area viewed from south-east.
Photo by Björn Nilsson.

& Wrentner 1996; Knarrström 2000a:27ff, 2001: 24ff; Karsten & Knarrström 2003:38). The majority of the flakes are characterised by pronounced bulbs of percussion with bulb scars and mostly relatively small rhomboid platform remnants. The blades are irregular in shape and can be classified as several morphological types, such as sturdy blades, long blades with opposite distal scars and finally short and slender blades. There are also some blades that fall into the definition of a microblade (e.g. Vang Petersen 1993:54; Högberg et al. 2000:9). These, however, are to be considered as "trimming microblades", by-products of the preparation and trimming of cores (cf. Madsen 1996).

The blades mostly have small and thin, sometimes wide, rhomboid platform remnants, even though larger ones exist with partially or fully developed ring cracks, attributes generally seen as indicating direct hard hammer percussion technique (Knarrström & Wrentner 1996; Whittaker 1997: 14f; Sørensen 2001). Sometimes bulb scars are present, and in several cases, heavy grinding or abrasion can be observed on dorsal ridges. Moreover, some of the blades display cracked and splintered platforms. Sometimes the whole area of the bulb has collapsed. A minor element of faceted and in some instances finely retouched platform remnants can also be traced in the material, attributes that have been suggested as characteristic of the Federmesser culture (cf. Fischer 1988:17f; Fugl Petersen 1994:12ff; Degn Johansson 2000:31; see also Context 2 in this volume).

The variations in platform sizes can be explained in terms of the size and hardness of the hammerstones used. Danish experiments concerned with Late Palaeolithic knapping techniques have convincingly shown that use of small and soft hammerstones can result in both small rhomboid platform remnants and the more characteristic larger ones (Madsen 1992:106).

Taken together, the technological attributes on the flakes and blades indicate a direct hard hammer percussion technique. Moreover, some traces in the material point towards a hard "elastic" technique, which defines hard direct technology with the use of soft hammerstones of sandstone, chalk, or chalk-sandstone (Sørensen 2001:35).

However, it has to be mentioned that the use of antler punchers – mostly characterised by small pointed-oval platform remnants with a slight overhang, a "lip", on the ventral side (Crabtree 1972: 74; Andrefsky 1998:xxiv, 18) – can also result in small rhomboid platforms. This circumstance may in some cases cause confusion regarding whether direct hard hammer technique or indirect soft hammer technique was practised at a site. Therefore, it cannot be totally ruled out that indirect soft hammer technique was used during the Late Palaeolithic as well, a question especially interesting at sites where hammerstones are not present in the material (Andersson & Knarrström 1999: 96ff).

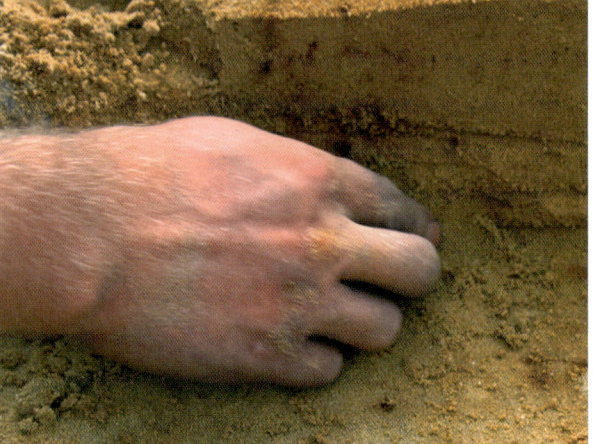

Figure 31. Sequence of a blade being uncovered after about 11,500 years, encapsulated in sand. Photo by Sven Waldemarsson.

In the case of Context 1, the find of a hammer-stone made of sandstone (fig. 32) supports the practice of a direct hard elastic technology at the site. This artefact is ellipsoid in shape and slightly larger than a baby's fist. It is worth noticing that the hammerstone displays knapping marks all around the edge, which indicates a technique whereby the core was struck with a more horizontal or sweeping, rather than a vertical or straight blow angle, thus resulting in a scratching-like contact with the hammerstone. Moreover, the hammerstone has markings on the flat sides, three (or possibly five) on one side and one on the other. A similar hammerstone of almost the same shape and with the same characteristics has been found in an Ahrensburg context in Kreis Soltau in Germany (Dürre 1971:7, Tafel X:23). The markings, which seem to be the result of some kind of wear and almost look like "finger marks", have been noticed on hammerstones from other Stone Age periods as well, on some also in groupings of three (e.g. Karsten & Knarrström 2003:90, fig. 60) as on the one from Årup. However, what exactly these markings represent is unclear.

The core remnants from the context are heavily reduced. The most intact examples have only a few scars left from blade detachment. However, the technological attributes correspond well with the types of blades. Roughly half of the cores have opposed single-face platforms with steep platform angles, and with distinct archaic features. The other group of cores consists of more or less conical examples with flat platforms. Both types of cores are distinct features of the flint craft during the Ahrensburg culture, even though the opposed single-face platform core appears on the "other side" of the traditional dividing line to the Early Mesolithic as well, and the conical core has a wide chronological spread into the Neolithic. However, the context, the technological attributes and the archaic features of the cores make them distinct Late Palaeolithic examples.

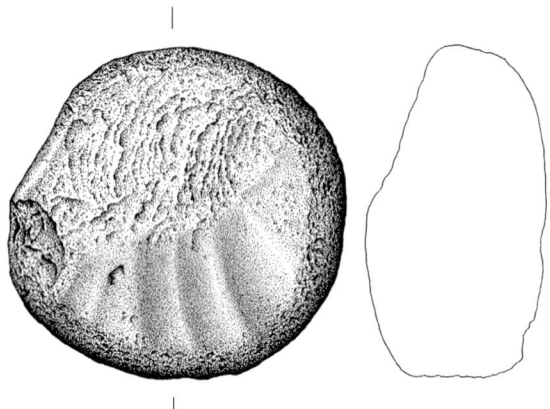

Figure 32. The hammerstone from Context 1. Drawing by Björn Nilsson. All forthcoming artefact drawings 67% of natural size.

The collection of artefacts includes several microliths and microburins. The microburins [by the way, a somewhat badly chosen term that is a little confusing, since they are not at all burins but "notch remnants" (cf. Vang Petersen 1993:88; Johansen & Stapert 2000:15)] constitute evidence of on-site production of microliths. Microburin technique has generally been associated with the Early and Middle Mesolithic periods but microburins have increasingly been observed also in Late Palaeolithic contexts (Madsen 1983:20; Vang Petersen 1993:88). Even if they have been described only rarely so far, and are thus interpreted as waste from the manufacturing of points (cf. Madsen 1996:69), the technique is no more to be considered as an "exception" or "accident" in Late Palaeolithic contexts.

The microliths found in the context have some features in common with Zonhoven points (Taute 1968), while others cannot easily be placed in either the Late Palaeolithic or Mesolithic culture groups. Two lanceolates found close together in the south-eastern part of the context are worth special mention (fig. 34:7–8). These are both made of distal parts of irregular slender blades, where the proximal end with the bulb of percussion has been removed by letting the retouch form the point in this part. They are retouched along one side with the distal end intact. The microliths show distinct archaic features and have parallels throughout the Late Palaeolithic – not least the so-called *Federmesser* points (e.g. Vang Petersen 1993:76; Johansen 1997; Degn Johansson 2000:30f) – into the traditional Early Mesolithic.

Moreover, a special type of microlith was found that could best be described as a barbed point (fig. 34:9). The point is made of Senonian flint and has retouch along both sides, with the point oriented to the distal end. On one side a marked barb can be noticed. This type of point occurs in Late Palaeolithic (e.g. Tromnau 1975) as well as in traditional Early Mesolithic contexts (e.g. Nordqvist 2000).

Also worth noticing is a transverse arrowhead – classified as such through a combination of morphological identification and use-wear analysis (see below) – of classical Late Mesolithic type (fig. 34:14). However, it is of course not a question of a Late Mesolithic mix-up, and this Late Palaeolithic transverse arrowhead from Context 1 gives another knockout blow to the assumption that the development of arrowhead technology proceeded from pointed tips to transverse tips (cf. Fischer 1994, fig. 1; Fischer & Malm 1997:80). One revision has already been made, when the many of the early Middle Mesolithic trapezoid microliths – the Blak microliths – convincingly were shown to have

Figure 33. A selection of blades and cores from Context 1. 1–5: Blades with opposite distal scars. 6–10: Blades. 11–12: Platform cores. 13–14: Opposed single-face platform cores. Drawings by Björn Nilsson.

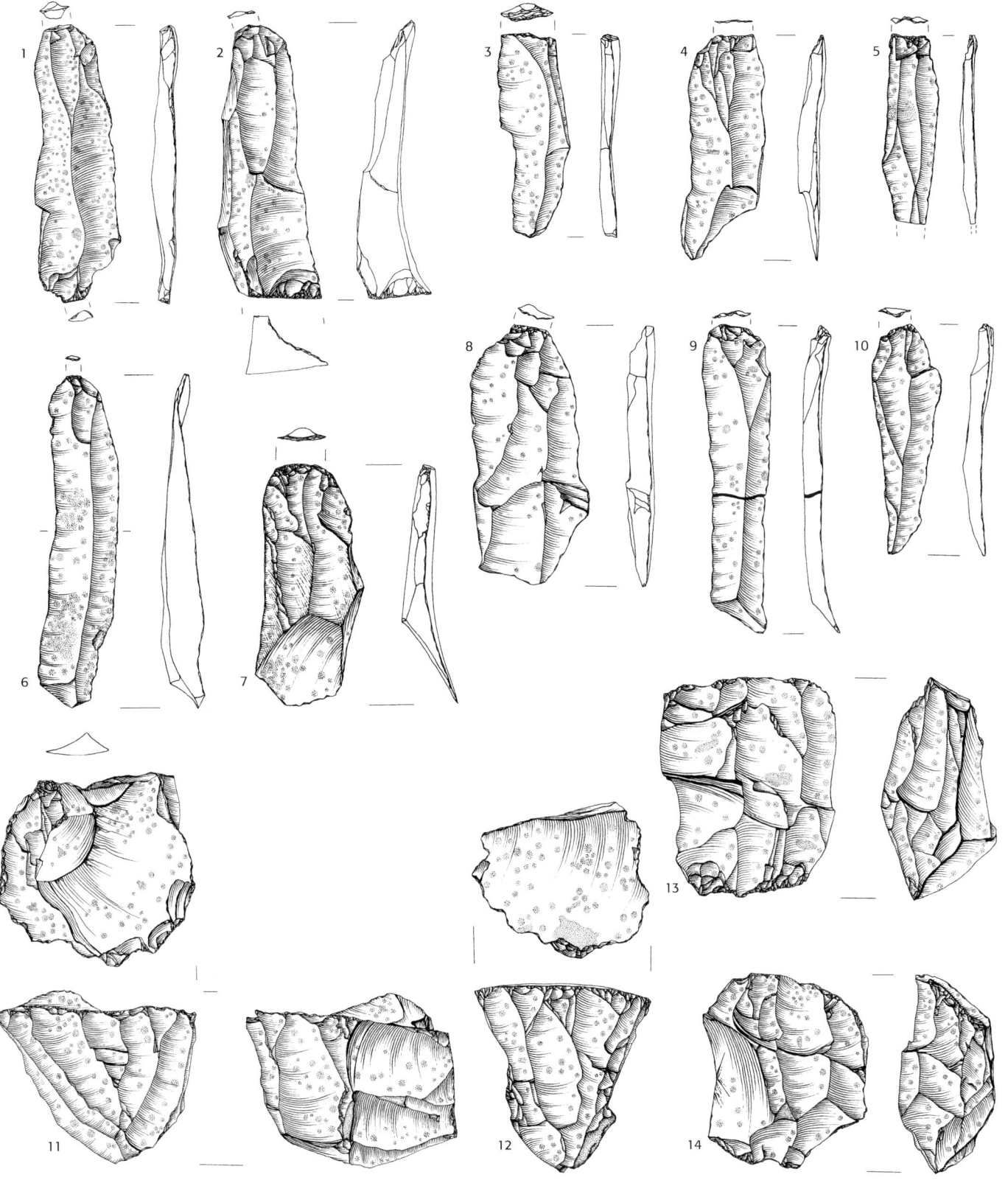

been used as transverse arrowheads (Karsten & Knarrström 2003:59ff). With the find from Context 1 the chronology of transverse arrowheads can be moved back to the Late Palaeolithic. However, the find in itself is not revolutionary in any way. Similar microliths can be found in almost every Ahrensburg context where microliths are present, though without being classified as transverse arrowheads, generally conjured away as Zonhoven points or trapezes (e.g. Taute 1968; Jöris & Thissen 1995:960, fig. 121:18–20; Johansen & Stapert 2000, fig 11:2, 68:8).

Furthermore, worth commenting are a few microliths, which to us seemed too small to have functioned as points and barbs on arrows. After having been subjected to use-wear analysis (see below) these artefacts, together with a few other microliths initially thought of as fragmented points and one small irregular blade with retouch in the distal end, formed a category that can best be described as awls or pricking tools (fig. 34:15–18).

The formal scrapers from the context are mainly made of sturdy blades, with the scraper-edge retouched at the distal end of the blade. There are also scrapers made of flakes. Two of the scrapers occur in a fragmented state. A majority of the scrapers have one or more areas with residual crust, indicating that the first removals from a core were extensively used for scraper production. One reasonable explanation could be that the first series of blades and flakes tends to be thicker, and perhaps a sturdier material was preferred for tools expected to last for heavy duty (cf. Knarrström 2000a:49, 2001:46).

Most of the scrapers have very steep edge angles, some almost 90 degrees. This characteristic seems to be a distinct feature of Late Palaeolithic scrapers (Andersson & Knarrström 1999; Larsson et al. 2002). One scraper is a double-edge scraper made of a flake (fig. 34:4). In this case the scraper-edges are located proximally and distally. This type

of scraper has been noted at many other Ahrensburgian sites (e.g. Rust 1943; Taute 1968; Tromnau 1975; Dürre 1971; Degn Johansson 2000; Johansen & Stapert 2000).

Three formal burins were retrieved. One is made of a small flake and one on a break of a fragmented blade. The third is made on a break of a sturdy blade, but has to be considered as unsuccessful as the burin blow obviously resulted in an overshot (cf. Vang Petersen 1993:70, fig. 31:C). It may be noticed that no burins of classical shape, made on a break from truncated blades, are present in the find assemblage. However, three large burin spalls (see example in fig. 34:5) give evidence of such having been manufactured on the site, but most likely eventually taken away.

Three formal blade knives were found. These all have one more or less straight edge on one side and partial retouches on the other, located at the distal end of the blades (fig. 34:6). Additionally, several retouched blades and flakes were found in the material.

Moreover, three finds, including one opposed single-face platform core and two points (fig. 35), were made 50 m to the north-east of the context. The finds are of the same good quality of Kristianstad flint and could very well be linked to the other finds. This indicates the presence of a number of remains from the same period in the immediate vicinity. The core displays characteristic features known from other Ahrensburgian contexts (e.g. Taute 1968). The points consisted of two lanceolates. One is made from a blade with opposite distal scars and had one side fully retouched with a straight broad retouch, resembling a backed point (=Federmesser). The other is only partly retouched. Both are made of very straight blades with the point oriented to the proximal end of the blade.

As mentioned earlier, there was no sorting effect of transgressions or erosion on the gentle slope, so the spatial distribution of the flint can be

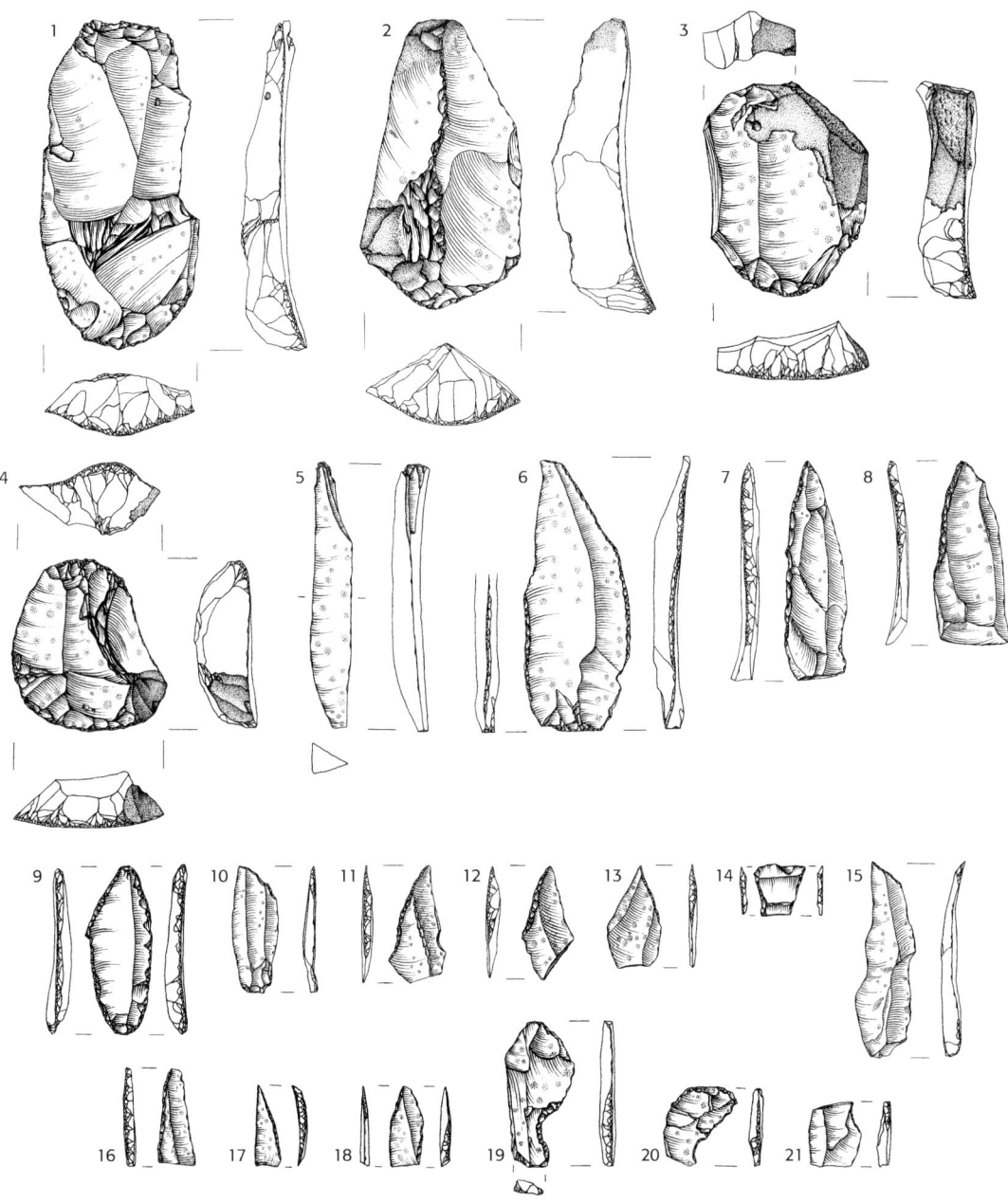

Figure 34. A selection of artefacts from Context 1. 1–4: Scrapers. 5: Burin spall. 6: Blade knife. 7–13: Microliths. 14: Transverse arrowhead. 15–18: Awls. 19–21: Microburins. Drawings by Björn Nilsson.

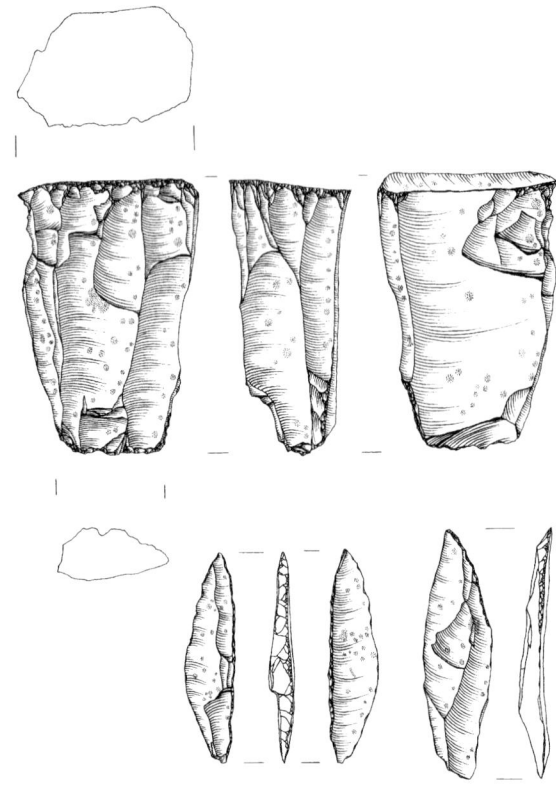

Figure 35. The three artefacts found 50 m north-east of Context 1. Drawings by Björn Nilsson.

considered correct. Although the lithics occurred over almost the whole excavated area, the find assemblage was well-defined with several very clear concentrations (fig. 36). The assemblage formed an almost rounded spatial distribution, which could be divided into two main flint-rich areas with three clearly visible concentrations of flint and with an empty area in the south-eastern central part of the site, containing no finds whatsoever. The two main areas have to be considered as knapping floors, indicated by a large amount of flakes and blades, but also a high density of splinters. The highest

incidences of burnt flint were concentrated in the north and south of the empty area (fig. 37). Due to the very small amount of burnt flint, a plausible interpretation would be that this represents a small and very temporary hearth located in the area.

In the southern part of the western flint-rich area a small accumulation of cores and rejuvenation flakes was present. Here we also found some formal scrapers and a knife, but above all a lot of splinters, flakes, and blades. In addition several microliths and microburins were retrieved from this concentration, indicating that microliths were manufactured in this part. In the northernmost part of the western area, another accumulation of flint was observed, consisting primarily of flakes, splinters, and blades, indicating knapping on site.

The only hammerstone found in the context was collected from the eastern flint-rich area, where a lot of splinters, flakes, and blades were also found together with some cores and rejuvenation flakes. Moreover, several of the formal scrapers were found in this area.

The limited number of Senonian flint occurred all over the site, although a small accumulation, with a high density of splinters, could be identified in the eastern concentration, indicating that knapping of Senonian flint took place in this part (fig. 39 & 40).

Taken together, the spatial distribution of the finds clearly shows structures at the site, with identifiable activity zones, especially noticed regarding accumulations of waste material, microliths, microburins and scrapers.

All the flints, with the exception of splinters and very small flakes, were subjected to comprehensive refitting. During one week of refitting, a total of 116 pieces were refitted into 27 units comprising two or more pieces, primarily constituting parts of cores and broken blades and artefacts (for details see Nilsson 2005). Most of the refitted units were highly concentrated in the spatial distribution, with the individual pieces lying close by each other (fig. 41). However, one unit (U. No 7), consisting of two flakes and three blade fragments of Kristianstad flint, constituting the outermost of a blade core and representing the initial phase of the blade production (fig. 42), shows a much wider and less concentrated spatial distribution. A use-wear analysis of the blade fragments showed that all three pieces had been used for different purposes, which could explain the spreading over the area. Moreover, the sequence confirms the contemporaneity of the material.

The largest unit consists of 26 flakes of Kristianstad flint (U. No 9) all coming from the northernmost concentration in the western part of the site. The unit represents the second outermost reduction of a flake core (fig. 43). The core had been worked from two opposite platforms which both display very steep edge angles. To judge from the structure of the flint, the nature of the cortex, etc., it is very likely that several of the refitted units as well as non-fitting flakes, blades, and some cores from this concentration derive from the dressing of one and the same nodule.

The second largest unit is made up of 24 pieces of Kristianstad flint (U. No 1), which were all retrieved from the southernmost part of the site. The sequence constitutes the most of a blade core with a fitting opposed platform single-face core (fig. 33:13), which has its face centred in the refitted unit (fig. 44). This unit presents the story of the individual core and gives interesting information about the raw material as well as the technological profile. The raw material probably came to the site in the form of a nodule that was not much worked or prepared previously but probably tested for quality (see also p. 161). On two sides, the front and the bottom, of the refitted unit, remnants of the natural outer surface of the nodule can be seen. These natural parts together with the shape of the whole unit indicate the original size of the nodule, which could be estimated at approximately 0.1 by 0.1 m.

The first knapping of the core seems to have been to create the platform. Then the core was prepared by removing most of the natural surface. During this procedure a large flake was removed, which took almost a third of the whole core. This large flake was broken into two pieces during the blow. The break of the distal part was used as a platform and some flakes were knapped off, of which three can be refitted, one worked into a microburin and one into a microlith (fig. 45). The proximal part of the large flake has been secondarily used, probably in a scraping manner, judging by macro use-wear on one edge. After this large flake had been removed, the core was trimmed on the sides by horizontal knapping. Then a few longer blades were unidirectionally struck off from the face of the core, six of which could be refitted. In the next step, a blow from the front of the core created an opposite platform, giving a steep angle. After this preparatory stage, several blades were struck off from the opposite platform. Four of these blades are possible to refit, of which two have direct contact with the opposed platform single-face core. However, most of these blades are obviously missing, giving a space in the middle of the refitted unit. A plausible interpretation would be that these blades, which seem to have been very straight in character, were used for arrowhead manufacturing and taken away from the site. To force this interpretation further, this space may represent the blades that left the site as the "missing" tanged points.

Several of the refitted units show a technological profile similar to the previous two examples, with the use of opposite platforms. One more example is shown in figure 46. A third example, worth commenting on, is a unit (U. No 4) including five flakes of Senonian flint, from the northeastern concentration (fig. 47). A noticeable detail is that the flakes display frequent occurrence of

FOR SPATIAL DISTRIBUTION

All forthcoming isarithms are made by hand and based on a combination of the actual number of finds per square and the archaeological field observations of the distribution of finds within each individual square. When more than one isarithm are present in a square, the highest one reflects the total number of finds in that particular square.

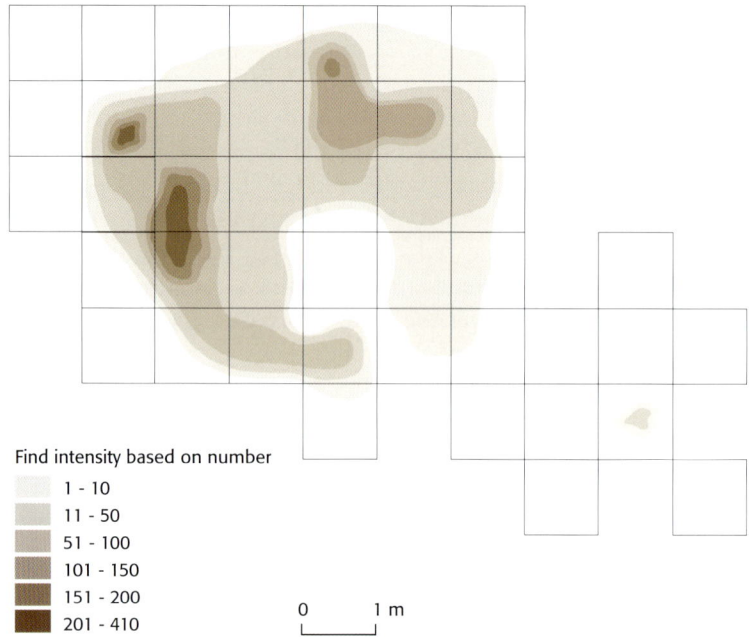

Find intensity based on number

    1 - 10
    11 - 50
    51 - 100
    101 - 150
    151 - 200
    201 - 410

0   1 m

Figure 36. Spatial distribution of the total amount of flint in Context 1 based on number.

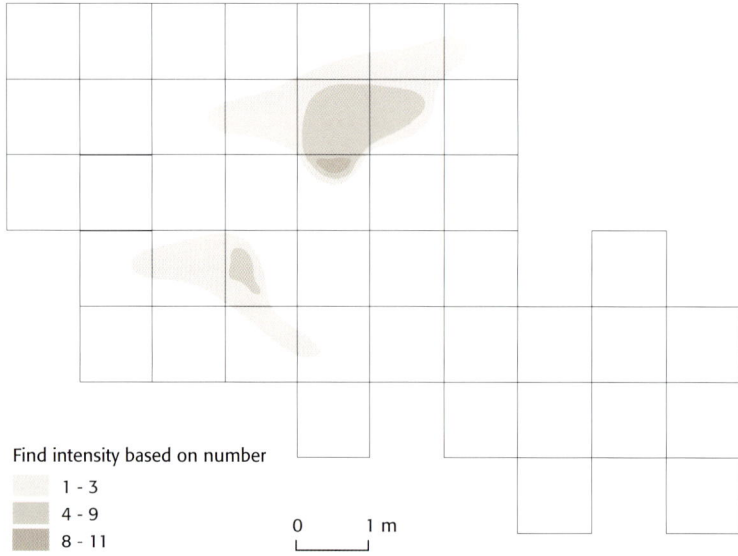

Find intensity based on number

    1 - 3
    4 - 9
    8 - 11

0   1 m

Figure 37. Spatial distribution of burnt flint in Context 1 based on number.

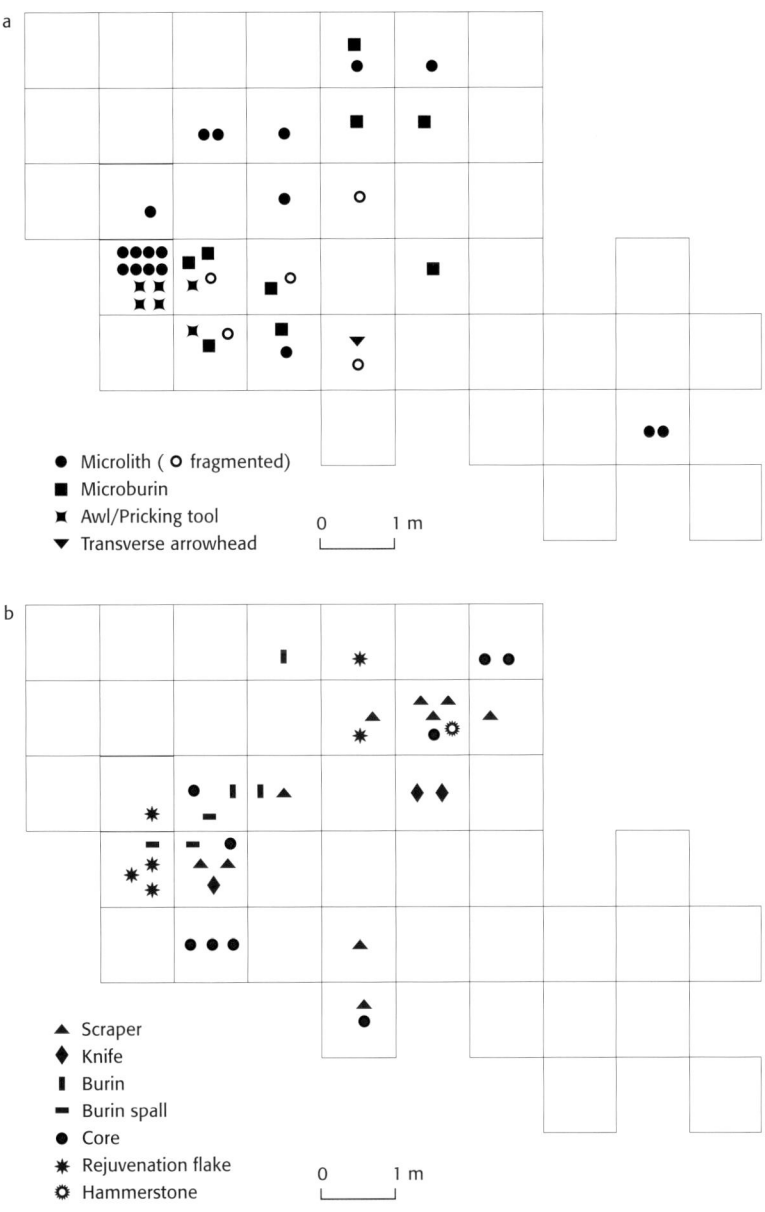

a

● Microlith (○ fragmented)
■ Microburin
✖ Awl/Pricking tool
▼ Transverse arrowhead

0   1 m

b

▲ Scraper
◆ Knife
▮ Burin
━ Burin spall
● Core
✳ Rejuvenation flake
✹ Hammerstone

0   1 m

Figure 38a-b. Spatial distribution of formal artefacts in Context 1 based on number. Symbols match the number of finds.

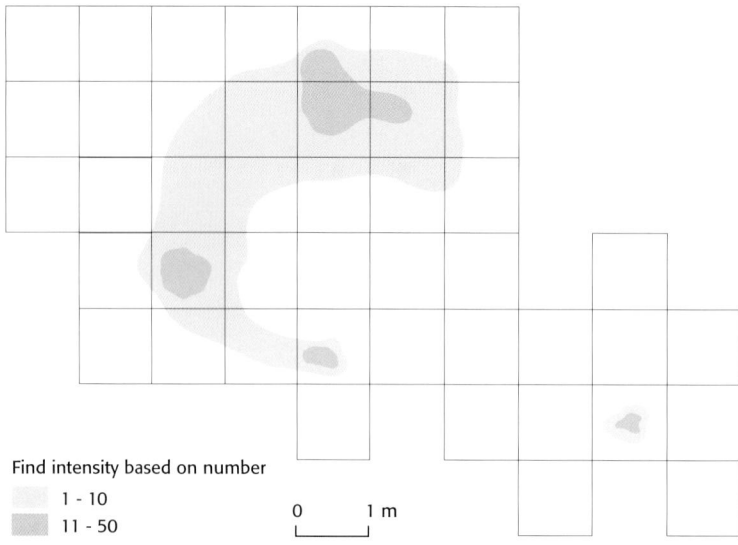

Figure 39. Spatial distribution of the total amount of Senonian flint in Context 1 based on number.

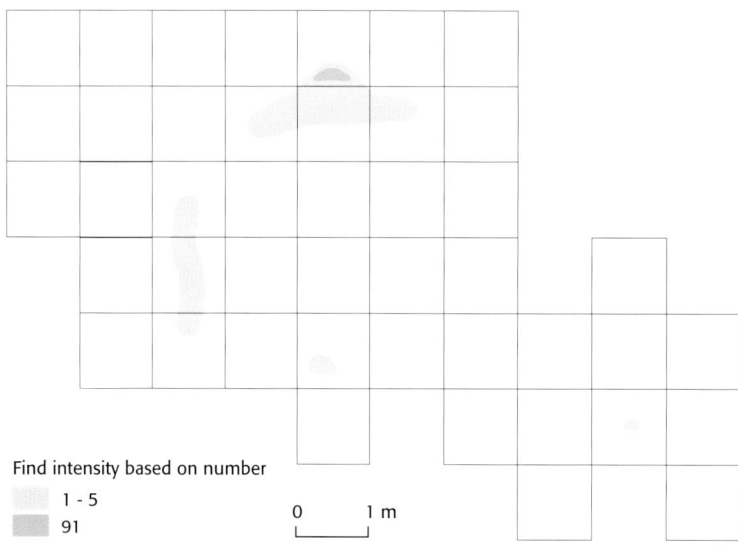

Figure 40. Spatial distribution of splinters of Senonian flint in Context 1 based on number.

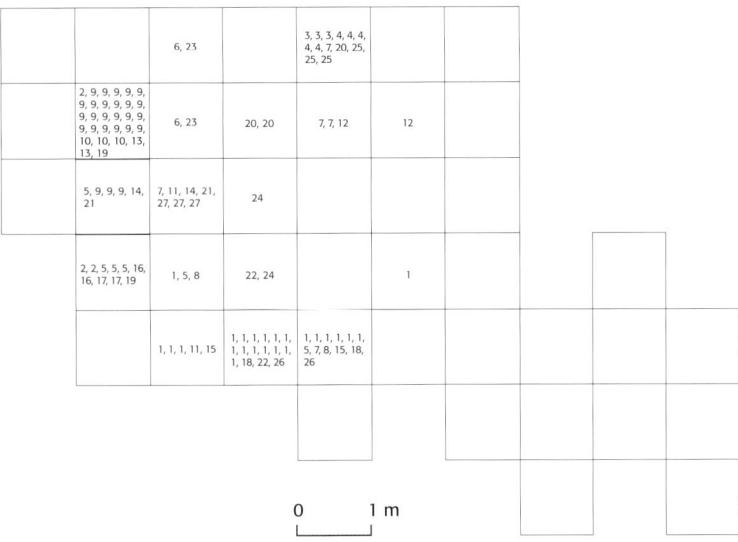

		6, 23		3, 3, 3, 4, 4, 4, 4, 4, 7, 20, 25, 25, 25		
	2, 9, 9, 9, 9, 9, 9, 9, 9, 9, 9, 9, 9, 9, 9, 9, 9, 9, 9, 9, 9, 9, 10, 10, 10, 13, 13, 19	6, 23	20, 20	7, 7, 12	12	
	5, 9, 9, 9, 14, 21	7, 11, 14, 21, 27, 27, 27	24			
	2, 2, 5, 5, 5, 16, 16, 17, 17, 19	1, 5, 8	22, 24		1	
		1, 1, 1, 11, 15	1, 1, 1, 1, 1, 1, 1, 1, 1, 1, 1, 1, 1, 18, 22, 26	1, 1, 1, 1, 1, 1, 5, 7, 8, 15, 18, 26		

0   1 m

Figure 41. Plan illustrating the distribution of pieces of flint possible to refit into units. Unit numbers match the number of pieces. Several of the units lying close by each other most likely belong to the same core judging by similarities in distinctive features such as flint quality, colour, texture, and cortex. If you want to see the connections between each unit more explicitly, take a copy and draw your own lines.

faceted and finely retouched ("prepared") platform remnants, in accordance with what has been described earlier. This unit, together with two other short sequences of Senonian flint from the same concentration (U. No 3 and 25), indicates that the collection of Senonian flint derives from a small moraine nodule knapped on the site, even though parts of it seem to have been taken away.

Regarding formal tools refitted into units, the scrapers deserve special mention. In one short sequence (U. No 8) a blade scraper can be refitted from two fragments (fig. 48). Use-wear analysis showed that the scraper edge had not been used. Due to the steep edge angle and what seems to be an unsuccessful heavy retouch at the edge, a plausible

interpretation would be that the edge was resharpened and that the scraper was broken during this act. However, along one of the sides the scraper displays dorsal use-wear indicative of having been used as a butchering knife, cutting meat/hide. It is hard to tell whether the scraper was used as a combination tool in a scraping and cutting manner, or if it became a scraper from a blade already used as a butchering knife. What can be said, though, is that use-wear can be identified along the edge on both sides of the break, indicating that the edge was intact when used.

Moreover, a scraper made of a sturdy blade and the double scraper can be refitted in sequence (U. No 12), with the platform remnant of the

Figure 42. Refitted sequence (U. No 7) of two flakes and three blade fragments (two from the same blade), constituting part of the outermost of a blade core (note the steep platform angle). The spatial distribution of the unit makes a connection over the whole area. A use-wear analysis of the blade fragments clearly shows how these were used in different activities on the site. The first blade fragment found in the northern part of the site (2) displays micro-detachments and polish along one of the edges, suggested as caused by working of wood (cf. Knarrström 2001:122, fig. 109). The second blade fragment (4a), found in the southern part, displays clearly visible micro-detachments along the proximal edge. The third blade fragment [4b (distal end of 4a)] displays micro-detachment and polish confined to the edges on a break, indicating working of bone/antler in a planing manner. Numbers represent the order of flaking. Drawings by Björn Nilsson.

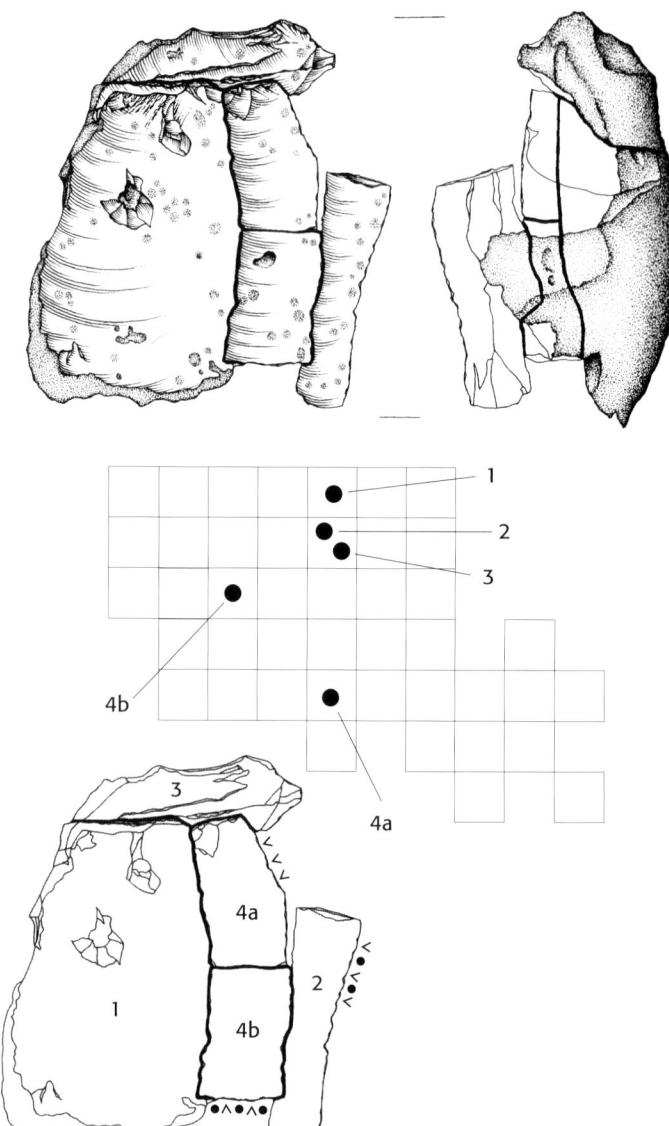

Figure 43. The refitted sequence of flakes (U. No 9). Photo by Staffan Hyll.

3 cm

e

a

b

Figure 44a–f. Refitted blade core (U. No 1).
Photo by Staffan Hyll.

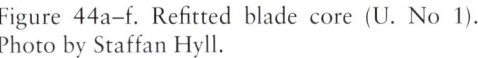
3 cm

f

c

d

Figure 45. The microburin and the micro-lith refitted to the core. Photo by Staffan Hyll. Drawings by Björn Nilsson.

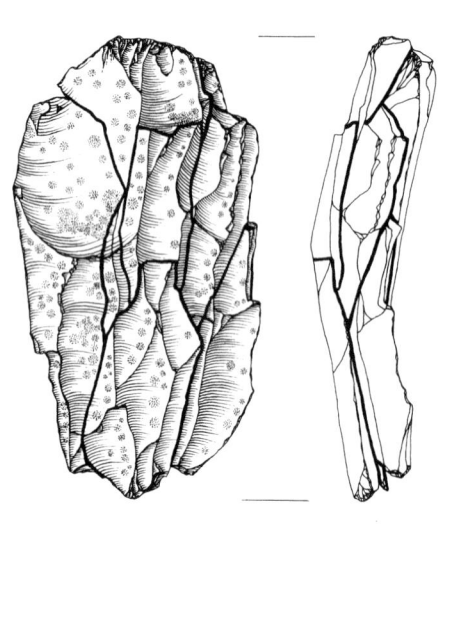

Figure 46. Sequence of a larger flake refitted with four blades and one flake (U. No 5), representing part of an opposed platform (single-face) core that was refreshed by striking the larger flake off. Drawing by Björn Nilsson.

blade scraper fitting the ventral side of the double scraper (fig. 49). Furthermore, a flake scraper can be refitted with a flake (U. No 24), with the ventral side of the flake to the dorsal side of the scraper (fig. 50). Judging by similarities in the flint structure and cortex, these two short sequences involving scrapers consist of artefacts from the same flint nodule. Several other pieces of flint, with the same characteristic, including three more scrapers, occurred on the site, and it seems quite reasonable that most of the scrapers derive from the same nodule and were produced on the site. A few more days of analysis would probably have resulted in more pieces being refitted.

To summarise, the refitting analysis has given a good glimpse of the technology practised at the site. It seems obvious to us that the flint knapper was skilled in the technological tricks of the Ahrensburgian flint-working tradition. He or she used two opposite platforms, prepared and repaired the core front, and used quite steep core angles.

Several of the groupings are very similar with respect to flint structure and cortex. A plausible interpretation is that the material derives from the working of three nodules of Kristianstad flint and one of Senonian flint at the most. Several sequences are rather short, however, and many blades cannot be fitted into sequences at all. This state of affairs

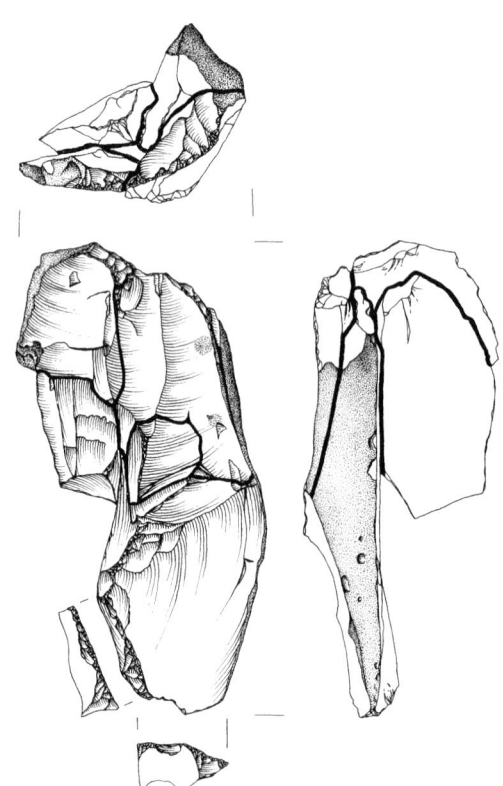

Figure 47. A refitted sequence of Senonian flint (U. No 4). Note the faceted and finely retouched ("prepared") platform remnants. Drawing by Björn Nilsson.

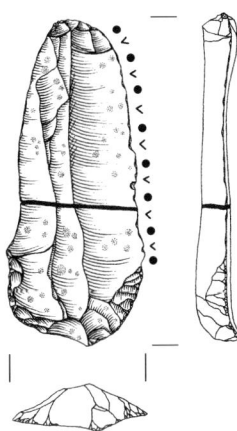

Figure 48. Blade scraper refitted from two fragments (U. No 8) with the distribution of use-wear indicated. Drawing by Björn Nilsson.

along the edges, with occasional striations indicating that some hides were fresh or at least moistened (see fig. 51). Two scrapers have only generic polish confined to the edge with a soft rounding not possible to assign to material, indicating light use and short duration. A fair guess, though, is that they

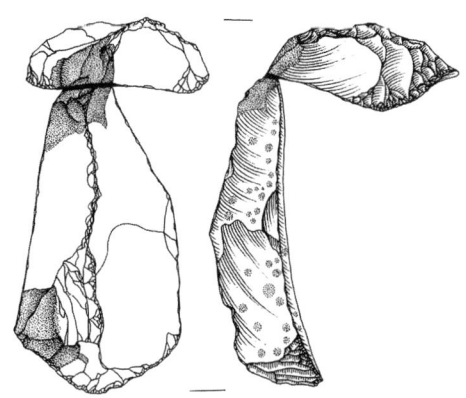

Figure 49. Sequence including two scrapers (U. No 12). Drawing by Björn Nilsson.

suggests that some blades may have been imported to the site, but also that many blades produced on the site were subsequently taken away. Moreover, the spatial distribution of the refitted pieces correlates with the results from the spatial distribution based on the total number of flints.

As mentioned above, use-wear analysis has been carried out on the material and some results have already been commented on. In total, 76 pieces of flint were analysed for traces of use-wear. Of these 39 show no signs of having been used at all, 34 pieces display use-wear indicating the material worked and/or the function, and 3 pieces display use-wear that is not possible to assign to either material or function (for details see Nilsson 2005).

All formal scrapers were analysed for traces of use-wear. Of these two display no use-wear whatsoever, probably representing re-sharpened edges. Four scrapers have been used for hide working. The polish on these scrapers is evenly distributed

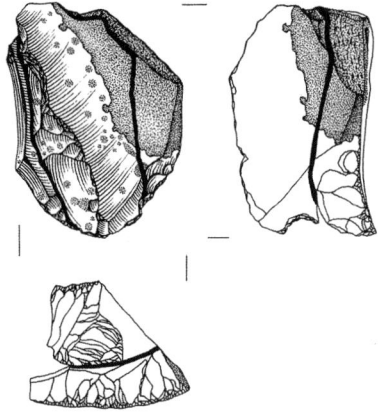

Figure 50. Sequence including a scraper and a flake (U. No 24). Drawing by Björn Nilsson.

too were used on hides, possibly in combination with wood. A large flake scraper shows polish confined to the higher parts of the micro-topography, with several striations perpendicularly oriented to the edge (fig. 52), indicating working of harder organic material such as antler/bone. A fragmented blade scraper displays polish confined to the edge, mostly on the higher parts of the surface, and small striations a little way up on the ventral side of the edge. Moreover, a soft rounding of the edge is visible (fig. 53). Taken together, these attributes indicate that the scraper was used to work harder organic material such as wood, possibly in combination with hide, considering the rounded edge.

Not only were all the scrapers subjected to use-wear analysis, so too all the microliths. As mentioned earlier, a few microliths display traces of use-wear indicating that they had been used as awls or pricking tools. This is indicated by micro-detachments and generic polish confined to the pointed edge. Moreover, two of the microliths (fig. 34:16–17) display explicit signs of having been hafted (see example in fig. 54). Judging by the position of the wear traces, these pieces have not been any longer and should be considered as intact.

The microliths thought of as having functioned as points and barbs on arrows display no traces of use-wear whatsoever, with one exception – the transverse arrowhead. They had obviously been discarded in an unused state for reasons unknown. One plausible interpretation could be that the more time-consuming work of preparing arrow shafts was performed before the manufacturing of microliths, which in comparison can be seen as an easier task. Therefore, it may be supposed that the microliths had to fit the arrow instead of the other way around. This could explain both the morphological variation and why seemingly perfect but never shafted microliths were left lying on the ground. The transverse arrowhead (see fig. 34:14), however, displays impact damage on the dorsal side of the edge and clearly visible striations perpendicularly oriented along the ventral surface (fig. 55), showing that it had evidently been shot.

The three formal blade knives were all analysed for use-wear as well. The result from this analysis revealed that all three knives had been used for cutting. Common features are micro-detachments and generic polish confined to the edges. One knife has the polish concentrated on the higher parts of the micro-topography, indicating contact with hard organic material. This knife also shows some horizontal striations at the distal end, indicating that it was used as a plane as well. The tool is interpreted as having been used on antler/bone in a cutting and planing manner.

Another knife displays plenty of small bifacial micro-detachments as well as several striations at an angle somewhat removed from the edge, indicating use as a butchering tool for cutting fresh meat/hide (fig. 56).

Methods

FOR MICRO-WEAR ANALYSIS

The use-wear analysis within the framework of this particular study was conducted with a modified Nikon Optihot-100S metallurgical microscope (50–200x). The study object was prepared with a detergent consisting of ethanol, water and surfactants.

The distribution and type of micro-wear found on tools in this study are shown with four symbols in connection with the drawings of each artefact. A v-sign (<) denotes the presence of double-sided micro-retouches, solid dots (●) represent ordinary polish, circles (o) generic polish, and lines (–) symbolise the occurrence of striations.

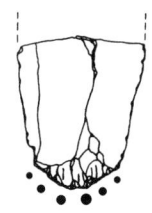

Figure 51. Use-wear (50×) on a fragmented blade scraper of Senonian flint. The polish and pronounced striations are interpreted as being caused by the processing of hides. Photo by Bo Knarrström.

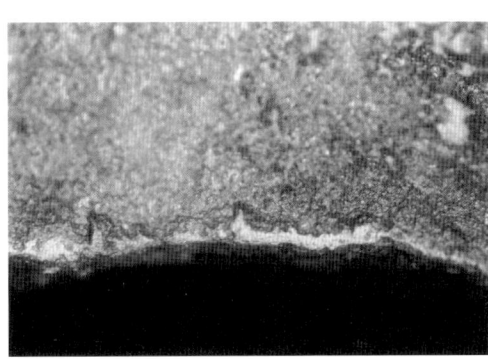
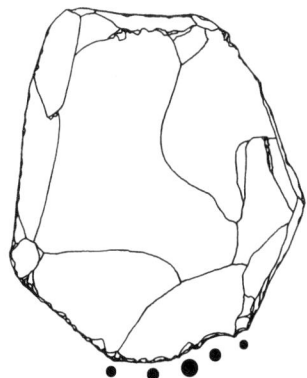

Figure 52. Use-wear (100×) on a flake scraper of Kristianstad flint. The polish has not affected the depressions in the micro-topography, thereby indicating contact with hard organic material such as bone/antler. Photo by Bo Knarrström.

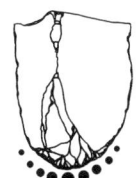

Figure 53. Use-wear (100×) on a section of an edge of a fragmented blade scraper of Kristianstad flint, indicating working of wood. The somewhat soft rounding of the edge may indicate that the scraper was used on hide as well. Photo by Bo Knarrström.

Figure 54. The base of an awl of Kristianstad flint (200×). Generic polish and small striations, probably deriving from the wood in a haft. Photo by Bo Knarrström.

Figure 55. The picture (50×) shows striations perpendicularly oriented along the ventral surface of the transverse arrowhead, probably caused by flint debris from the impact damage on the edge. Photo by Bo Knarrström.

Figure 56. Use-wear (100×) on the edge of a blade knife. The polish follows the micro-topography of the flint surface, interpreted as a result of contact with soft organic material, most likely meat/hide. Note the striations at an angle somewhat removed from the edge, which indicate that the knife had cut deep into the material. The striations are suggested to have been caused by small splinters of flint having struck into the material, thereby scratching the tool during the continued cutting (cf. Knarrström 2000a:47, 2001:43). The tool is interpreted as a butchering knife. Photo by Bo Knarrström.

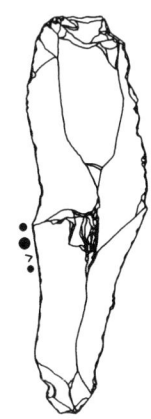

Figure 57. Use-wear (100×) on a cutting tool made of Kristianstad flint. The polish (gloss) is interpreted as caused by sturdy grass or similar plant fibres. Photo by Bo Knarrström.

Thirteen of the blades were selected for micro-wear analysis. Of these, three display no use-wear whatsoever. Two had obviously been used, indicated by micro-detachments along the edges, but are not possible to assign to either function or material. One blade displays micro-detachments along one edge and polish (gloss), which can be linked to plant material with high content of silica (fig. 57), probably some sort of sturdy grass or sedges (cf. Meeks et al. 1982:317ff). In other words, this particular tool most likely was used for cutting reed or sturdy grass.

The remaining seven blades had all been used for cutting (fig. 58). Common features for these blades are micro-detachments and polish, concentrated on what is believed to have been the active cutting edge. There are also striations running parallel at an angle somewhat removed from the edge. The polish usually follows the surface structure of the flint, thus indicating contact with soft organic material. However, sometimes the polish is combined with bifacial micro-detachments, which would imply contact with a harder material. The activity that will actually leave a combination of such use-wear is butchering of larger animals (cf. Knarrström 2000a:47, 2001:43), and our suggestion is that the blades should be interpreted as butchering knives.

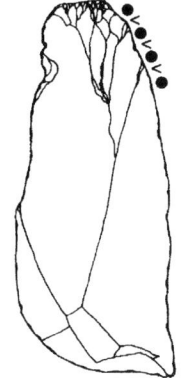
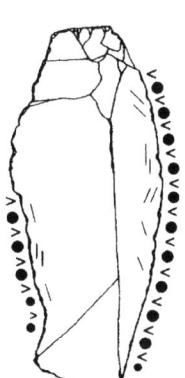
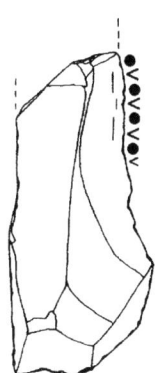

Figure 58. Examples of blades used as butchering knives.

The seven blade fragments selected for analysis all show, with one exception, traces of use-wear. Two indicate use as butchering tools and one displays micro-detachments along one of the sides and clearly visible polish confined to the edge on a break indicative of working of antler/bone. The remaining three are part of the refitted unit no. 7, and have been commented earlier.

Of nine flakes analysed, only three display traces of use-wear, two indicative of working of antler/bone and one of cutting meat/hide.

Taken together, the use-wear analysis must be considered successful, as it clearly indicates the different activities performed. Moreover, it shows that not only were the tools made at Årup, they were actually used at Årup as well. The results suggest the performance of activities such as cutting of meat/hide, scraping of hide, and working of antler/bone and wood. In addition, the use-wear analysis made it possible to identify new artefact categories which probably would not have been observed otherwise.

Regarding the spatial distribution of the artefacts subjected to use-wear analysis, a result worth noticing is that the scrapers indicative of working of hide were all concentrated in the north-eastern part of the area. Moreover, the identified awls were all concentrated in the western flint-rich area, where several pieces indicative of working of antler/bone and wood were also accumulated. The butchering tools seem to follow the inner line of the spatial distribution of the total number of flints. This is an interesting observation considering the empty area in the south-eastern central part of the site. We can imagine the big game on this area, lying butchered on the bloodstained fine-grained sand, with the butchering tools spread around the body. Moreover, a conspicuous fact is that the only shot arrowhead found on the site showing wear consistent with having been shot – the transverse arrowhead – was lying close by this area as well.

Stressing the interpretation further, the results of the use-wear analysis can be linked with the results of the refitting analysis and the spatial distribution of the finds. By doing this, a rather detailed picture of the activity zones emerge (fig. 59).

What conclusions can be drawn from Context 1? The stratigraphy provides the find material with a *terminus ante quem*, no later than *c.* 8800 BC, given by the radiocarbon date from the layer overlying the assemblage. However, as no material suitable for radiocarbon dating was found in the stratigraphical sequence of Context 1, on average 0.1 m beneath the dated layer, the finds themselves have to guide us in the dating.

In our opinion, both the technological and morphological profile of the material is based on the traditions of the late-glacial Ahrensburgian culture. The flints show distinct archaic features and clear parallels to other finds of the Ahrensburgian culture in north-west Europe (e.g. Rust 1943, 1958; Taute 1968; Tromnau 1975; Jöris & Thissen 1995; Johansen & Stapert 2000). The context comprises several well-known attributes and key artefacts, such as opposed platform single-face cores with steep platform angles, microliths with features in common with Zonhoven points, a double-edged scraper, and scrapers made of sturdy blades with steep edge angles. It is also worth noting that no axes were found in the context.

Furthermore, it is worth comment that some traits in the material are common to the Federmesser tradition, which is interesting as there have been hypotheses put forward implying that the Ahrensburgian culture derived from the Federmesser tradition (e.g. Paddayya 1971).

However, the material comprises several artefacts, such as the opposed platform single-face cores, the platform cores, and different types of microliths, that have parallels in the earliest postglacial south Scandinavian material as well. To some researchers this would probably be regarded as a chronological problem, in view of the material being of Late Palaeolithic or Early Mesolithic origin. In accordance with Knarrström (2004) it is our firm conviction that this is really not a problem – the formal artefacts belong to the same cultural unit. The traditional linking of the Paleolithic/Mesolithic division to the Late Glacial/Post-Glacial transition is misleading. We believe that the traditional supra-regional definition should be given up in order to define regionally specified units instead (cf. Jöris & Thissen 1995).

The only conceivable "problem" with dating the material to the Ahrensburgian culture would, from a traditional point of view, be that the projectile inventory comprises only microlithic points and totally lacks the so-called "Ahrensburgian point" [a tanged point of moderate size which, according to the prevailing view, had the bulb of percussion at the pointed end – although this morphological attribute has proved to be less than the whole truth (Knarrström 2004:63)]. In a traditional way of looking at chronology and typology the Ahrensburgian point has always been regarded as a key artefact of the Ahrensburgian culture, and the presence has long been considered imperative for ascribing any site to this tradition (e.g. Andersson & Knarrström 1999:8; Johansen & Stapert 2000: 1). Even if Ahrensburgian sites such as Stellmoor (Rust 1943), up to the end of the Younger Dryas and the earliest Preboreal, are dominated by tanged points, different kinds of microliths were present from the beginning. Moreover, it is a fact that at many Ahrensburgian sites tanged points are rare or even absent, while different types of microliths occur in large quantities (Johansen & Stapert

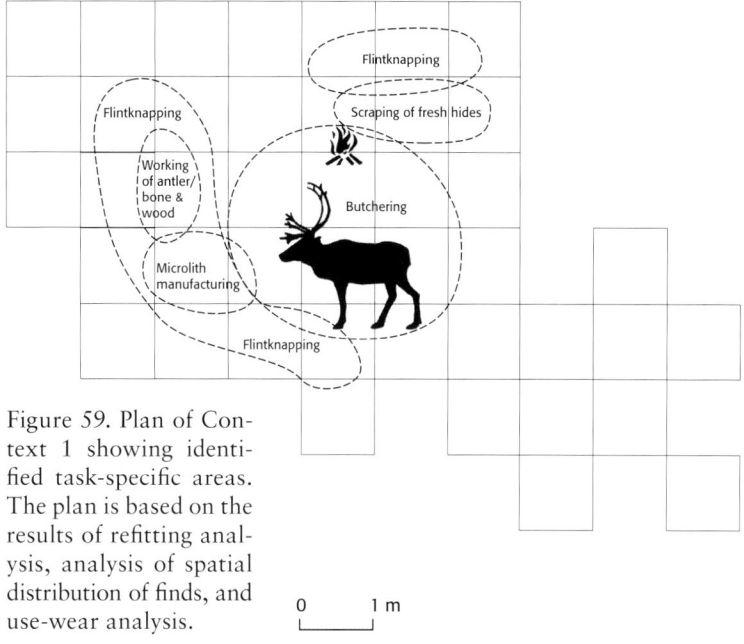

Figure 59. Plan of Context 1 showing identified task-specific areas. The plan is based on the results of refitting analysis, analysis of spatial distribution of finds, and use-wear analysis.

2000:2). Wolfgang Taute included in one of his great works several sites with only a few or no tanged points in the Ahrensburgian culture, especially because of the characteristics and archaic features of the blade technology (1968:220f). Instead of relating such sites to the Mesolithic – which many other archaeologists probably would have done – Taute suggested that this phenomenon might represent a late phase of the Ahrensburgian culture (1968:236).

Later on the term Epi-Ahrensburgian has been introduced to denote find spots in north-west Europe which have been found to contain Late Palaeolithic flint technology but where tanged points are rare or absent (Knarrström 2004:70), as in Context 1. However, we will not use this term to label Context 1. The Ahrensburgian sites that we occasionally find are very often smaller camps for hunting, butchering and perhaps fishing, representing a very short time-span. *What are the odds that only a few hours of activity would always leave traces with the whole lithic form spectrum represented in every single material?* The term Epi-Ahrensburgian focuses on one single artefact, quite regardless of the comprehensive picture and context. In our opinion, this term is yet another reflection of what we see as a general trend within archaeology, namely to put a unique definition on each deviation that is observed, instead of considering that we are in fact dealing with human behaviour, characterised by an often unpredictable variability.

Dating back to the Late Palaeolithic and the Ahrensburg culture, the site is of great archaeological value as it constitutes the first excavated site containing artefacts indicative of the culture in Scania, from where previously only stray finds were known, represented by a few points (Larsson 1996:153; Andersson & Knarrström 1999).

The Ahrensburgian culture is the last of the "classic" Late Palaeolithic cultures, preceding the Early Mesolithic. The culture is generally regarded as spanning *c.* 10,600–8900 BC, which includes the Younger Dryas, the transition to and the beginning of the Preboreal (Fischer & Tauber 1986; Vang Petersen 1993; Andersson & Knarrström 1999; Degn Johansson 2000).

As in the earlier Hamburgian and Bromme cultures, the settlement pattern of the Ahrensburgian culture seems to have been fairly complex. The excavated sites testify to family camps, sometimes isolated, sometimes several together, and smaller camps for specialised activities such as hunting and butchering. The society was probably built on the nuclear family as the centre and with multifamilies or amalgamations of several units as an alternative when hunting or when moving the settlements. The Ahrensburgian people seem to have moved over large areas of land on a seasonal basis between different sources of food. They lived in an environment consisting of tundra, park tundra, and also forest. They were mainly reindeer hunters, but did also hunt animals such as elk and wild horse and several other species as well. Moreover, it has been suggested that fishing and hunting of seal, as well as collecting, also contributed to the diet (e.g. Andersson & Knarrström 1999:100; Knarrström 2004:60). To this it could be added that the way of life of the last foraging peoples of the late-glacial period does not differ to any greater extent from the way of life of the Preboreal hunting families. They shared much the same way of life, the same material culture, and economy. The Late Palaeolithic way of life continued for hundreds of years into the Preboreal times (Knarrström 2004:69f).

Context 1 fits this Late Palaeolithic life-pattern well. Our interpretation is that the site was briefly occupied in connection with hunting activities, by only a few individuals (see landscape reconstruction in fig. 22). The flint inventory indicates a very short stay, perhaps representing just a few hours of activity. It is notable that the tools were made, used, and to a very great extent discarded and left on the site, although some artefacts were obviously carried away. Moreover, the material clearly illustrates a specific hunting situation where a big game animal, presumably a reindeer, was skinned and dismembered in order to be carried home. In addition, hunting equipment was repaired and manufactured in preparation for new hunting expeditions.

The site should probably be seen as part of a system of settlement which, in addition to considerable land masses, also included the lakes in the interior as well as the coastal region, which both could be reached via the River Skräbeån.

Irrespective of whether a more exact dating would have placed the material on this side or the other of the dividing line between the Younger Dryas and the Preboreal, or on the "right side" or the "wrong side" of the traditional dividing line between the Late Palaeolithic and the Early Mesolithic, Context 1 represents the first glimpse of behaviour and way of life in a hitherto little known and archaeologically almost invisible epoch of the Scanian Late Palaeolithic

Context 2
A HUNTING STATION IN THE TWILIGHT ZONE

Context 2 was situated in the north-eastern part of the investigation area, close by the fossil Skräbeån river bank, approximately 5–5.3 m above present sea level. The context was observed as a cultural deposit, approximately 0.1–0.3 m thick, consisting of greyish-brown fine-grained sand containing large amounts of knapped flint covering an area of approximately 26 m². Artefacts were also found in the underlying subsoil, indicating action by post-depositional processes. The deposit was partly covered by peat, which in this area was heavily decomposed and mixed with sand. The flint assemblage was primarily concentrated in an area between two naturally occurring boulders, interpreted as an activity area where flint knapping was evident.

In the eastern part of the area, a pit containing fragments of brick, slag, pottery and glass had disturbed the context. The pit, clearly of modern origin and associated with a mill pond close by, also contained flint that was judged as originating from the context of the hut and activity area.

Adjacent to the two boulders and the knapping floor, we uncovered a 5.9 m long and 1.6 m wide brownish-grey colouring and four postholes encompassing an area of roughly 10 m². The postholes consisted of brownish-grey to blackish-grey sand with sporadic occurrences of soot, the depths varying between 0.12 and 0.34 m and the diameters between 0.20 and 0.28 m. A centrally situated concentration of soot and some fire-cracked flint, measuring approximately 0.6 m in diameter and 0.06 m in depth, was seen as the remains of a hearth.

The structure which had clearly been erected in relation to the water was oval in form and oriented in a SW–NE direction. In the longitudinal direction of the hut floor, two separate blackish-grey colourings were distinguishable. The thickness of

Hard facts
OF CONTEXT 2

In total 3,552 pieces or 5,984 g of flint are associated with the context. Of these, 1,518 pieces or 1,512 g are burnt. The assemblage is dominated by 3,448 pieces or 5,866 g of Kristianstad flint, while 104 pieces or 118 g are of Senonian flint. Divided into categories, the assemblage comprises 1,392 flakes, 1,119 splinters, 103 blades and blade fragments, 33 microblades, 11 cores, 3 rejuvenation flakes, 11 formal scrapers, 2 formal knives, 4 formal borers, 1 flake axe, 1 combination tool, 10 microliths, 7 microburins, 3 worked pieces, and 849 other flints.

the floor deposit varied between 0.02 and 0.15 m, the thickest part appearing in the south-western section in which direction the inclination of the slope was steeper. This observation indicates that the floor had been counter-sunk into the slope in order to make the hut floor more level.

Taken together, the context is interpreted as the remains of a windbreak with a preserved floor deposit and an opening facing an activity area/knapping floor to the south.

Context 2 was well preserved. However, the vertical distribution of the artefacts spanning approximately 0.3 m indicated that the site had been subjected to turbating activities dispersing the artefacts in a vertical direction. Given the permeable quality of the subsoil at the site, the processes responsible for the vertical dispersion can be explained by frost heaving as well as bio-turbation, in the form of the action by roots and burrowing rodents (cf. Fischer 1990:35f).

Artefact categories such as flakes, blades, microblades, and splinters made primarily of the locally

Figure 60. Context 2 during excavation. Note the colouring between the two boulders. Photo by Conleth Hanlon.

derived Kristianstad flint dominate the flint assemblage. Only a limited amount consists of formal tools. The material displays considerable variations in quality, from a coarse to a fine texture. To a very limited extent, the inhabitants had used Senonian flint, a fact indicating essential reliance on local procurement of lithic raw material.

The flint material is well preserved and no signs of water rolling or wind polishing are evident, indicating that the material had been covered by windblown sand very soon after abandonment. Parts of the material display colour patination most likely caused by secondary inundation and peat growth (cf. Vang Petersen 1993:31).

Weathering and partial crushing of the natural surfaces of some of the knapped flint indicate that secondarily deposited moraine flint was the main source of raw material. The Kristianstad flint was most likely collected in the vicinity of the knapping site. The Senonian flint, naturally occurring

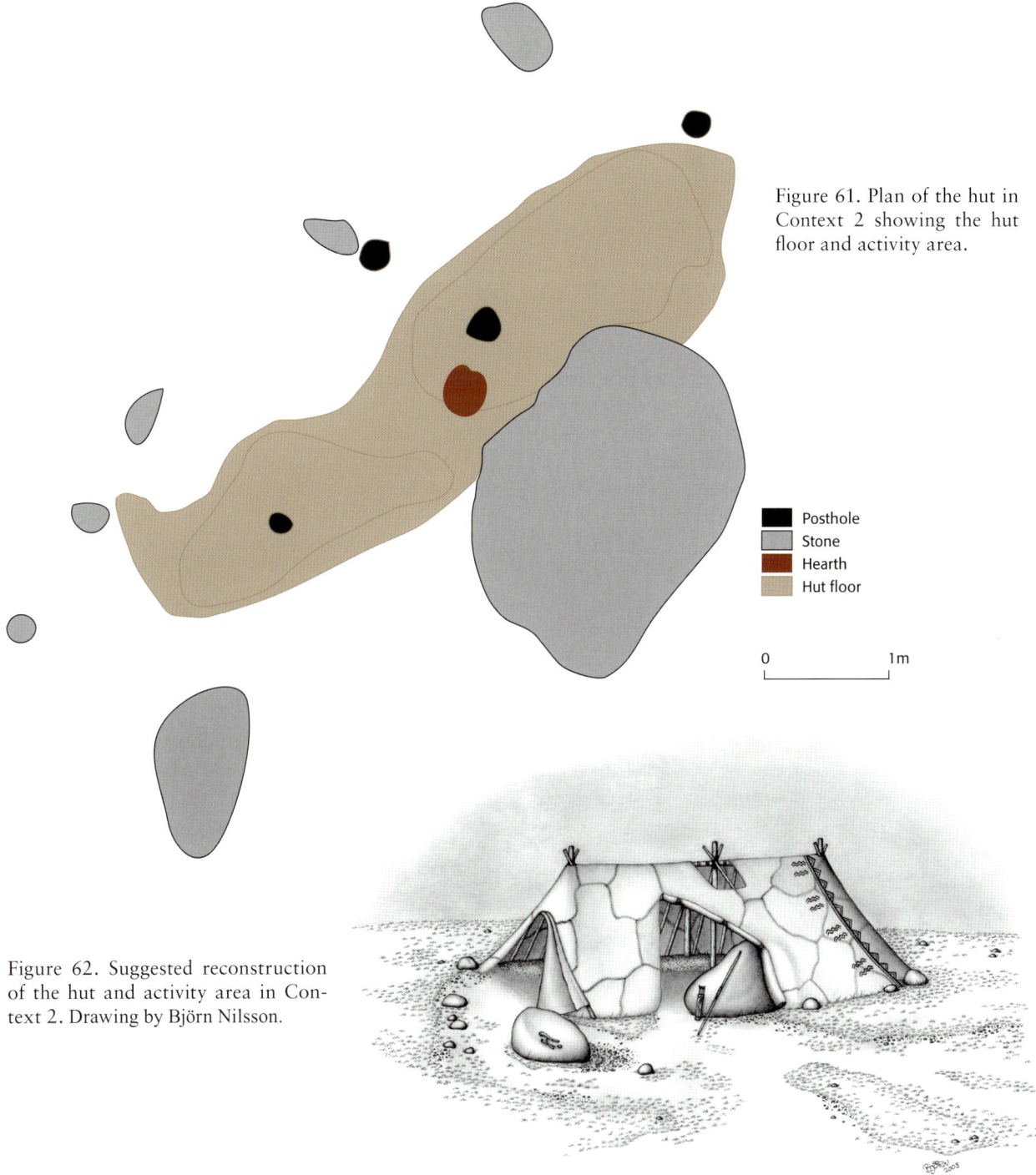

Figure 61. Plan of the hut in Context 2 showing the hut floor and activity area.

■ Posthole
▧ Stone
■ Hearth
▧ Hut floor

0   1m

Figure 62. Suggested reconstruction of the hut and activity area in Context 2. Drawing by Björn Nilsson.

in the south-western part of Scania and Zealand (Knarrström 2000a:26, 2001:20ff), must have been imported to the site.

Generally, secondarily deposited moraine flint is of much poorer quality than primarily deposited flint, as moraine flint to a large extent has been subjected to mechanical damage and weathering. Frost fractures and cracks therefore make these flints less suitable for advanced flint knapping (cf. Whittaker 1997:70; Knarrström 1999:9f). As parts of the flint from the context had been subjected to frost weathering before being worked, it was clearly of inferior quality.

The flint assemblage is characterised by simple flaking technology. The greater part of the material is crudely worked, as evidenced by the irregular shape of the cores, blades, microblades, and flakes. In addition, the blades and flakes are characterised by pronounced bulbs of percussion and larger rhomboid platform remnants, some with completed ring cracks, indicating direct hard hammer percussion technique (cf. Knarrström & Wrentner 1996; Whittaker 1997:14f; Eriksen 2000:42; Knarrström 2000a:27ff, 2001:24ff; Sørensen 2001).

However, there is an element of blades with smaller rhomboid platforms and not so distinct bulbs of percussion, as well as platforms of other shapes. This variability can be explained in terms of the size and hardness of the hammerstones used (cf. Context 1). Regarding the predominantly irregular shape of the blades and the microblades, some of these just barely fit the traditional definition of a blade, that is, a flake that is more than twice as long as it is wide, with more or less parallel edges (e.g. Crabtree 1972; Andrefsky 1998). Rather, these blades can be more correctly described as blade-like flakes or blade-flakes (cf. Whittaker 1997:33). However, from the point of view of manufacturing and function there are no differences between the two types (cf. Karsten & Knarrström 2003:139ff).

The hammerstones associated with Context 2 consist of secondarily used exhausted flint cores. These confirm the use of direct hard hammer percussion technique on the site, but do not exclude the use of antler punchers. Furthermore, the major part of the material displays no evidence of trimming of the platforms, a fact that can be explained by use of expedient technology, in turn possibly indicating a good supply of flint, although of rather poor quality. On the other hand, there is a minor element of faceted and in instances finely retouched platform remnants present in the material. Chronologically, these attributes have been suggested as characteristic of the Late Palaeolithic Federmesser culture (cf. Fischer 1988:17f; Fugl Petersen 1994; Degn Johansson 2000:31; see also Context 1). This is not to say that the material in question represents the Federmesser tradition, but the presence of these attributes could indicate that older traits are represented in the flint assemblage.

The cores from the context are irregularly shaped and maximally exhausted. The principal way of working the cores was by unipolar or polygonal reduction. Some of the cores are so fragmented that it is impossible to decide the primary type of reduction. The blades present in the context are also primarily produced by unipolar reduction. A small conical and irregular microblade core is worth special mention (fig. 63:2). This type is generally seen as characteristic of the early part of the Early Mesolithic, but appears sporadically in Late Palaeolithic contexts as well (e.g. Vang Petersen 1993:58).

Regarding the formal artefact categories, a small symmetrical side-trimmed flake axe deserves special comment (fig. 63:1). The axe in question is of a shape primarily seen as a key artefact of the Late Mesolithic. However, flake axes are also known from very early Maglemose contexts, such as the Barmose site on Zealand (cf. Degn Johansen 1990). Although these early flake axes often display a

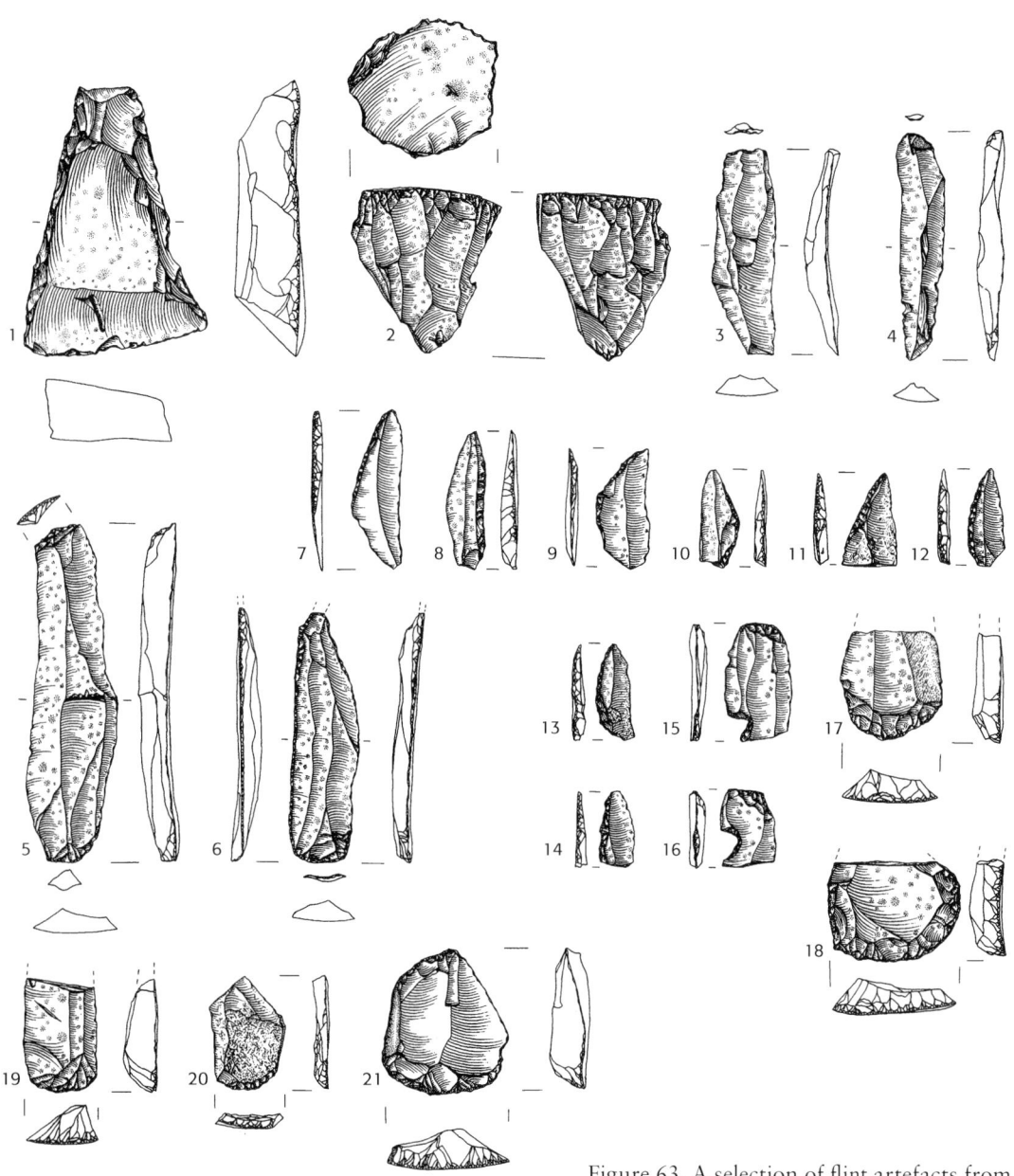

Figure 63. A selection of flint artefacts from Context 2 and the knapping floor. 1: Flake axe. 2: Core. 5: Blade knife. 6: Borer. 7–14: Microliths. 15–16: Microburins. 17–21: Scrapers. Drawings by Björn Nilsson.

Figure 64. A fellow archaeologist sitting on the same small boulder as a flint knapper 11,000 years before him. Photo by Sven Waldemarsson.

superficial likeness to core axes due to their thickness, narrowness, parallel or convex sides, flat-trimming, and side trimming, there are also specimens with diverging side-trimmed sides like the one from Context 2.

The introduction of the flake axe has long been seen as the event that distinguishes the Early Mesolithic from the Late Palaeolithic. It seems that the introduction of the flake axe has been perceived largely as a cultural adaptation to the spreading of the forest, beginning in the Preboreal (e.g. Fischer 1978; Vang Petersen 1993:13). Assigning contexts containing flake axes to the Late Palaeolithic has long been taboo, perhaps because it has been difficult to explain the presence of flake axes in the absence of expanding forests. Thanks to use-wear analysis we today know that flake axes were used to perform a vast variety of activities other than chopping wood (cf. Knutsson 1982; Juel Jensen 1988; Forsström 1996). Essentially this means that the flake axe could have been introduced before the development of wooded areas with other primary functions. It was not long ago that the presence of flake axes in the Hensbacka Culture in western Sweden was recognised, a culture which today is regarded as Late Palaeolithic (Fischer 1993; Kindgren 1996; Nordqvist 1997; Knarrström 2000b:152, 2004:61; Larsson 2001:26).

The scrapers in Context 2 consist of small flake scrapers as well as a few fragmented blade scrapers. Morphologically these correspond well with both Late Palaeolithic and Early Mesolithic typology (cf. Vang Petersen 1993:68).

Of the few borers found, one fragmented blade borer displays full retouching along one edge and partial retouching on the opposite edge. However, it is worth special attention that it exhibits a zinken-like retouch at the distal end of the blade (fig. 63:6).

The finds of microburins constitute evidence of on-site production of microliths. The blades were notched on one side and then snapped off at the narrowest part. That this was not always successful is illustrated by the microburin in figure 63:16. The microliths from Context 2 can primarily be classed as simple lanceolates, some of which display heavy retouching. This type of microlith is characteristic of Early Mesolithic contexts, but is also common during the Late Palaeolithic (cf. Vang Petersen 1993:84; Taute 1968).

On both technological and morphological grounds, the material from Context 2 can be dated to the transitional period between the Late Palaeolithic and the Early Mesolithic. The technological attribute analysis has shown that the lithic technology practised undoubtedly falls within the variation range of a South Scandinavian Late Palaeolithic/Early Mesolithic techno-complex. The question of whether the material should be considered Late Palaeolithic or Early Mesolithic is irrelevant, as we do not see the transition as a static dividing line. However, in our opinion the material has much more in common with a Late Palaeolithic, rather than an Early Mesolithic techno-tradition. What is regarded as the Early Mesolithic and the Maglemosian culture is in fact made up of at least two totally different traditions, the early part being of a Late Palaeolithic tradition and the later part being of a more specialised Mesolithic tradition with the introduction of an advanced microblade technology and high-quality production of regular blades (cf. Karsten 2004).

The major part of the flint was concentrated in the activity area in front of the opening of the hut between the two boulders. By the smaller of the two boulders, a concentration of unburnt flint of the same type and quality was found, giving rise to the idea that a flint knapper could have used the boulder as a seat while working the flint.

The finds of five cores at the northern side of the boulder further strengthen the notion of the presence of a flint knapper. If we picture a right-handed flint knapper sitting on the smaller of the two boulders, facing the north-east, the core will be held in the left hand with the right hand striking it. Consequently the cores are likely to be dumped on the left-hand side when exhausted and the flakes will naturally end up in front of and somewhat to the right of the knapper (cf. Newcomer & Sieveking 1980; Fischer 1990:39). The highest incidence of burnt flint was concentrated in an area between the two boulders, in all probability indicating that a hearth was located there, although no soot or charcoal was observed in this connection. On the other hand, the concentration of flint can also be seen as the result of dumping of flint waste produced elsewhere. Nevertheless, the most probable explanation is that we are dealing with an activity area and a hearth situated in front of the opening of the hut, where the main part of the flint knapping was performed. Formal artefact categories recovered from the knapping floor are: lanceolates, microburins, scrapers, a knife, borers (one of which could be characterised as zinken-like), cores, and a flake axe.

The spatial distribution of the flint in the hut floor was clearly defined by a marked decrease in intensity at the northern limit of the floor. Towards the activity area, the finds were more evenly distributed and it was not possible to distinguish clearly between the finds from the floor and the activity area. This indicates that the hut construction and the activity area in front of it should be interpreted as one context in use contemporaneously. The striking similarities seen in the flint assemblage regarding choice of material, artefacts, and flint waste further strengthen this assumption.

The flint material from the hut floor is dominated by informal artefact categories such as flakes, blades, and splinters primarily concentrated in the western part of the hut. Apart from the centrally placed hearth, a concentration of burnt flint was also found in the western part of the hut floor, possibly indicating the presence of yet another hearth. Formal artefact categories present in the hut were lanceolates, microburins, scrapers, a knife, borers, cores, and a microblade core.

Apparently, there were no obvious differences in the spatial distribution of the formal categories between the hut and activity area. However, the frequency of some of the categories differed somewhat between the two areas, pointing to some interesting

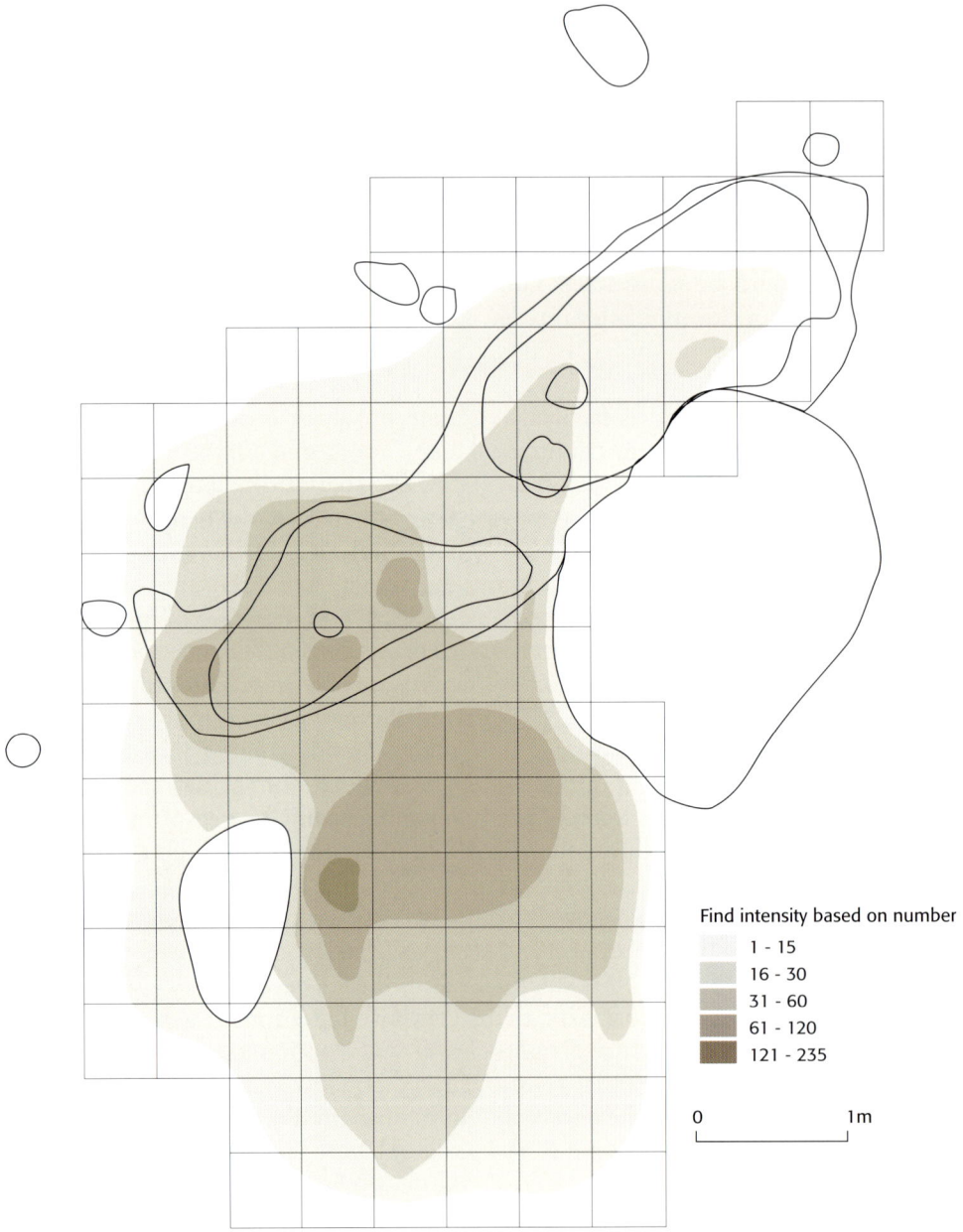

Find intensity based on number

- 1 - 15
- 16 - 30
- 31 - 60
- 61 - 120
- 121 - 235

0   1m

Figure 65. Distribution of total amount of
flint in Context 2 based on number.

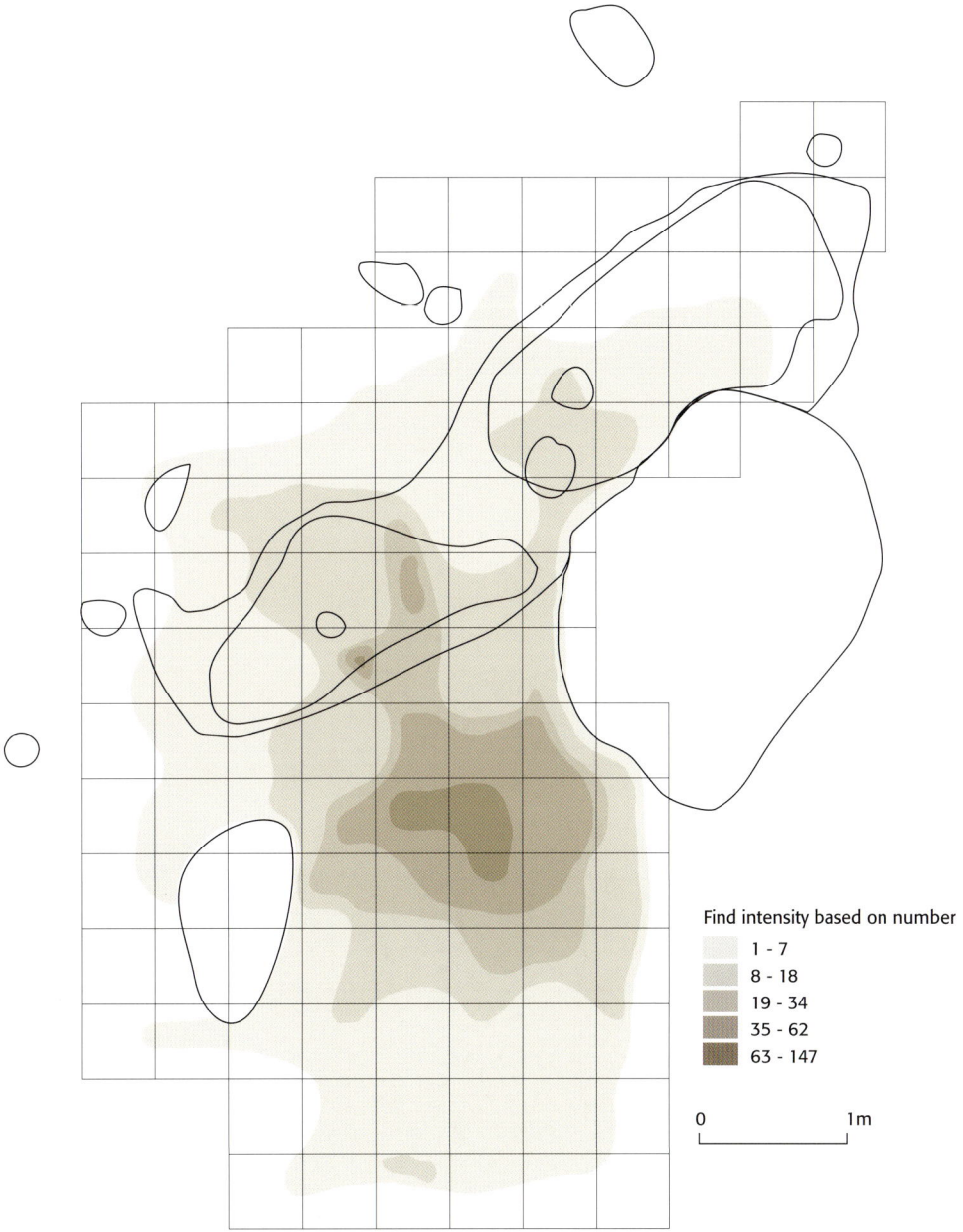

Figure 66. The spatial distribution of burnt
flint in Context 2 based on number.

Find intensity based on number

1 - 7
8 - 18
19 - 34
35 - 62
63 - 147

0　　　　　　　1m

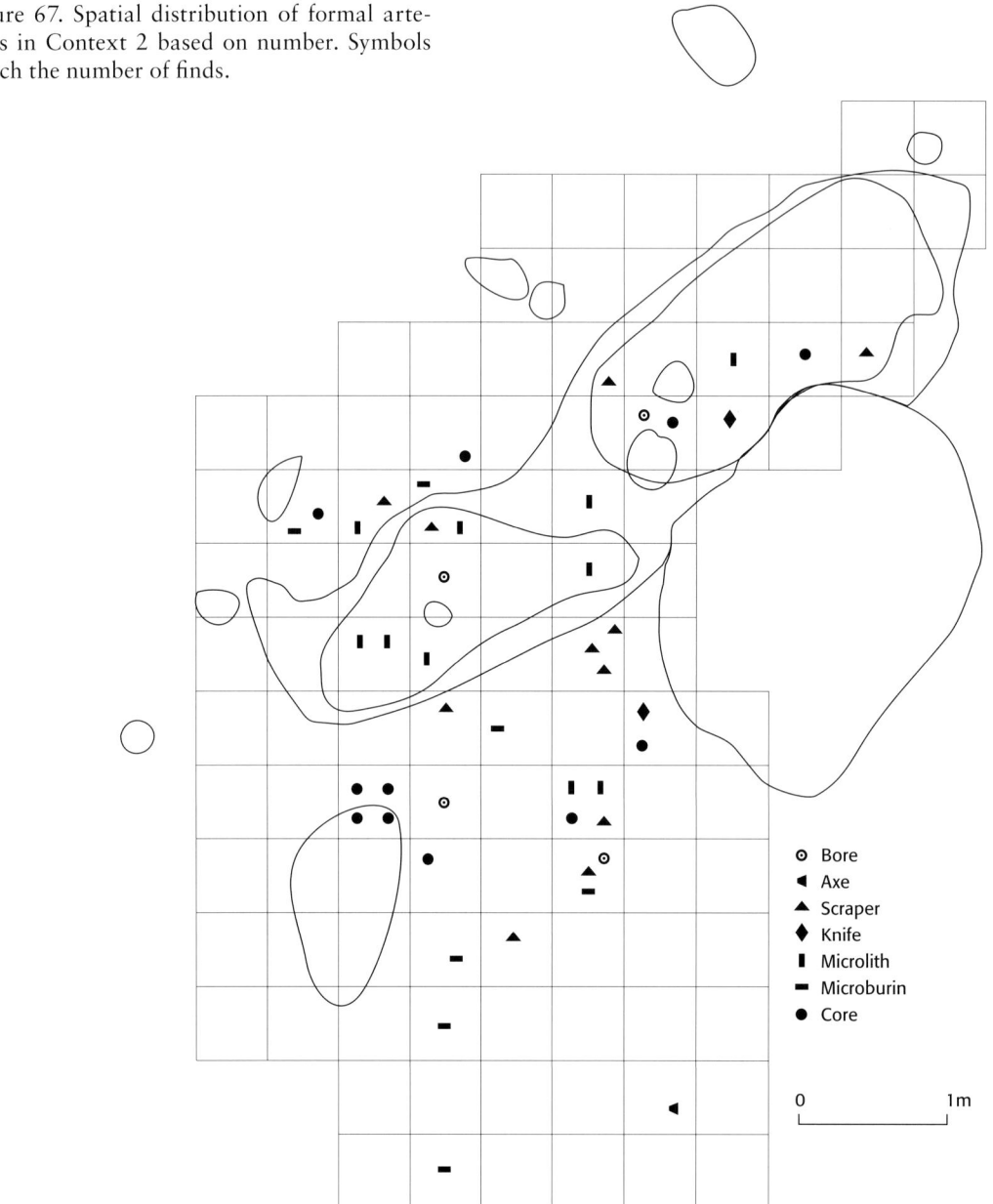

Figure 67. Spatial distribution of formal artefacts in Context 2 based on number. Symbols
match the number of finds.

⊙ Bore
◀ Axe
▲ Scraper
♦ Knife
▮ Microlith
▬ Microburin
● Core

0   1m

Figure 68. Plan illustrating the distribution of pieces of flint possible to refit in Context 2. Note the connection between the hut floor and the activity area proving contemporaneity. Eight of the nine units most likely belong to the same core judging by similarities in distinctive features such as flint quality, colour, texture, and cortex. The ninth unit (U. No 9), which consisted of two microburins, deviates in colour and quality, so it cannot with any greater degree of certainty be associated with the other units.

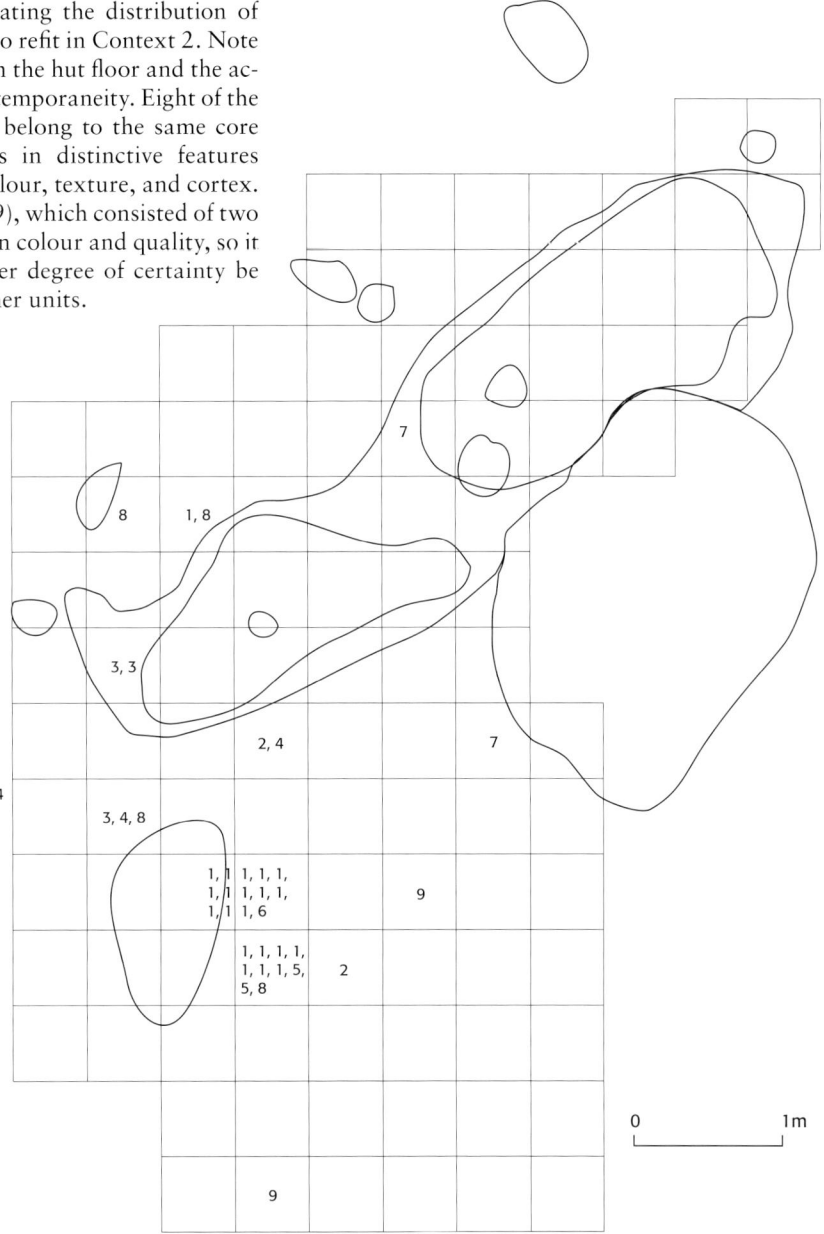

results. Of the total ten microliths associated with the hut and activity area, eight were found in the western part of the hut floor. That microliths were actually made on site was evidenced by microburins found together with the microliths, in both the hut and the activity area. However, five of the total seven microburins were found in the activity area close by the smaller boulder, indicating the primary place of microlith manufacture. The concentration of microliths found in the hut floor is taken as evidence of retouching and/or shafting or re-shafting of microliths inside the hut.

An interesting observation was that the technology practised inside the hut was of a much finer character than that of the knapping floor. This may indicate that the primary knapping took place in the activity area and the secondary knapping, entailing the finer and more detailed handicraft, was performed inside the hut.

Another category displaying differences in distribution was formal scrapers. The majority of these were also found in the activity area, which contained seven of the total eleven scrapers. Five of these were grouped by the larger boulder and opening of the hut, indicating the primary place of activities involving scrapers. In this connection the boulder may very well have functioned as a back-rest.

In conclusion, the flint assemblage displayed a high degree of similarity between the hut floor and the activity area regarding the categories represented. However, differences become evident from studying the frequencies of distribution, especially noticeable regarding the microliths, microburins, and scrapers.

The authors spent one week refitting flints from Context 2. A total number of 41 individual pieces were refitted into nine units consisting of two or more pieces, primarily constituting parts of flake cores (fig. 68). The largest unit (U. No 1) is the better part of a rather large and chunky flake

3 cm

Figure 69. The refitted core from the knapping floor. Photo by Staffan Hyll.

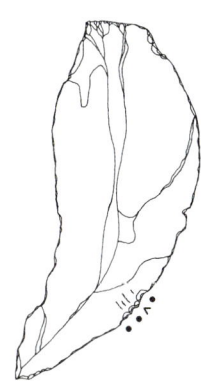

Figure 70. The retouched flake from the hut floor of Context 2, which was used in a planing/scraping movement on bone, refitted to the core from the activity area, thereby showing that the two areas were in use contemporaneously. Photo by Staffan Hyll. Drawing by Björn Nilsson.

core made up of 21 pieces of rather poor-quality of Kristianstad flint (fig. 69). At the other end of the scale are two microburins refitted into a notched blade.

The majority of the refitted units (U. No 1–8) are made of the same type of flint and display similar distinctive features as regards quality, colour, texture, and cortex as the flake core, indicating that the units belong to this. However, it was not possible to fit these to the core, obviously showing that crucial pieces are missing or have not been identified. The spatial distribution of the refitted pieces demonstrates that the flint knapping was concentrated in the activity area and especially at the smaller boulder.

A fascinating discovery was that in four instances there is a match in fit between flints from the hut floor and the activity area (U. No 1, 3, 7 and 8). One of these is a retouched flake found in the hut floor, which fits on to the core (fig. 70), clearly illustrating that flakes produced on site also had been used as tools. Use-wear analysis showed that the flake had been used in a planing/scraping movement on bone. These facts provided the link between the activity area and the hut construction, showing that they had been in use contemporaneously.

Furthermore, the analysis provided insight into the technological aspects of the flint knapping practised on site. Judging by the refitted flake core as well as the other refitted units, the knapping technique can be characterised as crude. Large, irregularly shaped thick flakes with rhomboid platform remnants display extensive crushing of the edges, clearly indicating the use of direct hard hammer percussion technique. The striking pattern observed on the refitted core shows that it had been worked from all directions and that the rather poor quality of the flint had resulted in spontaneous fracturing.

As no organic materials had been preserved in the context, the only way of throwing light upon questions regarding economy and subsistence was by use-wear analysis. In total, 34 pieces of flint were analysed for traces of use-wear. Of these, 10 pieces show no signs of having been used at all, 21 pieces display use-wear indicating the material worked and/or the function, and three pieces display use-wear which was not possible to assign to either material or function. In conclusion, the use-wear analysis indicated that bone, hide, meat, wood, and possibly antler were worked in the context of the hut.

The formal scrapers analysed show that they have been used to work bone, dry hide, fresh hide, and wood in a scraping manner. Two scrapers display wear indicative of hafting. A very interesting result is that five scrapers in front of the opening of the hut display the same type of use-wear indicative of working of bone. The fact that the individual scrapers display identical use-wear makes a strong case for these representing a singular event of bone working, perhaps performed by one person. Some of these also display use-wear indicative of scraping of bone on edges produced on a break, very much in the fashion of how a burin is used (fig. 71). One of the scrapers also displays edge-wear indicative of a cutting movement. Regarding

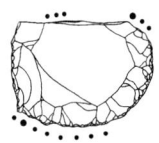

Figure 71. Example of a scraper from Context 2 with the distribution of the use-wear indicated.

the working of bone, the retouched scraping edge was most probably used in the initial phase of scraping in order to shape the object. The edge on a break was likely used in the final stage to smooth the surface of the object worked.

The flakes analysed had been used to work bone in a planing or scraping manner and in a cutting manner. The blades had been used to cut meat, hide, and wood as well as having been used on bone and wood in a scraping or planing fashion. A borer had been used to work wood, the formal flake axe had been used in a planing movement on bone, and lastly a microlith had been used as a knife on hard organic material. Whether the microlith in question functioned as an arrowhead as well is hard to tell, but is of course feasible. Secondary use of stone points as knives is known from ethnographic examples (cf. Ellis 1997:53f). Only one of the microliths displays wear indicative of shafting.

The use-wear analysis must be considered successful as it clearly illustrated that several activities were performed in the hut context. Furthermore, a most fascinating discovery was that not only were tools made on site, they were actually used on site as well. This further stresses the contemporaneity of the activities performed.

As has been demonstrated, the typological classification, which most often implies the function of an artefact, in quite a few cases differ dramatically from the function indicated by the use-wear analysis. This fact gives rise to questions regarding the function of various formal artefact categories which traditionally are interpreted as indicating a certain way of use without the aid of use-wear analysis. How representative and real are such interpretations of prehistory in reality?

Three samples of charcoal collected from the floor layer had been identified as being of pine (*Pinus silvestris*). Unfortunately, the amount of charcoal in one of the samples turned out to be insufficient for dating. The remaining two samples produced the dates of 9650 ± 140 ^{14}C-years BP in the interval 9350–8600 cal. BC and 7395 ± 60 ^{14}C-years BP in the interval 6400–6080 cal. BC with 2 sigma. The later of these dates puts the hut in the Middle Mesolithic and the Atlantic chronozone, while the earlier puts the context in the transitional period of the Late Palaeolithic and Early Mesolithic, i.e. the transition between the Younger Dryas and the Preboreal chronozones.

As mentioned earlier, Context 2 was partially covered by an organogenic deposit, which was dated to *c.* 8800 BC; accordingly the older date fits very well in the stratigraphy and chronology of the area. The later date, on the other hand, probably originates from more recent bio-turbating activities, so it is not seen as representative of the context. These facts, in combination with the flint assemblage associated with the context, without any doubt support the earlier date.

To summarise, the context is interpreted as a small settlement unit consisting of a windbreak and an adjoining activity area. The oval and symmetrical shape of the hut structure gives the impression of a well-thought-out construction. The south-western part of the long side of the windbreak was open towards the activity area and the waterside. The opening most probably had a roll-up front or a flap enabling closing of the entrance. This was primarily indicated by the limitation of the floor deposit, but also by a decrease in the distribution of finds at the southern long side of the windbreak. An opening was probably also located to the western short side, judging by the somewhat drawn-out shape of the floor and distribution of flints in this part of the hut. The eastern and larger of the two boulders constituted an integrated part of the hut, in fact making up a part of the southern wall. Since the hearth was placed close by the boulder, this most probably doubled both as a heat reflector and as radiator, reflecting and storing the heat from the fire at the same time.

Even today, this is a practised survival skill taught for example by the Swedish Army. In their survival handbook (*Handbok överlevnad* 1999:152, 176), boulders or rocks are recommended for use as heat reflectors in order to maximally utilise the heat radiation from a fire, exactly like the windbreak.

Regarding the roof-supporting posts, these are assumed to have been standing upright as no signs of a positioning of these at an angle were observed during excavation. Three of the four posts were positioned in a straight line with an equal distance between each one of them, the fourth being somewhat displaced in relation to the central post, most likely in order to create more living space. The position of the displaced post indicates a primary function of supporting the northern wall/side of the windbreak. Therefore, this post most probably was shorter than the others. In order to stabilise the construction, a ridge beam must have been placed on top of the three centrally placed roof-supporting posts. Rafters positioned at an angle against the ridge beam supported the walls/sides of the construction. Hide, a material that is tough, easy to weatherproof with grease, and easy to transport, most likely covered the windbreak. The material needed to complete the dwelling was collected locally. Allowing for the space created by the angle between the outermost posts and the covering material, the total size of the windbreak is estimated as having been approximately 6.2 m long and 2.5 m wide, encompassing an area of roughly 13.5 m².

The windbreak and the activity area have been convincingly shown to be contemporaneous, a fact supported by similarities in the flint assemblage and evidenced by refitting analysis as well as use-wear analysis.

The amount of flint associated with the context could be taken as evidence of repeated visits to the same dwelling, although the authors believe that this is not the case. Rather, the amount of flint present could have been accumulated during a very short time-span. Repeated habitation would have generated a far more voluminous amount of flint as well as a more marked diversity in the material and a less well delimited spatial distribution of finds. Furthermore, repeated habitation would have been indicated by a greater amount of features as well as disturbed structures.

The number of formal tool and artefact categories associated with the context indicated quite a varied repertoire of activities performed on the site. By linking the results of the use-wear analysis with the results of the refitting analysis and the spatial distribution of the formal artefacts, a rather detailed picture of several activity zones emerged in the context (fig. 72).

The interpretation of the results from the windbreak can be translated into the following activities:

- whittling, boring, and scraping of wood, possibly indicating manufacturing of arrow shafts;
- shafting and reshafting of microliths;
- softening of hide by scraping;
- cutting of soft organic material, possibly meat;
- working of antler/bone.

The results suggest the performance of fine handicraft and ordinary household activities, primarily concentrated in an activity zone in the south-western part of the construction. As indicated by the low intensity of finds, the northern and eastern part of the dwelling may have been used primarily for sleeping and storage purposes.

The interpretation of the results from the activity area can primarily be translated into the following activity zones:

- butchering zone, comprising the activities of scraping of hide and partitioning of meat;
- bone-working zone, comprising the activities of removing membranes and making bone tools;
- knapping zone, comprising the activities of general knapping and tool manufacturing, especially giving an on-the-spot account of a few hours in the life of a flint knapper.

The results have in common that the activities executed outside the windbreak were of a nature requiring a great deal of space, or the activity was messy, potentially smelly, or dusty. The former is primarily true of activities comprising butchering, scraping of hide, and bone working, and the latter is true of flint knapping.

In conclusion, the context is seen as a singular event of short duration, most probably representing a couple of days' stay. The activities performed in connection with this visit were undoubtedly associated with hunting. The material clearly illustrates that hunting equipment was manufactured in preparation for hunting as well as showing that killed prey was taken care of at the site. Thus, the context in question should be viewed as a hunting station occupied by no more than 2–3 people making up a task group which procured natural resources to be brought to the residential location. This all took place during a few days in the twilight zone between the Late Palaeolithic and the Early Mesolithic.

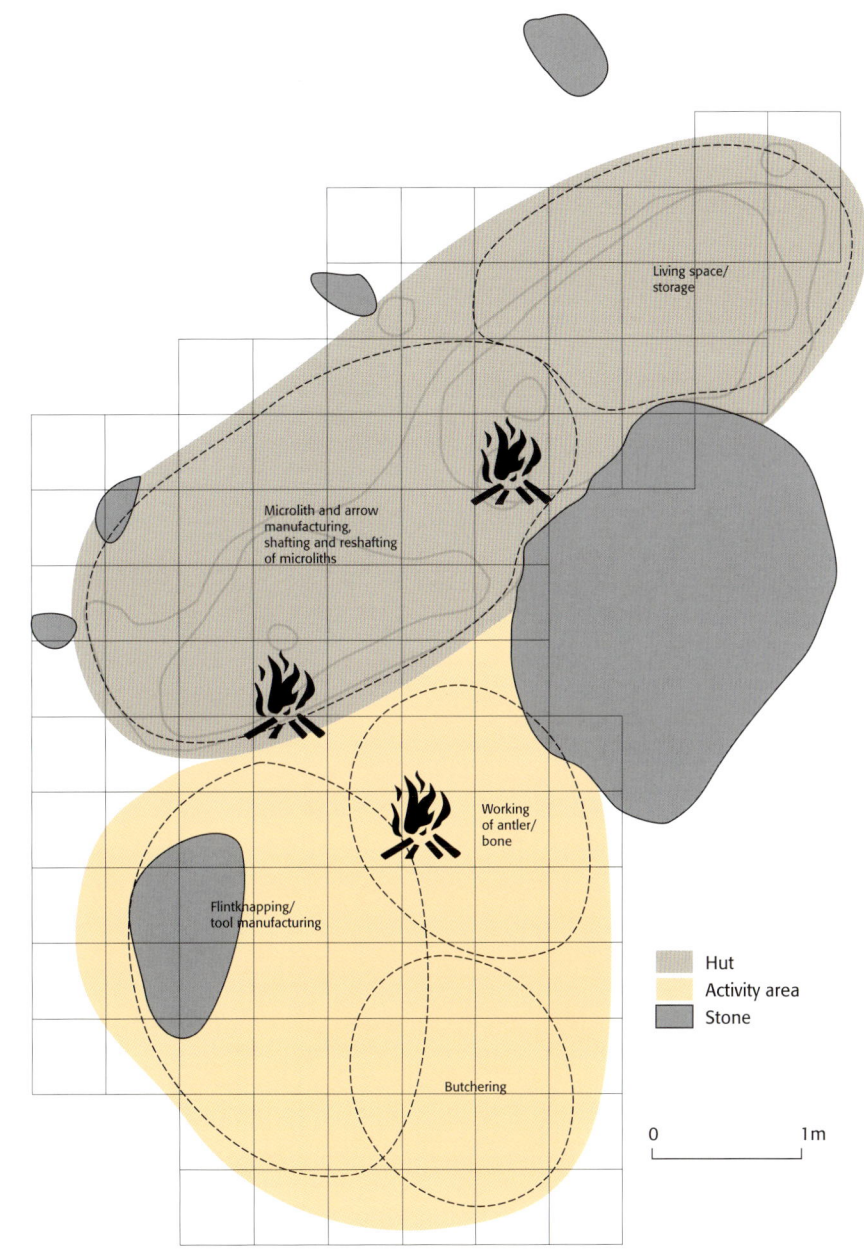

Living space/
storage

Microlith and arrow
manufacturing,
shafting and reshafting
of microliths

Working
of antler/
bone

Flintknapping/
tool manufacturing

Butchering

Hut

Activity area

Stone

0   1m

Figure 72. Plan of Context 2 showing identified task-specific areas. The plan is based
on the results from refitting analysis, use-
wear analysis, and analysis of spatial distribution of formal artefact categories.

Context 3

An Early Mesolithic field camp

Context 3 was situated in the south-eastern part of the investigation area and was initially detected by concentrations of knapped flint on a slight sandy elevation approximately 5.2 m above present sea level, close by the fossil Skräbeån river bank. The flint material appeared in an area of 30 m². Clearing by hand revealed the remains of a roughly 4.5 m long and 2.5 m wide hut consisting of four postholes, two furrows, a couple of stones and a few clay deposits encompassing an area of about 11 m². A hearth, approximately 0.4 m in diameter, containing burnt flint, soot and charcoal, was located outside the hut entrance.

The structure had clearly been erected in relation to the water and was oval in form with a WNW–ESE orientation. The postholes, the fillings of which consisted of black-greyish sand, were concentrated in the inner part of the structure. The depths varied between 0.06 and 0.20 m and the diameter between 0.15 and 0.30 m. The two furrows at the western short side of the structure were interpreted as having made up part of the wall in this section. This assumption was supported by the presence of a clearly visible posthole in the larger of the two furrows.

Three clay deposits and a couple of stones indicated the outline of the northern long side and the eastern short side. The clay deposits were slanting slightly towards the inner part of the hut. The middle part of the southern long side lacked any structural elements, indicating an open construction as well as the location of the entrance.

The inner part of the structure, delimited by the furrows, stones, and clay deposits, consisted of yellow-whitish sand and did not distinguish itself from the surrounding subsoil. In the light of this, it was somewhat uncertain whether the hut floor had been lowered or not. However, the slanting of the clay

of Context 3

In total 129 pieces or 1,318 g of flint are associated with the context. Of these, 28 pieces or 23 g are burnt. The assemblage is dominated by 104 pieces or 1,188 g of Kristianstad flint, while 25 pieces or 130 g are of Senonian flint. Divided into categories, the assemblage comprises 74 flakes, 6 splinters, 24 blades and blade fragments, 5 microblades, 5 cores, 2 rejuvenation flakes, 1 formal borer, 2 flake axes, 1 formal burin, 2 microliths, 1 strike-a-light, 1 hammerstone, and 3 other flints.

deposits indirectly indicated that this was the case. Presumably, the floor had been countersunk into the slope in order to obtain a level surface. Given this, the floor could be estimated as having been lowered by approximately 0.1–0.15 m.

The rather scanty quantity of flint is dominated by informal artefact categories such as flakes and blades made primarily of the locally derived Kristianstad flint. This type of flint varies considerably in quality, from a very coarse to a very fine and dense texture. The flint material is well preserved and no signs of water rolling or wind polishing are evident.

The cores, blades and microblades are predominantly irregular in shape. In addition, the blades and flakes are characterised by pronounced bulbs of percussion and larger rhomboid platform remnants with ring cracks, indicating direct hard hammer percussion technique (cf. Knarrström & Wrentner 1996; Whittaker 1997:14f; Sørensen 2001). This is further supported by the find of a

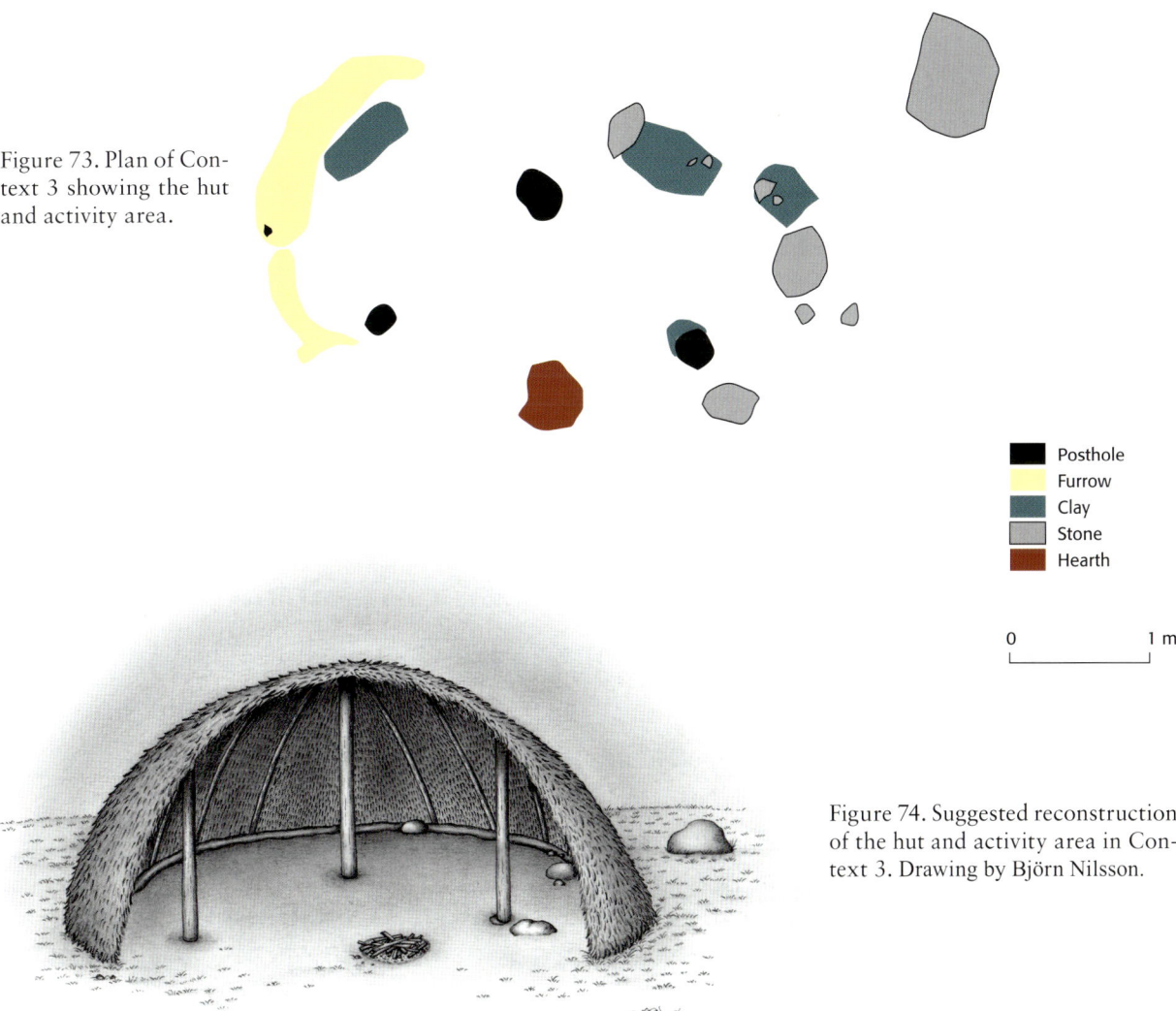

Figure 73. Plan of Context 3 showing the hut and activity area.

⬛	Posthole
🟨	Furrow
🟦	Clay
⬜	Stone
🟫	Hearth

0   1 m

Figure 74. Suggested reconstruction of the hut and activity area in Context 3. Drawing by Björn Nilsson.

Figure 75. The hut in Context 3 during excavation. Photo by Conleth Hanlon.

Figure 76. Close-up of the hearth. Photo by Conleth Hanlon.

small hammerstone of Senonian flint, made from an exhausted core.

The formal tools and artefacts found include two flake axes of which one is fragmentary, two lanceolates of which one is burnt and fragmentary, one fragmented flake borer, and one burin. Moreover, worth commenting on is a core found close to the hearth, which displays traces of use-wear on the opposite platform edges indicative of being secondarily used as a strike-a-light.

On both technological and morphological grounds the find material can be tentatively given a dating to the Early Mesolithic.

The small amount of finds present in the context of the hut may or may not be an effect of the machine stripping. However, had the context contained a much larger amount of finds these would surely have been detected early on in the process of machine stripping. Since all finds present were clearly concentrated in the area of the hut, with space devoid of finds surrounding the features, these were all associated with the dwelling.

As can be seen in figure 78 and 79, the majority of the knapped flint, burnt as well as unburnt,

was concentrated around the hearth. Flints were also found in the hearth, the furrows, and the postholes. It was not possible to identify any task-specific areas in the hut context, apart from the general flint knapping, which was concentrated to the hearth and opening of the hut. An interesting observation is that two cores were found in the larger furrow. This can be seen as the result of a wall effect where heavier objects tend to end up deposited to the sides of a dwelling.

A couple of metres to the east of the hut construction the two small flake axes, the intact lanceolate, and a few flakes and blades were found beside the fossil riverbank. These artefacts are very likely the remains of a dump zone interpreted as being contemporaneous with the hut. Taken together, the spatial distribution of flint indicates that the flint knapping took place both inside and outside the hut, but centring on the hearth and the opening.

The mere presence of the formal artefacts indicates that some task-specific activities took place in and around the hut. The exact nature of these tasks is more difficult to pinpoint, however.

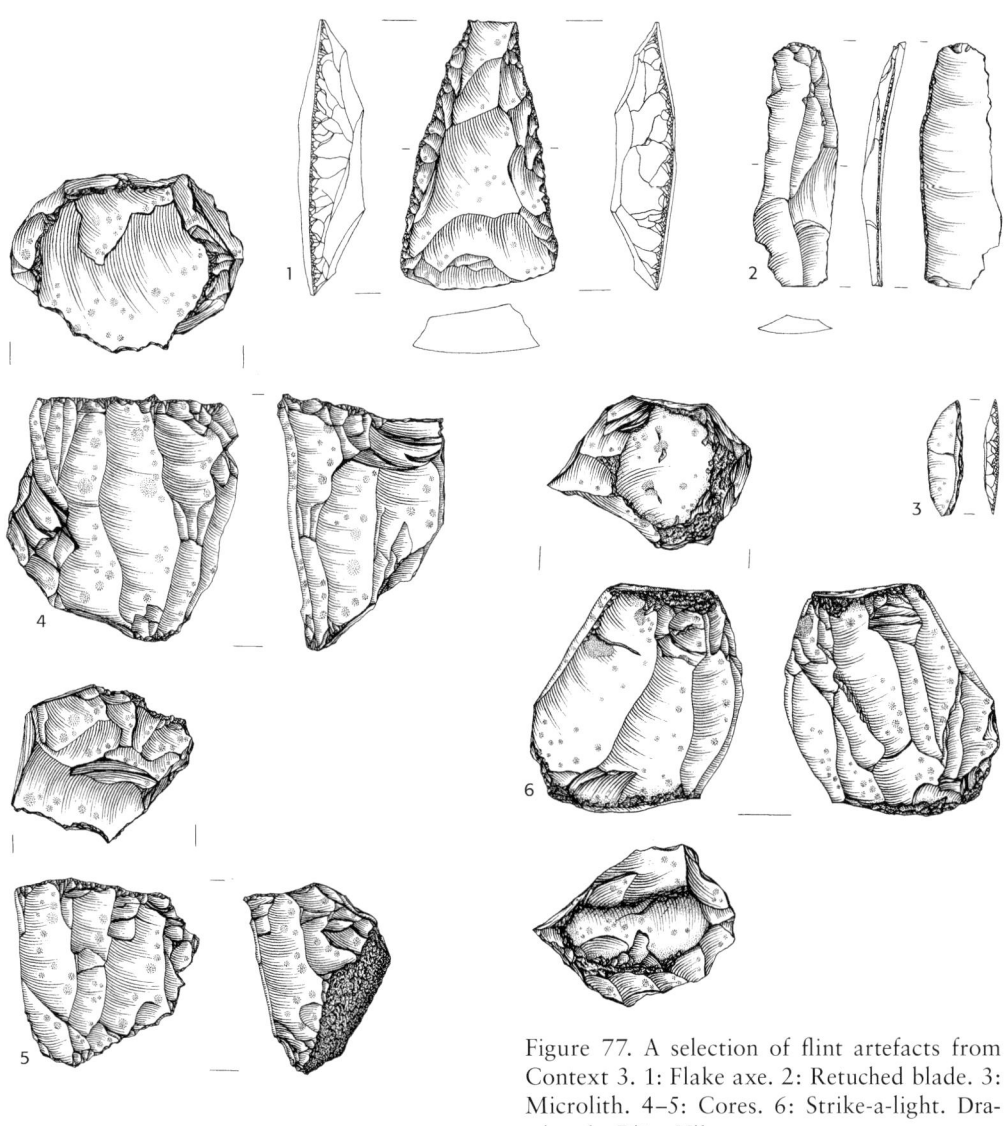

Figure 77. A selection of flint artefacts from Context 3. 1: Flake axe. 2: Retuched blade. 3: Microlith. 4–5: Cores. 6: Strike-a-light. Drawings by Björn Nilsson.

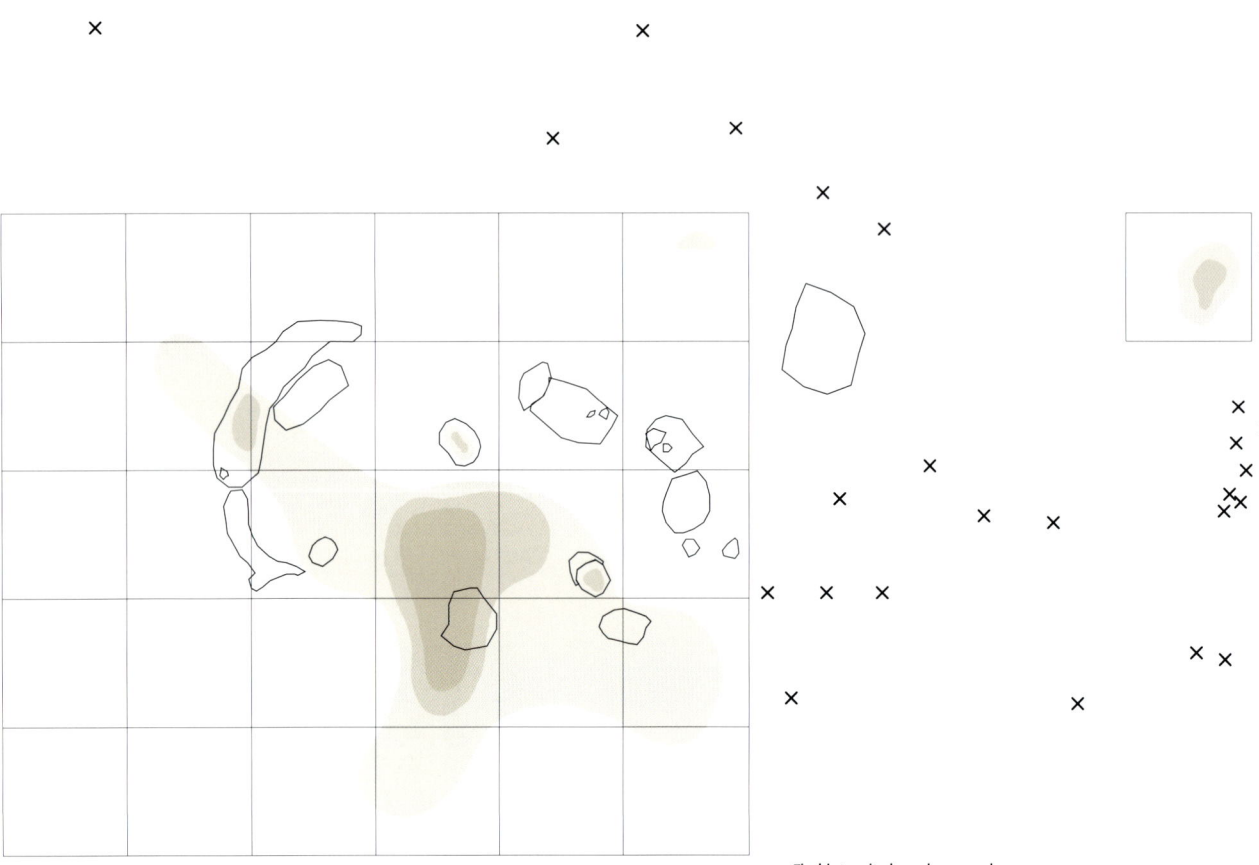

Figure 78. Distribution of total amount of flint in
Context 3 based on number.

Find intensity based on number

✕   1 (digitaly registered by total station)
     1 - 3
     4 - 10
     11 - 22

0   1 m

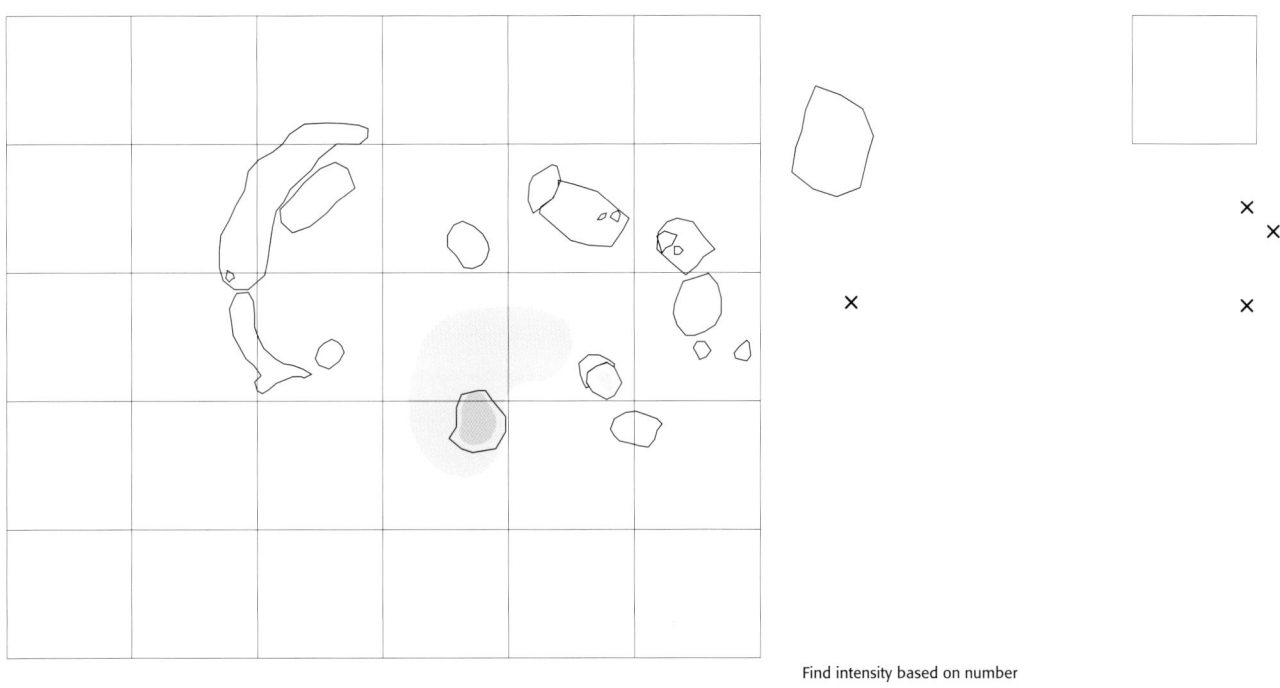

Figure 79. Distribution of total amount of burnt flint in Context 3 based on number.

0   1 m

Find intensity based on number
×   1 (digitaly registered by total station)
     1 - 3
     15

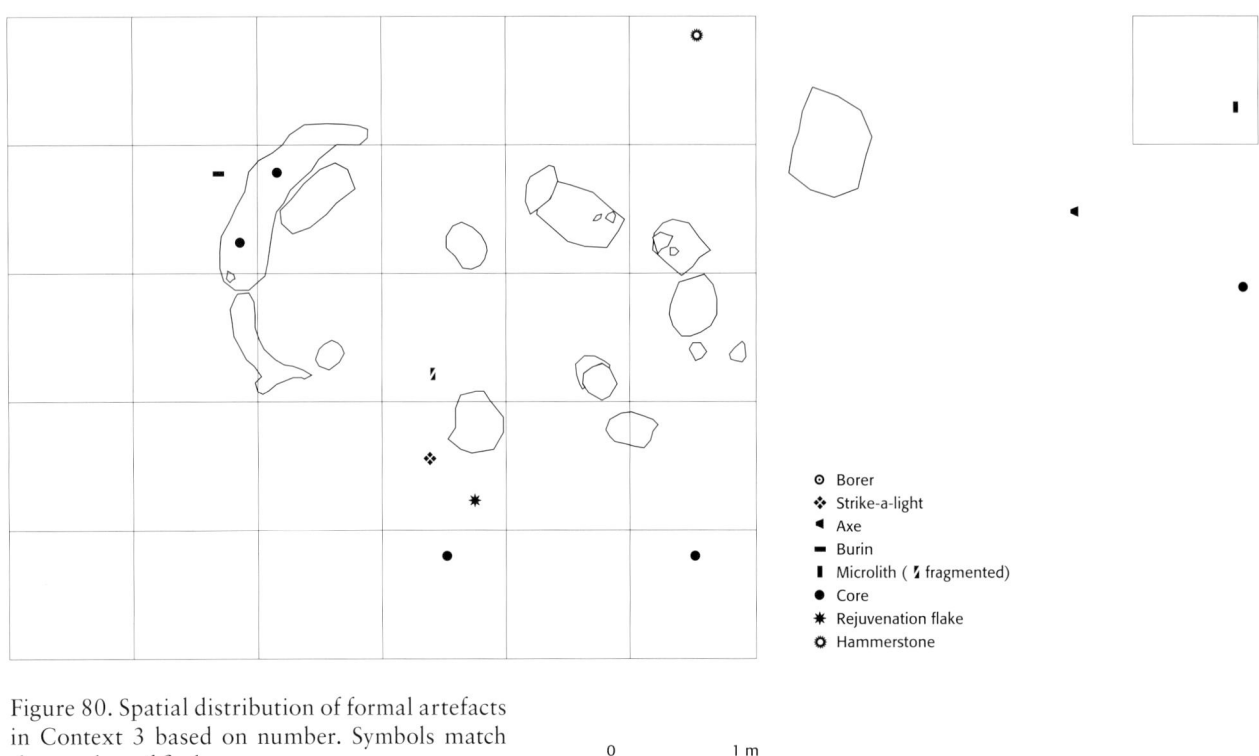

Figure 80. Spatial distribution of formal artefacts in Context 3 based on number. Symbols match the number of finds.

◉ Borer
✤ Strike-a-light
◀ Axe
━ Burin
❙ Microlith (⸺ fragmented)
● Core
✳ Rejuvenation flake
✪ Hammerstone

0   1 m

In general, flake axes can be used to chop, cut, and scrape with; lanceolates can be used to cut, bore, punch, and carve with and can be fitted as projectiles. Borers can be used to bore and punch with, and lastly burins can be used to scrape and incise with. In short, we are left with a vast range of possible uses for the formal tools found in the context of the hut. Luckily enough, the materials available to work during the Mesolithic are roughly limited to antler, bone, meat, plants, hide, and wood.

Ten pieces of flint were analysed for traces of use-wear. Only two pieces, a burin and a flake, show any signs of use. The burin displays polish and micro-detachments confined laterally to the edge indicative of contact with antler or bone in a planing movement. The flake in question displays generic polish on the ventral side of a distal break and is interpreted as having been in contact with wood in a planing movement.

The rather limited tool inventory primarily suggests woodworking and antler or bone-working. The presence of the two lanceolates in combination with the flake and burin may indicate preparation of new arrow shafts and shafting of microliths.

The intact and perfectly finished flake axe made from high-quality Kristianstad flint turned out not to have been used at all. The axe may very well have been deliberately deposited in an unused state by the water to the east of the hut just because it was an unusually nice specimen out of the ordinary. Compared to the fragmented flake axe, which was of a much sturdier design and made from Kristianstad flint of inferior quality, this was apparently used until it broke and was then simply discarded on the ground. Clearly, there is a difference in how these two objects were viewed and treated.

Since the hut construction was found beneath an organogenic deposit dated to *c.* 8800 BC, the construction theoretically should be older than that age. However, as the dated samples were not taken from the peat deposit straight above the hut construction, but from a section south of it, where the peat and gyttja deposit was considerably thicker and possibly older, it could not be entirely ruled out that the hut was in fact somewhat younger.

This assumption turned out to be correct. Two samples of charcoal collected from the hearth and the furrow had been identified as being of pine (*Pinus silvestris*) before being radiocarbon dated. Unfortunately, the amount of charcoal from the furrow turned out to be insufficient for dating. However, the dating of the sample from the hearth showed that the hut had an age of 8980 ± 80 ^{14}C-years BP in the interval 8300–7800 cal. BC with 2 sigma, thus putting the context in the late Preboreal – early Boreal chronozone and the Early Mesolithic. The flint material corresponds well to this dating.

Taken together, the dwelling is viewed as a simple and temporary construction representing a singular event of very short duration. As regards construction, the southern long side lacked any features and therefore seems to have been open. This fact demonstrates that we are dealing with what can best be described as a windbreak. The lack of any visible soil coloration indicating a floor formation in combination with a limited amount of artefacts further strengthens the temporariness of the construction. Especially the few artefacts present suggest a very short occupation as well as a limited range of activities. However, due to unfavourable conditions of preservation, we do not know whether tools made of organic materials such as antler, bone, or wood were also used on the site. Although bone and woodworking were indicated by use-wear analysis it does not tell us anything about the use of tools made of bone or wood as such. This of course constitutes a problem, albeit one we have no control over. Still, the few tool categories present limit the number of tasks possibly executed on site, thus further strengthening the assumption of a temporary and short occupation. If we consider what we do know, the tool inventory and use-wear analysis indicate with some confidence that the occupants repaired and manufactured equipment associated with hunting activities.

Put in a larger context, the windbreak fits in a logistical movement pattern in which small task groups leave a residential location or base camp to procure specific resources in specific contexts. While away from the residential location the groups make use of special field camps (Binford 1980:10ff). The windbreak in question is thus seen as a temporary field camp used seasonally in connection with hunting and/or fishing activities in the area (see landscape reconstruction in fig. 23).

THE ARROWS FROM LILLA LOSHULT

By Björn Nilsson & Conleth Hanlon

*I*n May 1951, a remarkable discovery was made during peat cutting in the bog of Lilla Loshult, approximately 50 km north-west of Årup. The find consisted of two wooden arrow shafts with adherent microliths. The find is unique, as it contains the only known intact wooden arrow with inserted microliths from the Early Mesolithic in Northern Europe.

The first arrow found had two microliths conjoined to the wooden shaft with birch resin: a triangle-like microlith inserted as a point and a lanceolate as a barb. The lanceolate was found separated from the shaft, but impressions in the resin showed its original position (Malmer 1969:252f). The shaft was found in seven pieces, making up a total length of 88 cm. Presumably a small piece of the shaft was missing, but the original length may have been at the most a few centimetres longer. At the end of the arrow shaft a notch had been made for the bowstring (Petersson 1951:123ff; Malmer 1969:249ff). The cross-section of the shaft was completely circular and it had been carved from a larger piece of pine wood (*Pinus*). Moreover, the surface of the arrow shaft had been finely worked with no traces of cutting marks (Petersson 1951:124ff).

Approximately 2.5 m away from the first arrow, an additional find consisting of two lanceolates and a badly fragmented wooden shaft was found. The microliths were not attached to the shaft, but were originally most probably fitted in the same way as the microliths of the well-preserved arrow. The fragmented arrow shaft consisted of ten pieces, making up a total length of 58 cm. The original length was probably the same as that of the more complete arrow (Petersson 1951:123ff; Malmer 1969:249ff).

The better preserved arrow was lying in a securely fixed horizontal position in the geological layer in which it was found. Peat from the layer produced a pollen diagram indicative of the pollen flora of the early Boreal (BO1) (Nilsson 1968:539).

The context of the second arrow was somewhat uncertain, as its original position had been disturbed in the process of the peat digging. Despite this, both arrow finds were interpreted as contemporaneous (Nilsson 1968:541).

The finds from Lilla Loshult could perhaps be considered as a hoard find (cf. Larsson 1978a:163). Most likely, we are dealing with the traces of a hunting scenario in which the two arrows were shot at a game animal, but missed their target and were lost (cf. Petersson 1951:128). Clear parallels to such a hunting scenario are illustrated by the Danish bog finds of the two intact aurochs skeletons from Prejlerup (Aaris-Sørensen 1984) and Vig (Hartz & Winge 1906), which were both found together with microliths.

The Lilla Loshult arrows are important in many respects. They provide us with first-hand information regarding how Early Mesolithic microliths could

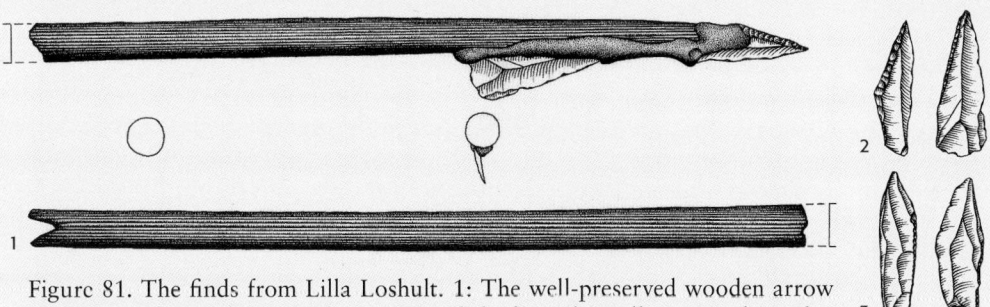

Figure 81. The finds from Lilla Loshult. 1: The well-preserved wooden arrow with inserted microliths. 2: The two microliths from the well-preserved wooden arrow separated from the shaft. 3: The two microliths of the fragmented wooden arrow (redrawn by Björn Nilsson from Malmer 1969).

have been shafted and functioned as part of arrows. They also give evidence of the material used in shaft making as well as the manufacturing technique and the size and shape of complete arrows.

Of special interest is the way in which the microliths of the well-preserved arrow were attached to the shaft. Although the shafting of the triangle microlith making up the point of the arrow is not entirely clear, it seems as if it has been inserted into a groove and fixed with resin. The barb was fitted to the shaft with the retouched long side orientated inwards, no groove was observed, and the barb was fixed in position with resin only (Petersson 1951:126).

Another interesting observation is the morphology and the position of the microliths, with a triangle microlith fitted as a point and a lanceolate inserted as a barb. Despite the existence of the well-known Loshult arrow, these types of microliths have in most instances been interpreted as having been positioned the other way around with lanceolates as points and triangles as barbs (cf. Vang Petersen & Brinch Petersen 1984:177f; Vang Petersen 1993:84). The example of the Lilla Loshult arrow clearly shows that no such general rule regarding the shafting of microliths existed. However, some archaeologists seemingly have a hard time accepting this fact. Reconstructions evidently based on the arrow from Lilla Loshult can be seen in which the triangle microlith has been replaced by a lanceolate as a point (Andersen 1981:44, 2001:48). The reason why such overtly faulty measures have been considered necessary is hard to understand indeed.

Morphologically, the Lilla Loshult microliths correspond well to microliths from several other South Scandinavian contexts of the Preboreal and the early Boreal, such as Klosterlund in Jutland (Mathiassen 1937), Linnebjär in south-western Scania (Salomonsson 1965), and Henninge Boställe in central Scania (Althin

1954). The Loshult arrows should therefore be seen as part of the south Scandinavian Early Mesolithic tradition. The morphology of the microliths in question is also represented at Årup and the arrow from Lilla Loshult constitutes an excellent example of how these could have been shafted.

Fragments of arrow-shafts are known only from a few Early Mesolithic sites in south Scandinavia, as for example Holmegård IV (Becker 1945) and Prejlerup (Vang Petersen & Brinch Petersen 1984) on Zealand. However, the closest parallel to the Lilla Loshult find is the well-preserved arrow shaft from the Vinkel bog in Denmark. Through pollen analysis the Vinkel arrow has been dated to the early Boreal. It was made from pine and measures approximately 101 cm in length. The shaft had been carefully rounded and smoothed down so that any traces of cutting were discernible only at either end of the arrow. The most interesting aspects of the Vinkel shaft, however, are the shape of the tip of the shaft and the lashing present by the nock. The tip of the shaft had been bevelled flat so that a microlith could be easily glued to the shaft (Troels-Smith 1961:129). This way of shafting the point could be true of the Lilla Loshult arrow as well. At the nock end of the arrow a notch had been made for the bowstring and a well-preserved lashing extended from the end of the notch to about 17 mm down the shaft with traces of this continuing a further 5 mm. There were traces of yet another lashing in an area 15.8 cm down the shaft. As there were no traces indicating that the two areas of lashing could be associated with fitting of fletching, the lashing at the nock end could instead have functioned as a grip, facilitating an easier hold of the arrow when pulling back the bowstring (Troels-Smith 1961:130f). Neither lashing nor fletching are evident on the Lilla Loshult arrows, possibly indicating a different shooting technique (cf. Troels-Smith 1961:142f).

Right from the age of the reindeer hunters, some 12,000 years ago, up to the longbow archers of the Middle Ages, hunting and warfare with bow and arrow have been of vital importance. During these millennia thousands of millions of arrows must have been manufactured and shot. In spite of this, we know of very few examples today, mostly in the form of fragments. The majority is long gone but many may still be preserved in bogs and marshes. Now and then specimens will certainly turn up when a ditch is dug or a bog exploited. However, a qualified guess is that only a few will actually be properly recognised and identified as arrows.

In this perspective the unique find from the Lilla Loshult bog has been, and will continue to be, a very important piece in the jigsaw puzzle of our understanding of prehistoric man and the manufacture and use of arrows.

Context 4

A MICROLITH MANUFACTURING SITE AND AN UNEXPECTED HUT

In the western part of the Årup site, an area of white sand, quite reminiscent of a beach, covering approximately 1,000 m², stretched along the eastern side of a drained wetland. This was indicated by the occurrence of a very thin layer of peat as well as the presence of several ditches. The original small lake must have been rather shallow judging by the thinness of the peat deposit as well as the depth of the basin, which only amounted to approximately 0.3 m. According to older maps, the draining enterprise most likely took place in connection with agricultural work or the laying out of the park of Årup Manor sometime during the later part of the eighteenth century (Palmgren 1728; Mogren 2003:48). Plenty of finds of worked flint and artefacts as well as the presence of a few features such as pits and furrows indicated Early Mesolithic activity adjacent to the former lake or wetland. The finds and features were clearly oriented in relation to the water as they were evenly spread along the former shore. Despite the features present, it was not possible to identify any complex structures or dwellings during the excavation.

Primarily two activity zones, Contexts 4 and 8, were identified in the area. Context 8 was situated in the northern part where activities involving ritual burning of flint were evident (see Context 8: "Ritual Årup"). Context 4 was located in the southern part where several blades, microburins, and microliths were found scattered over an area comprising approximately 100 m². The microburins, dominated by proximal parts of small blades, clearly indicate on-site production of microliths. In combination with several small blades and finished microliths, this demonstrates that we are possibly dealing with a specialised site for manufacturing microliths.

OF CONTEXT 4.

In total 1,876 pieces or 4,298 g of flint are associated with the context. Of these, 115 pieces or 297 g are burnt. The assemblage is dominated by 1,582 pieces or 4,053 g of Kristianstad flint, while 294 pieces or 245 g are of Senonian flint. Divided into categories, the assemblage comprises 911 flakes, 754 splinters, 109 blades and blade fragments, 34 microblades, 7 cores, 1 rejuvenation flake, 3 formal scrapers, 14 microliths, 7 microburins, 1 worked piece of flint, and 35 other flints.

The assemblage of worked flint consists of both Kristianstad and Senonian flint. Although Kristianstad flint dominates the material, only a limited amount of this can be identified as Mesolithic in character or for that matter associated with manufacturing of microliths. The Senonian flint, on the other hand, displays characteristic Mesolithic morphological and technological attributes as well as similarities in colour and texture. The small and short blades of Senonian flint have an irregular shape, indicating direct hard hammer percussion technology with the use of a small hammerstone. Unfortunately, no cores were found in the context.

Against this, it can be concluded that the material most distinctly associated with the production of microliths is dominated by imported Senonian flint, perhaps deriving from only one or two nodules. Some of this displays a characteristic element of bryozoans (Bryozoa) (Whitten & Brooks 1972:357), which make the finds stand out from the surrounding material. The assemblage is well preserved and no visible signs of water rolling or wind polishing

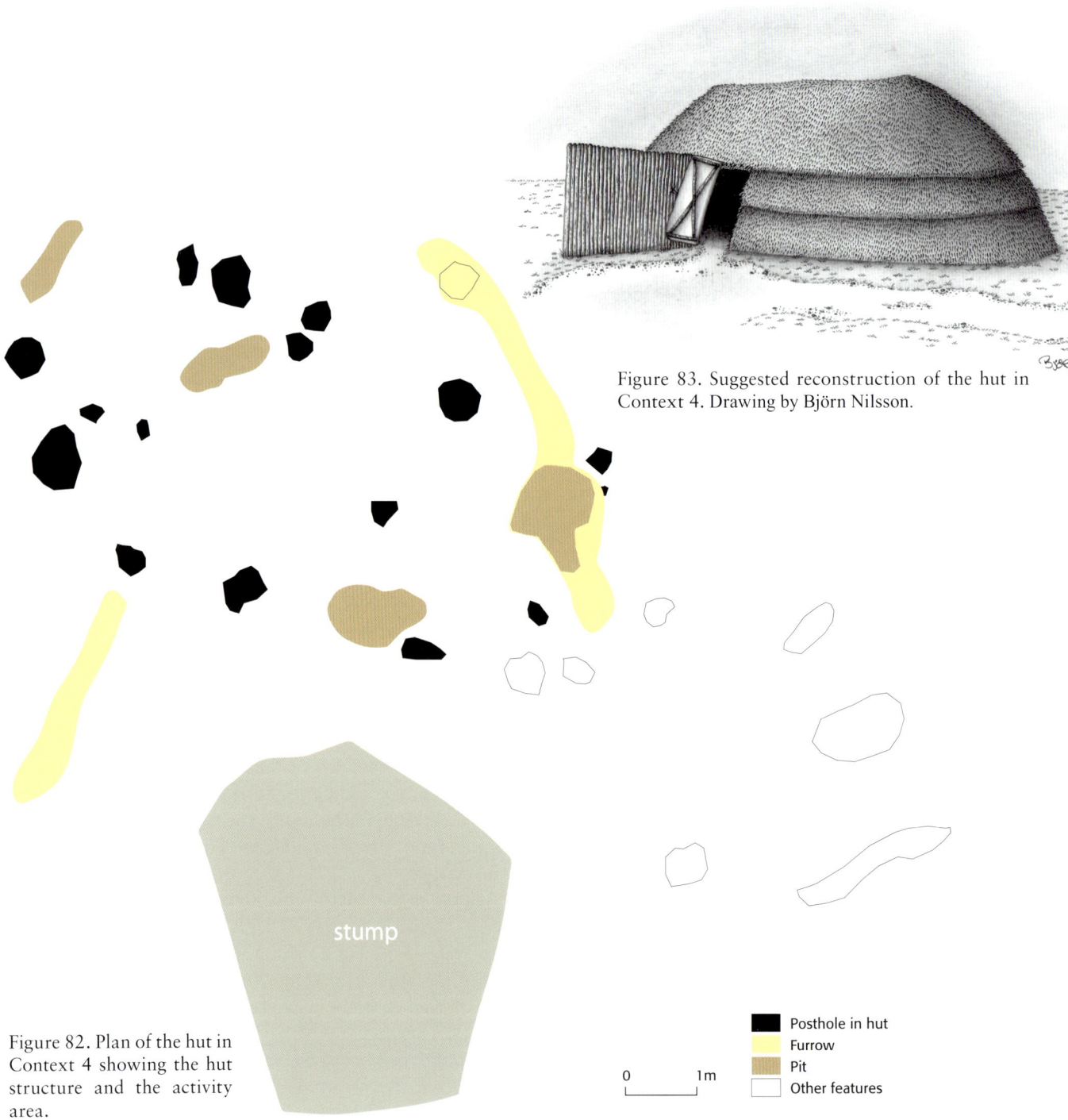

Figure 83. Suggested reconstruction of the hut in Context 4. Drawing by Björn Nilsson.

Figure 82. Plan of the hut in Context 4 showing the hut structure and the activity area.

stump

■ Posthole in hut
Furrow
Pit
☐ Other features

0   1m

Figure 84. The "beach". Photo by Sven Waldemarsson.

3 cm

Figure 85. A stone axe, a burin and some microliths from the western area by the drained wetland. Photo by Staffan Hyll.

are evident, although the material displays an un-mistakable orange-red patination caused by the occurrence of ferric oxide in the groundwater and subsoil.

The results of a simple refitting analysis of only a couple of hours' duration clearly indicate con-temporaneity in the assemblage. A few small and short blades of Senonian flint can be refitted, illus-trating that they had in fact been detached in se-quence from the same core. In total, it was possi-ble to refit two individual units consisting of seven blades and two parts of a single blade. The former unit involves a connection over a distance of ap-proximately 10 m (fig. 86).

A concentration of 11 microliths primarily comprising lanceolates was found close to a very large stump. Apart from lanceolates, two of the microliths are triangle-like in shape. Four micro-liths were found within features, two in a furrow, one in a pit, and one in a posthole. Unfortunately, the stump seemed to cover the central part of the concentration of microliths, so it was suspected that only the peripheral part of the context could be investigated properly.

The morphological variation of the microliths in Context 4 can be explained in terms of func-tion. Possibly, the variations correspond to a pre-conceived conception of how the microliths should be fitted on arrows, with some meant to function as points and others as barbs (cf. "The arrows from Lilla Loshult" in this chapter).

In trying to explain exactly why the lanceo-lates were discarded, several possibilities are feasi-ble. Initially it was thought that the microliths had been discarded in an unused state, as a result of not fitting into shafts in connection with the manu-facturing of arrows (cf. Context 1). However, we came in for a surprise when the microliths of the concentration found by the stump were subjected to use-wear analysis. Of the total eleven micro-liths analysed, the surfaces of three microliths had been subjected to mechanical alteration, one by fire and two by sand blasting, thus rendering iden-tification of use-wear impossible. Five microliths display no signs of having been used whatsoever. However, the remaining three microliths display traces of use-wear. Two of these exhibit signs of having been shafted, one of which in addition dis-plays impact damage and the third microlith dis-plays distinct signs of impact damage only. In con-clusion, some of the microliths evidently had been both shafted and shot. In the light of this, a rea-sonable explanation not to be ignored is that the discarded microliths can be seen in the context of an ancient world of ideas where the boundaries between the spiritual and material realms were fluid. Possibly, the arrows after an unsuccessful hunt were perceived as cursed and bringing bad luck and thus had to be replaced with new ones to please the spirits and restore the order of things (cf. Karsten 2001:108). The fact that both fired and unused microliths were found together with microburins seems to make a good case for a site where manufacturing of microliths and reshafting of used microliths is evident.

The assemblage is in line with the general mor-phology of the South Scandinavian Early Meso-lithic. The long and slender shape of some of the lanceolates is similar in type to lanceolates of the middle and late Maglemosian tradition. However, it has to be mentioned that the traditional South Scandinavian chronology, where lanceolates are regarded as representing primarily the Early Meso-lithic and the Maglemosian tradition, does not seem to be completely valid in the case of Årup. As will be elaborated further on, in contrast to the general picture lanceolates seem to dominate the microlith assemblage at Årup throughout both the Early and Middle Mesolithic phases (see discus-sion Contexts 5 & 6).

Although no organic material suitable for radio-carbon dating was found, the material of Context 4

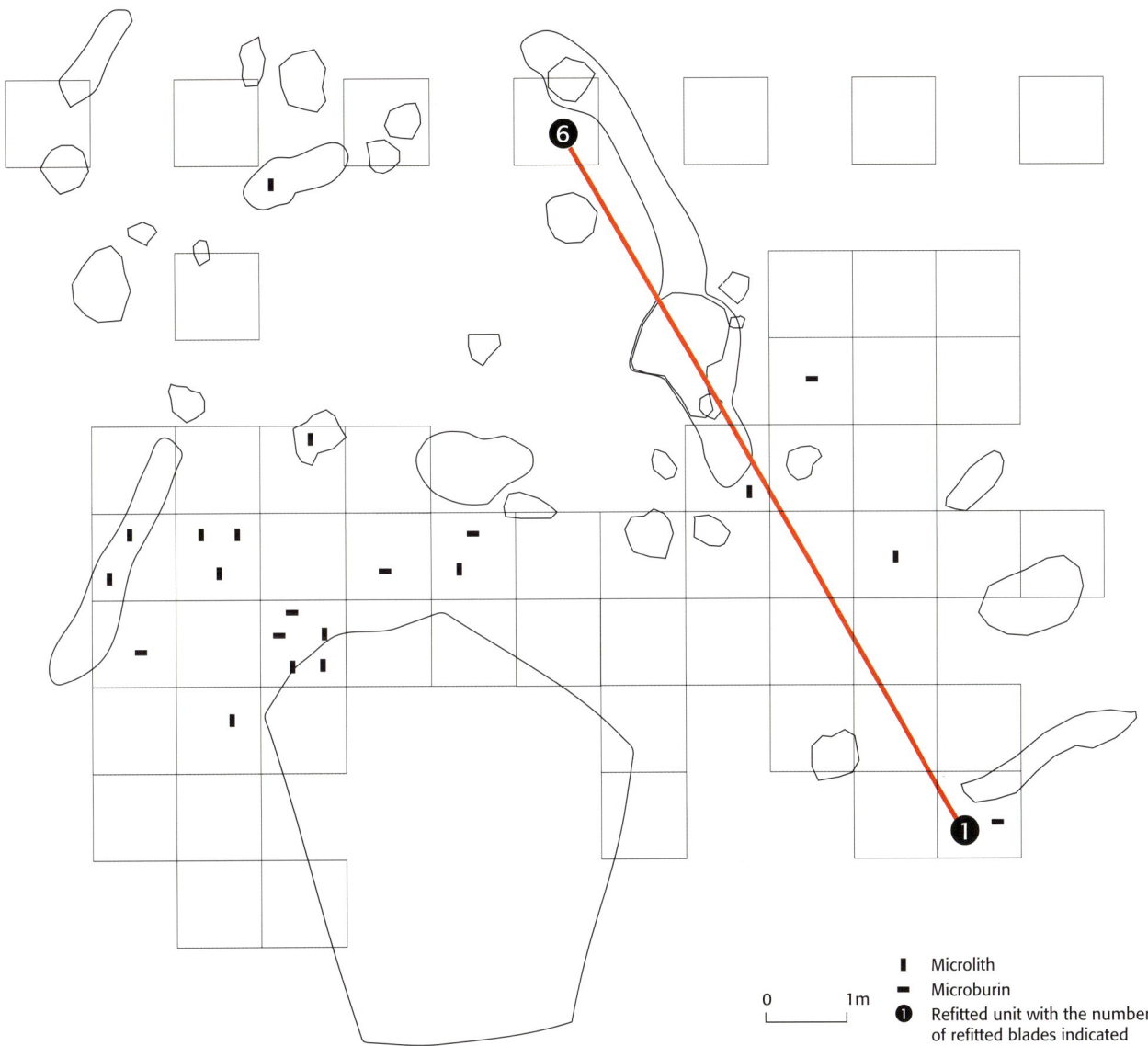

Figure 86. Plan showing the concentration of microliths and microburins and the spatial distribution of refittable blades. Symbols match the number of finds.

Microlith
Microburin
Refitted unit with the number of refitted blades indicated

0   1m

3 cm

Figure 87. A selection of microliths, micro burins
and blades from Context 4. Photo by Staffan Hyll.

Figure 88. Some refitted blades from Context 4. Photo by Staffan Hyll.

3 cm

can be suggested on technological and morphological grounds to belong to the middle/late Early Mesolithic. This is further strengthened by the fact that the material of Mesolithic character was dominated by Senonian flint which at Årup seems to be of chronological significance. While the older Contexts 1–3 by the riverbank belonging to the Late Palaeolithic and the early part of the Early Mesolithic are totally dominated by Kristianstad flint, the younger Contexts 5 and 6 situated in a higher part of the area contain a much larger amount of Senonian flint (see the "Hard Facts" of the respective contexts).

However, the story of Context 4 does not end with microlith manufacture. In addition, an unexpected discovery was made during the post-excavation analysis. The area of Context 4 was excavated under pressure, due to a very tight time schedule in this particular part of the investigation area forcing us into the difficult situation of setting priorities. In this case, as no explicit structures were identified in the field situation the priorities meant that we chose to focus on the flint concentrations at the expense of the features and latent structures. This choice had the result that the flint concentrations could be well defined during the excavation, but no structures whatsoever. During the post-excavation analysis, when all of the discarded features and disturbances had been removed from the plan, the remaining features were examined once again. Adjacent to the microlith manufacturing site a latent structure was identified on the plan. Further examination defined a round-oval structure, approximately 8.5 by 4 m oriented in SE–NW direction. This was made up of 17 postholes, 3 pits, and 2 furrows and was interpreted as the remains of a hut clearly erected in relation to the former shore. The postholes consisted of brownish-grey to greyish sand, varying in depths between 0.06 and 0.17 m. Three, possibly four, of the postholes were positioned inside the hut, interpreted as roof-supporting posts. The pits consisted of dark greyish sand and were all located inside the hut by the inner wall. All of the pits contained flint, primarily flakes, blades, and splinters. The pit at the southern long side also contained some fire-cracked stones on the surface. The furrow at the western short side of the feature was interpreted as having made up a part of the wall in this section. The function of the eastern furrow is unclear. However, it could very well have something to do with the eastern wall, maybe as drainage. No soil colouring indicating any floor formation was observed during the investigation. This in combination with a limited amount of artefacts indicates the temporary nature of the structure. A more permanent habitation would probably have generated a greater amount of artefacts.

As the hut was not observed during the excavation and due to the priorities mentioned above, it was not subject to proper contextual investigation. Test pitting dug inside the hut, when it was not known that there was a hut, did not reveal enough finds for it to be judged as a high-priority zone. This means that no spatial analysis of the interior is possible.

However, more than half of the features contained finds (fig. 89), which are in accordance with the surrounding material. This could be indicative for the dating of the hut, as no organic material suitable for radiocarbon dating was found in the features whatsoever. Moreover, three of the microliths were found in features related to the hut, which indicates contemporaneity in the assemblage from the activity area and the hut construction. The simple refitting analysis, which involves a connection that crosses over the eastern part of the hut, further strengthens such an assumption.

Taken together, Context 4 is interpreted as a small settlement unit consisting of a hut and an adjoining activity area. The round-oval shape of the hut, with no obvious breaks of posts in the wall-line, gives the impression of a closed structure with only a small entrance or a roll-up front. The activity area located to the south of the hut could be indicative of the entrance being oriented in this direction (cf. Contexts 2 and 3). Moreover, the adjacent furrow containing two of the microliths could very well be seen as the remains of a simple windbreak or a wall connected to the hut, maybe to support an entrance in this part of the structure. Two or three posts with a ridge beam probably supported the roof to stabilise the construction, which very well could have been built up of bent rods, giving the hut a somewhat rounded shape. The hut was most likely covered with hide, which is easy to transport, or locally collected reed. The total living space inside the hut encompasses an area of roughly 30 m², which would have made a living for five to eight people comfortable.

The amount of flint associated with the context indicates a short time-span, and could be taken as evidence of that we are dealing with a temporary camp, maybe for a two- or three-day stay.

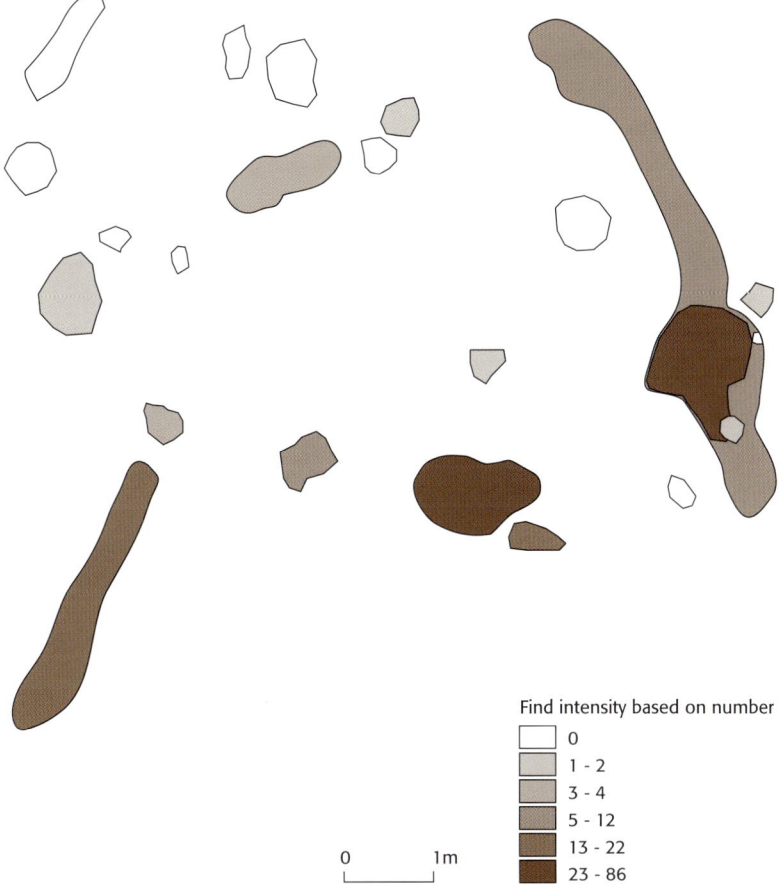

Find intensity based on number
- 0
- 1 - 2
- 3 - 4
- 5 - 12
- 13 - 22
- 23 - 86

0   1m

Figure 89. Plan of the hut with the features containing flint material marked and graduated based on number.

The evidence of on-site production of microliths and reshafting of used microliths suggests that the occupants were involved in hunting activities, giving a snapshot of how microliths were manufactured during the Early Mesolithic within the middle/late Maglemosian tradition of north-eastern Scania. In addition, it gives rise to some interesting questions regarding how to interpret the function and use of microliths and what finding them scattered on Mesolithic sites actually represents. In conclusion, Context 4 is seen as a temporary field camp used in connection with hunting in the land – or maybe the lifetime – of the Barum woman.

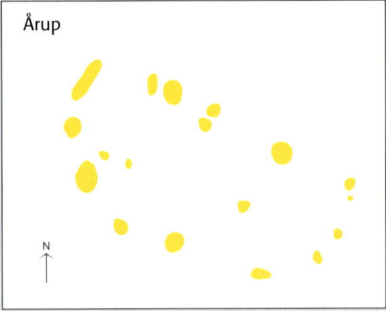

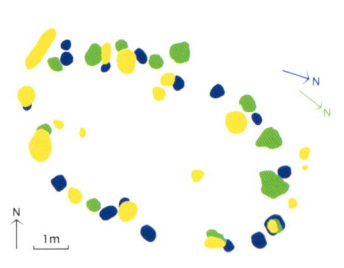

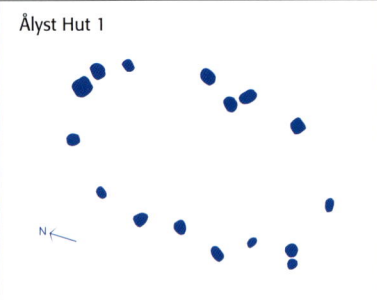

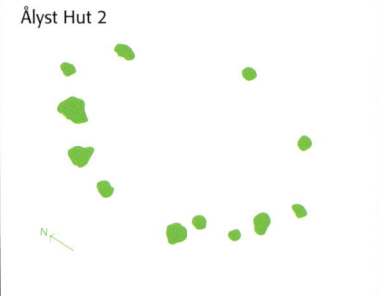

AS LIKE AS TWO PEAS: ÅRUP/ÅLYST.

When the local perspective of Årup was widened to a south Scandinavian perspective, a remarkable parallel to the hut of Context 4 was found. At Ålyst on Bornholm, two oval hut structures had been investigated simultaneously with the Årup hut. On technological and morphological grounds the huts can be suggested a dating to the middle and late Maglemosian culture (Casati et al. 2002; Sørensen 2002, 2003; Casati & Sørensen 2003; Casati & Sørensen personal communication). Even though the Ålyst huts are slightly shorter in size, the hut from Årup and the two hut structures from Ålyst show striking similarities in the size and position of the postholes.

The unmistakable parallel gives rise to interesting questions about cultural influences and regionality during the Early Mesolithic in south Scandinavia. The connection between Årup in north-eastern Scania and Ålyst on Bornholm has to be considered as more than a chance.

Figure 90. Outline comparisons of the huts from Årup and Ålyst. 1: The Årup hut. 2: Hut 1 from Ålyst (redrawn from Casati & Sørensen 2003, fig. 6). 3: Hut 2 from Ålyst (redrawn from Casati & Sørensen 2003, fig. 7). 4: The three huts when overlapped.

Figure 91. Årup and Ålyst in south Scandinavia.

THE EVER-CHANGING BARUM GRAVE

BY CONLETH HANLON & BJÖRN NILSSON

The Barum Woman, excavated by Folke Hansen in 1939, has since become a national treasure to be seen depicted in school books and on display in the Museum of National Antiquities in Stockholm. Until now, the grave has only been the object of critical questioning in relation to the revolutionary discovery that the skeleton, previously thought of as a man, in fact was a woman (Gejvall 1970).

Due to research in relation to the excavation at Årup, the authors had reason to examine the Barum grave goods, consisting of a slotted bone point and a bone chisel. In the process, the authors found some previously unobserved inconsistencies, which call for comment.

Let us begin with the slotted bone point. According to Hansen's written report on the excavation of the Barum grave, the point had five microblades inserted in their original position at the time of discovery. The sieving of soil produced additional microblades that were judged as belonging to the point (ATA 2584/1939). Since the excavation in 1939, the Barum point has been fitted with eight additional microblades and thus 13 microblades can be seen attached to the point today.

A closer examination of the slotted bone point revealed that the inserted microblades had been fitted with glue in a very haphazard and incorrect manner. No residue of resin was observed. As a general rule, Mesolithic slotted bone points as well as daggers have the microblades fitted with the ventral faces oriented upwards on one side and the dorsal faces oriented upwards on the other side (e.g. Voss 1961:156; Larsson 1973:8; Karsten & Knarrström 2003:64, 82). The reason for this is not quite clear, but could perhaps be explained in both functional and aesthetic terms. Regarding the function of slotted bone points they were associated early on with the hunting of waterfowl. The Swedish antiquarian Sven Nilsson used the term bird arrow (Sw. *fågelpil*) already in 1834 in analogy with points of some similarity used with throwing-boards by late hunters in Greenland and on the Kuril Islands. In a later work he expanded on the subject (Nilsson 1838–43:24; Edgren 1997:27). Other researchers have suggested that the type was used as a spear suitable for hunting in general, including the spearing of fish (e.g. Stenberger 1979:38), or primarily the hunting of mammals (Lidén 1948:101). In fact, the size and construction of the slotted bone point seems more suited for the hunting of big game. The long cutting edges are perfectly designed for causing long wound channels in prey. By opening blood vessels and cutting nerves, the type of projectile causes extensive bleeding in the prey (cf. Edgren 1997:31; Karsten & Knarrström 2003:65).

In connection with conservational measures and transferral to improved exhibition facilities in 1996, the Barum woman was subjected to a combination of renewed analyses, including osteological and odontological analyses as well as analysis of

Figure 92. The carvings and the microblade at the base of the bone point. Photo by Conleth Hanlon.

isotopic diet indicators and radiocarbon dating. Moreover, the artefacts from the burial were reconsidered. The results were published in an article in *Fornvännen* (Sten et al. 2000). In the article, the reconsideration of the bone point paid no attention to the actual insertion of the microblades. As the interpretation did not observe the problematic discrepancies in the depictions of the bone point over the years, the analysis uncritically took its starting point in the incorrect positioning of the microblades.

One of the microblades, which has been incorrectly inserted, is placed at the base of the point, where four small carvings can also be observed (fig. 92). The position of these carvings, close to the microblade in question, brought about a discussion of whether these markings had anything to do with the shafting of the point by lashing or if they represented some kind of sign or owner's mark. The conclusion arrived at by the author was that the carvings had to be interpreted as a sign or an owner's mark, since the lashing otherwise would have covered the microblade (Sten et al. 2000:83). The reasoning, which concentrated on the position of the microblade, is pointless since the microblade obviously was not present originally and therefore could not have had anything to do with the shafting of the point. Regarding the carvings, these could very well be interpreted as a sign or an owner's mark, and it is certainly a very plausible explanation.

Over the years different archaeological works have depicted the slotted bone point from Barum with variations in the numbers and positions of the microblades present (fig. 93). Hansen depicted the point with 11 microblades (1941:16, fig. 2), Oskar Lidén first depicted the point in the form of a drawing containing five microblades (1942:83, fig. 30) and in a subsequent article in a photograph with 13 microblades (1948:75, fig. 30a). Furthermore, only two or three of the microblades in Lidén's two depictions seem to be inserted at the same position. Since there are no records of exactly which five of the 13 microblades were attached to the bone point at the time of recovery, there is no way of deciding the original positions of the microblades. In conclusion, the Barum point on display in the Museum of National Antiquities in Stockholm is not presented in its original condition.

What did the point actually look like originally? Hansen seems to be the one to trust in this case. He excavated the grave and has to be regarded as the primary source in this matter. In his written report on the excavation, he described the slotted bone point as being 23 cm long (more exactly the point measures 23.5 cm) with five microblades still in their original position. There was no mention of any resin left in the slots of the point. If this was the actual case we do not know. Hansen also mentions that the sieving of soil produced additional microblades that were judged as belonging to the slotted bone point (ATA 2584/1939). When Hansen published the results from the excavation in 1941, the slotted bone point was depicted in a photograph with – what seems to be – 11 microblades present (Hansen 1941:16). As this must represent Hansen's own interpretation, it may be the closest to the original condition of the point we will ever get. Hansen was most probably one of very few who had the opportunity to study the point with the five original microblades still in their true position.

However, the story continues. The year after Hansen published his article, the Barum point showed up in Oscar Lidén's work on slotted bone points (1942). In a drawing, Lidén depicted the slotted bone point with the opposite side facing the viewer as compared to Hansen. If one compares the two depictions of the Barum point, Lidén depicted the point with only five microblades inserted and curiously enough in totally different positions from Hansen 1941. Furthermore, Lidén stated that the point was 18.5 cm, a reduction in length by 5 cm. He also compared the Barum point with a "point of precisely the same size and type" (1942:52) from Råbelövssjön. The two slotted bone points were depicted side by side as of identical size with their respective lengths clearly stated (Lidén 1942:83). What is very peculiar indeed is that the slotted bone point from Råbelövssjön, referred to by Lidén, measures 18.5 cm (cf. Ahlén 1879, fig. 283; Montelius 1917:7, fig. 63) and as previously mentioned, the Barum point measures 23.5 cm. Lidén certainly succeeded in confusing the facts.

When Lidén in his article of 1948 discussed the subject again, the bone point had gone through yet another metamorphosis. By now, the point displayed 13 inserted microblades and the very strangely positioned microblade by the markings at the base of the point had been added (Lidén 1948). This is also the current state of the point. The conclusion to be drawn from this run-through is that the spectacular changes to which the slotted bone point from Barum has been subjected took place between 1941 and 1948. Surprisingly enough, these facts have until

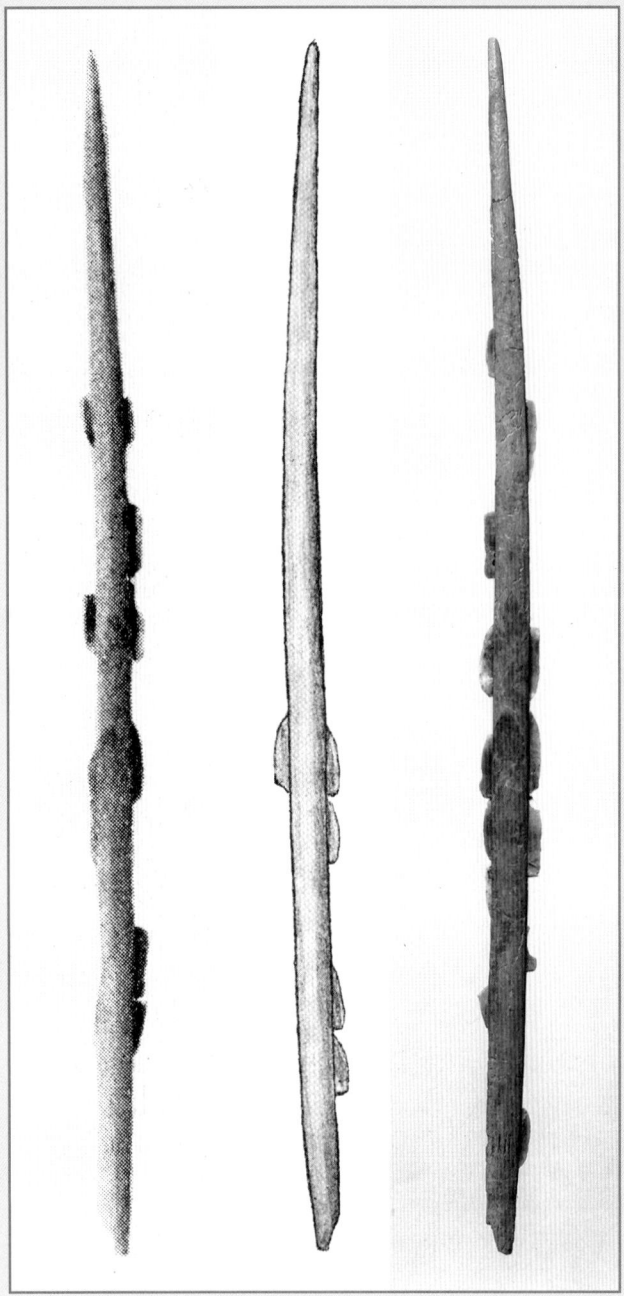

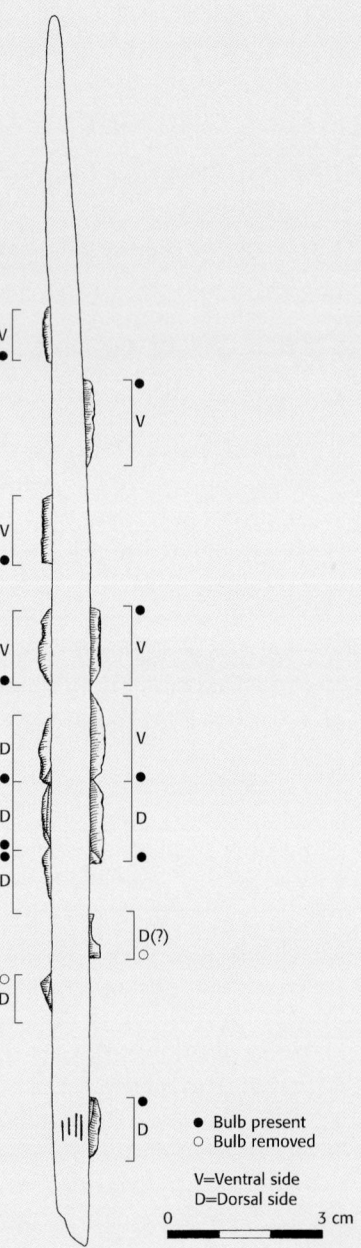

Figure 93. The changing Barum point with the different positioning of the microblades. 1: Hansen (1941). 2: Lidén (1942). 3: Lidén (1948)/Sten et al. (2000). Note that Lidén's drawings have been depicted from the two different sides of the bone point.

Figure 94. The current positioning of the microblades in the Barum point. Drawing by Björn Nilsson.

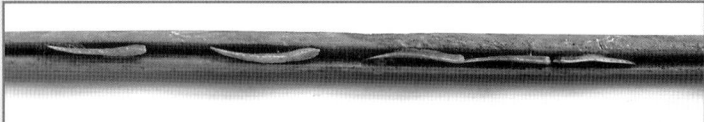

Figure 95. Close-up of some of the microblades inserted in the Barum point. Photo by Conleth Hanlon.

now never before been observed. Lidén certainly seems to have contributed substantially to the controversy over the Barum point. However, exactly how and in which way the point was changed, history does not tell.

The story of the slotted bone point from Barum does not end with the incorrect positioning of the microblades and the false portrayals. When we examined the facts more closely, the position of the bone point in the reconstructed grave struck us as oddly placed. This gave rise to questions regarding the reconstruction of the grave as such.

As previously demonstrated, not only the Barum point has undergone a most impressive metamorphosis; the Barum skeleton on display in the Museum of National Antiquities has also undergone considerable changes since the discovery in 1939. In connection with the various preservation measures taken over the years in the care of the Barum grave, the positions of the skeleton and the grave goods in the display case have been gradually changed. The most extensive change occurred in 1996 when the grave was totally reconstructed due to a new view of how the grave should be interpreted. As a curious fact, the stones present in the context of the original grave were not added to the reconstruction until 1996, and then they were incorrectly positioned.

Originally, in 1943 when the grave was exhibited for the first time, the skeleton was placed in an upright sitting position with the arms folded in a high position in front of the chest with the hands close to the shoulders (fig. 97:1). The slotted bone point was placed on the right pelvis in accordance with Hansen's excavation report of 1939 (ATA 2584/1939).

Sometime during the late seventies or early eighties the first changes of the grave are evident (fig. 97:2). The alterations

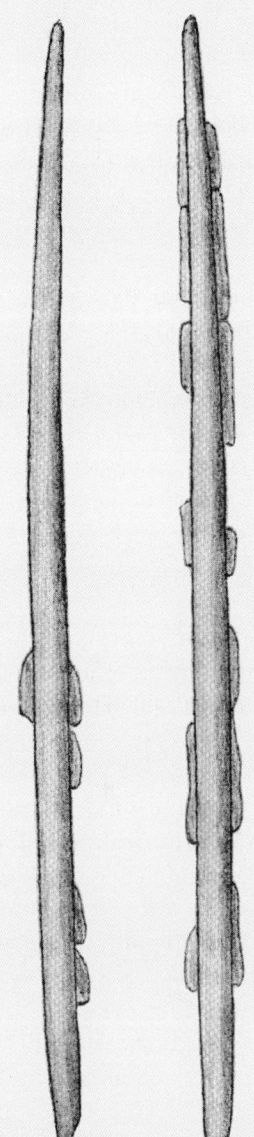

Figure 96. Liden's comparison between the slotted bone point from Barum and the one from Råbelövssjön (after Lidén 1942:83, fig. 30).

consisted of the lowering of the right arm and hand to a position in front of the chest and the slight changing of the left arm and hand to a position where it leaned against the left knee. The bone point was moved to an almost horizontal position on the right shoulder (Burenhult 1982:93, 1999:231). Burenhult seems to be the only one who explicitly has expressed the reasoning lying behind the changes of the grave in writing:

> *In a detailed study of the old excavation report it has also been established that the woman was sitting in a more reclined position than was previously reconstructed, and that the spear with flint insets rested against her right shoulder* (Burenhult 1982:90, authors' translation).

From this, we learn that the bone point indeed was seen as having been shafted when deposited in the grave and that it was perceived as a spear and not an arrow. We also learn that a detailed investigation took place which, however, apparently was never published, in any case we have not been able to find any references of it.

The repositioning in 1996 resulted in the skeleton being arranged in a slightly more reclining position with the arms folded in the lap (fig. 97:3). In the process, the slotted bone point was changed to an almost vertical position by the right shoulder of the skeleton, thus giving the impression that the point had been shafted. Why these changes were deemed necessary is hard to tell. In our opinion, the rearrangements of the grave have no support in the factual results as presented by Hansen in his report.

In Hansen's written report on the excavation the position of the slotted bone is described as being found inside the right part of the ribcage. However, a photo and a drawing from the excavation clearly show that the slotted bone point was lying just beside the ribs on the right pelvis with the tip pointing towards the head. The most important observation is, nevertheless, the indisputable fact that stratigraphically, the bone point is situated below both the arms and ribcage (ATA 2584/1939). This is also the region in which the point was originally placed in the display case in the Museum of National Antiquities. Had the point been shafted when deposited, the rate of decomposition of the wooden shaft would have been considerably slower than that of the body. This would have resulted in the point being situated stratigraphically above the arms and ribcage since the collapsing of the chest cavity would occur before the disintegration of the wooden shaft. Therefore, on stratigraphical grounds, the Barum point cannot have been shafted or placed by the right shoulder originally.

Over the years, the position of the bone point has been the subject of discussion. One view that has been expressed is that the bone point possibly killed the woman (Larsson 1982a:9; Edgren 1997:32; for a critical discussion cf. Karsten & Knarrström 2003:127). This hypothesis was primarily based on the comparison

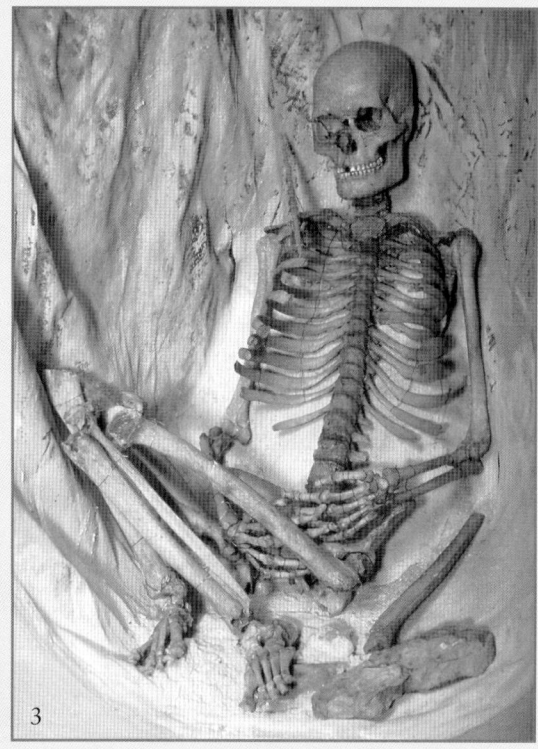

Figure 97. 1: The original positioning of the Barum woman at the Museum of National Antiquities in Stockholm in 1943. Note the position of the slotted bone point as well as the position of the hands. No stones are present (photo by ATA). 2: An intermediate positioning of the Barum woman at the Museum of National Antiquities in Stockholm after 1970. Note the position of the slotted bone point as well as the position of the hands. No stones are present (photo by Göran Burenhult). 3: The positioning of the Barum woman at the Museum of National Antiquities in Stockholm after 1996. Note the changed positions of the slotted bone point and hands. One has the impression that the slotted bone point is shafted and that the skeleton is in fact holding a shaft. All of a sudden, the stones have appeared (photo by ATA).

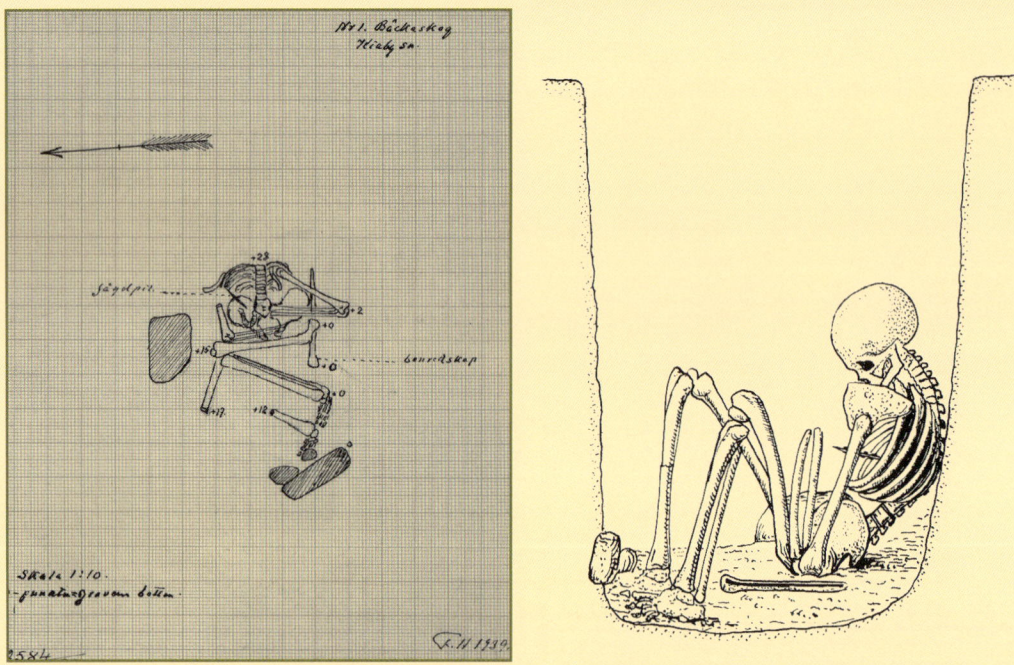

Figure 98. The original drawings from Hansen's excavation in 1939 showing the position of the slotted bone point *in situ* and a suggested reconstruction of the grave. The slotted bone point is marked with black (ATA 2584/1939).

with the male burial from Stora Bjärs on the island of Gotland, in which a fragment of a slotted bone point was found. Injuries to the jaw and skull of the deceased were taken as proof of the man having been deliberately killed, and that the slotted bone point could have been the cause of death. The fragmentation of the slotted bone point in combination with the well-preserved skeleton supports such an interpretation (Arwidsson 1979; Larsson 1982a). If we compare the Barum burial to the one from Stora Bjärs the Barum point is intact, a fact that speaks against a violent death of the woman. Had she been shot, the point would most likely have been fragmented, given the brittle nature of the point. No further evidence of the Barum woman having been deliberately killed is evident (Sten et al. 2000).

A brief examination of other parallels where slotted bone points have been present in graves indicates an interesting pattern to be observed in Mesolithic burial practice.

One example comes from the Tågerup excavation where a slotted bone point was found in a double burial, placed in the abdominal region of a man with the

Figure 99. A photo from Hansen's excavation in 1939 showing the position of the slotted bone point *in situ*. The slotted bone point is marked with an arrow (ATA 2584/1939).

tip pointing towards the head. At a glance, the placing of the object might suggest that it had caused the man's death, like the interpretation of the burial from Stora Bjärs. However, in this case, it was seen as unlikely since the point was found directly on top of a sooty, humic layer, which covered both bodies. The find was interpreted as a grave gift and a last gesture towards the couple before the grave was filled in (Karsten & Knarrström 2003:81).

Another parallel is grave 4 at the Bøgebakken cemetery on Zealand, Denmark. There a slotted bone dagger was found placed on the lower part of the chest of the deceased with the tip pointing towards the head (Albrethsen & Brinch Petersen 1977:7f; Sørensen 1996:73). When one compares the positioning of the slotted bone points and the slotted bone dagger from the Barum, Tågerup, and Bøgebakken burials, the similarity is indeed striking and indicates that we are in fact dealing with a repetitive Mesolithic burial custom. In this tradition, the slotted bone point can be seen as a status symbol, used by both men and women (cf. Karsten & Knarrström 2003:84f).

Thus, a common denominator can be seen in the positioning of the slotted bone points in graves during the Mesolithic. The placing of unshafted points on the lower part of the chest with the tip pointing towards the head may be interpreted as the material expression of cultural tradition and conceptual ideology.

However, the general picture of the positioning of grave goods in the region of the lower part of the chest during the Mesolithic is not reserved solely for slotted bone points. Grave gifts such as bone spatulas and flint blades have also been found in this region (e.g. Albrethsen & Brinch Petersen 1977; Larsson 1984b; Kjällquist 2001:51ff; Karsten & Knarrström 2003:80ff).

In conclusion, there are few facts or parallels in support of the present reconstruction of the national treasure in the Museum of National Antiquities in Stockholm. Furthermore, the reconstruction gives rise to problems of a more ethical nature. How unrestrained can archaeologists and curators be in their interpretations of the archaeological record without explicitly presenting the line of thought leading up to a certain reconstruction? The present reconstruction in which the woman seems to be holding a shafted point constitutes a static picture, which in the eyes of the public, no doubt, is perceived as the unadulterated and true picture of the grave. From a scientific point of view, the reconstruction can be seen as the uncritical transfer of modern values and beliefs to Mesolithic humans, thereby intensifying the notion of the Barum woman as an active hunter. The problem is not the perception of the Barum woman as a hunter – for she most probably was involved in hunting activities of some sort – rather it is the uncritical way this conclusion was arrived at. The distortion of facts in order to convey a certain message is not good conduct. Statements about the past must be firmly rooted in the archaeological record.

Context 5

Two inverted Middle Mesolithic dwellings

On the highest point of the eastern slope down towards the River Skräbeån at a level of approximately 6.5–6.8 m above present sea level, signs of repeated Mesolithic habitation were evident. In the northern part of this area the stratigraphy was quite complicated since the Mesolithic level was covered by a roughly 0.3 m thick cultural deposit dating to the Bronze Age, primarily indicated by the presence of typical pottery and an abundance of knapped flint. During the investigation, it was established that the Mesolithic level in parts had been disturbed by Bronze Age activities, mainly by the presence of several rather large cooking pits as well as hearths and various smaller pits. Furthermore, the area had been heavily affected by bio-turbating activities in the form of roots and burrowing rodents as well as farming activities of the eighteenth century (Palmgren 1728). These activities had resulted in Mesolithic material partly being mixed up with Bronze Age material. However, through a combination of test pitting and machine stripping it became clear that undisturbed Mesolithic remains existed under the Bronze Age layer.

In order to uncover the Mesolithic level, we let the machine totally remove the Bronze Age layer. On the undisturbed Mesolithic level two structures were discovered, interpreted as the remains of huts. The find material at this level was very limited. This, in combination with the degree of disturbance and mixed up material, makes a more detailed spatial analysis of the material rather pointless. For this reason, we will focus on the constructions with only a generic overview of the find assemblage.

The northerly of the two huts stood out as a large blackish-grey feature against the yellow sandy subsoil in and around which 10 postholes, a

Hard facts

OF Context 5.

In total 2,097 pieces or 8,981 g of flint are associated with the context. Of these, 569 pieces or 826 g are burnt. The assemblage is dominated by 1,264 pieces or 6,985 g of Kristianstad flint, while 829 pieces or 1,945 g are of Senonian flint and 4 pieces or 51 g of Danian flint. Three pieces or 294 g of stone and 2 pieces or 247 g of quartz were found. Divided into categories, the assemblage comprises 1,309 flakes, 204 splinters, 263 blades and blade fragments, 146 microblades, 23 cores, 4 rejuvenation flakes, 27 formal scrapers, 8 formal knives, 3 formal borers, 1 flake axe, 3 core axes, 1 combination tool, 1 formal burin, 20 microliths, 2 tanged points, 2 transverse arrowheads, 5 microburins, 1 hammerstone of flint, 10 worked pieces and 52 other flints, 3 hammerstones, 1 shale pendant, 1 flake, and 2 hammerstones of quartz.

pit, and a hearth were observed. The blackish-grey feature was interpreted as a floor layer with a thickness varying between 0.01 and 0.16 m, thicker and wider in the southern part with a gradual narrowing and thinning out to the north. In the southern part, a concentration of soot appeared which was interpreted as a hearth. The postholes varied between 0.08 m and 0.15 m in depth and in width between 0.8 and 0.16 m. The fillings consisted of brownish-grey to blackish-grey sand. Of the 10 postholes, 9 were regarded as constituting part of the hut construction thus, making up a round construction, approximately 3.7 m in diameter, with a centrally placed hearth.

Initially, the entrance of the hut was thought to have been located to the north due to the elongated shape of the blackish-grey floor layer and the

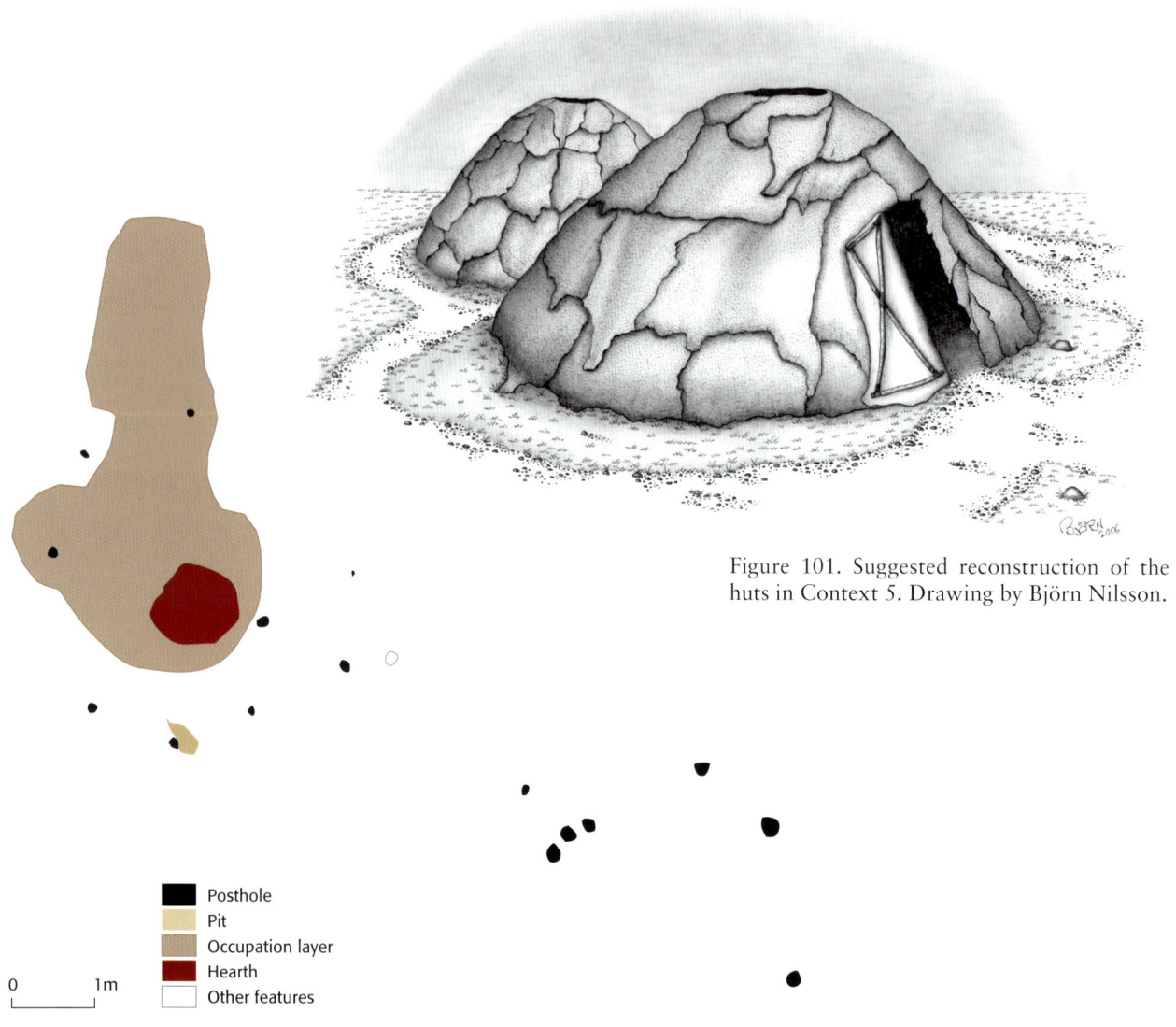

Figure 101. Suggested reconstruction of the huts in Context 5. Drawing by Björn Nilsson.

Posthole
Pit
Occupation layer
Hearth
Other features

0   1m

Figure 100. Plan of Context 5 showing the huts and activity area.

distribution of flint. However, the simple spatial analysis of flint shows a weak tendency to be somewhat drawn-out in the south-eastern part as well, which may indicate the entrance being located in this part. Of the two alternatives, the former seems most plausible.

Directly to the south-east of the northern hut construction the remains of an additional structure were found. Unfortunately, this structure was only partly identified as such during the excavation. The structure was made up of eight postholes and a pit, interpreted as a hut construction of the same diameter as the northern hut. Interestingly enough, this construction also displayed similarities in layout as it had three postholes retracted in the same way as one of the postholes in the northern hut. Moreover, a simple spatial analysis of burnt flint from the digging of squares shows a tendency to a concentration being located close to the retracted postholes. This may indicate the remains of a hearth, placed close to the retracted posts just as in the northern hut. No floor layer was observed during the investigation whatsoever, although the spatial analysis of the total number of flints indicates an increase in number inside the hut.

Unfortunately, the soil samples taken from the various features in the two constructions turned out not to contain any datable substances at all. One sample of charcoal of poor quality taken from a posthole in the northern hut had been identified, with some doubt it should be added, as being of hazel (*Corylus avellana*). The sample was used for radiocarbon dating, but regrettably, the amount of charcoal in the sample turned out to be insufficient for dating.

From the southern hut, two samples of charcoal taken from postholes had been identified as being of oak (*Quercus sp.*) and pine (*Pinus silvestris*). The first sample failed in the process of dating. Nonetheless, the sample from the second posthole produced an age of 7410 ± 40 ^{14}C-years BP in

Figure 102. The area of Context 5 had been heavily affected by bio-turbating activities in the form of roots and burrowing rodents. Picture shows part of a section from one of the test pits. Photo by Helén af Geijerstam.

Figure 103. One of the postholes in the northern hut. All the postholes were very similar in character, only varying somewhat in width and depth. Photo by Helén af Geijerstam.

the interval 6390–6210 cal. BC with 2 sigma, which puts the date in the early Atlantic chronozone and the early Middle Mesolithic.

As mentioned above, the layout and size of the two huts shared striking similarities. In a detailed analysis of the plans and layouts of the two

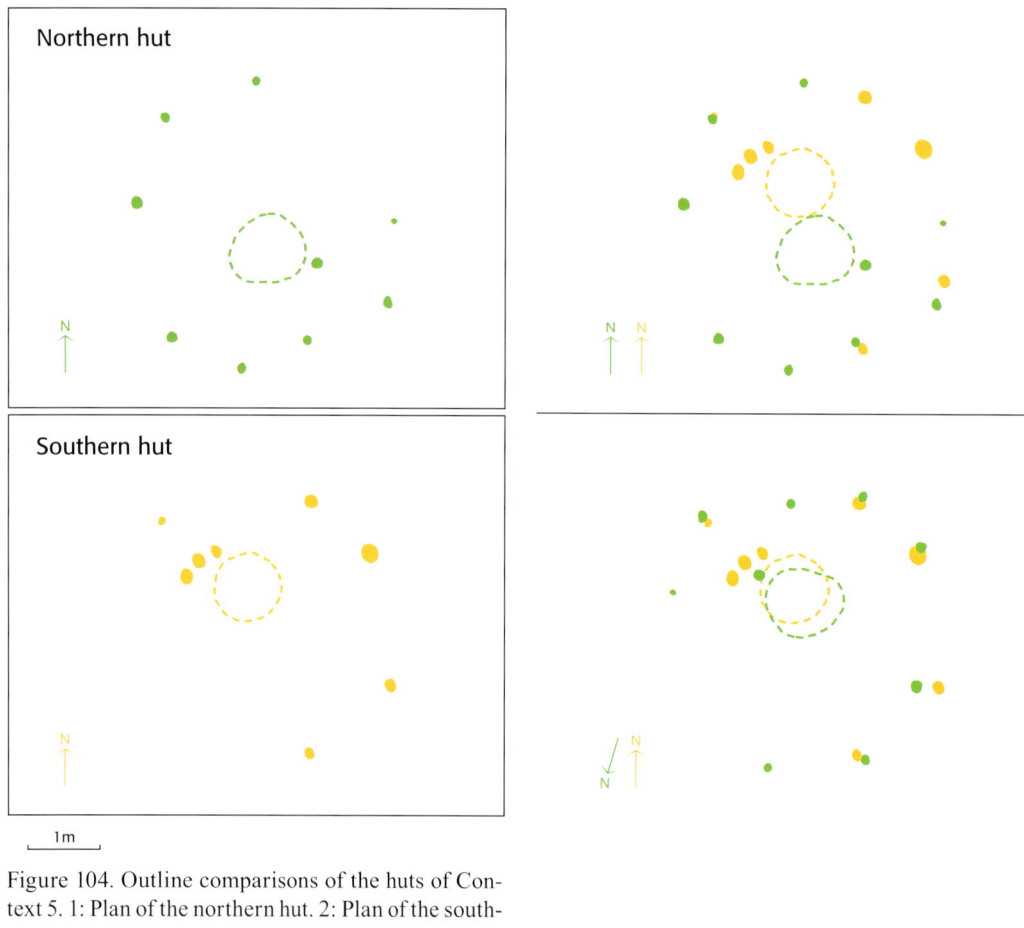

Figure 104. Outline comparisons of the huts of Context 5. 1: Plan of the northern hut. 2: Plan of the southern hut. 3: Outline comparison of the huts when overlapped. 4: Outline comparison of the huts with the northern hut turned clockwise through 180°.

structures, it was completely clear that the layouts were almost identical (fig. 104). Especially the fact that both huts had postholes that were retracted in relation to the others seemed to indicate that they were the result of the same planning. The primary difference was the number of postholes and that the huts apparently were orientated somewhat differently. However, if one turns the northern hut clock-wise through about 180° the postholes will overlap in a way that has to be considered as more than a mere chance. In the light of this, the two structures can be regarded as contemporaneous. Without doubt, the people who built the huts had knowledge of one hut at the time when the other was erected.

Quite possibly, the huts represent the replacement and improvement of a dwelling that had fallen

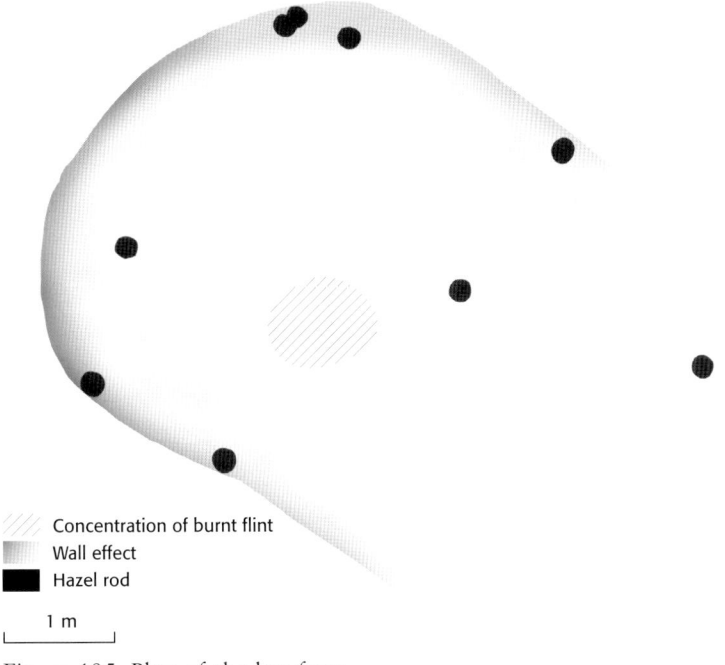

Concentration of burnt flint

Wall effect

Hazel rod

1 m

Figure 105. Plan of the hut from
Rönneholm 6 (redrawn from Sjöström 2000:22).

into disrepair, although it cannot be ruled out that the two inverted huts in fact were in use simultaneously. A perhaps more plausible explanation is that the people used standardised mobile constructions, which had to be erected in a certain manner, due to the spatial organisation of the dwelling space and social psychology of the spatial organisation of small groups, which may have been following culturally specific rules (cf. Grøn 2003: 698ff).

However, the striking similarities of the two structures of Context 5 indicate that the dating of the southern hut to the early Atlantic period and the Middle Mesolithic is valid for the northern structure as well.

As a curiosity, it is worth mentioning a parallel to the huts of Context 5, which has been excavated at the site Rönneholm 6 located in central Scania (Sjöström 2000). Within a concentration of flint and stones the remains of nine hazel rods driven into the ground were discovered. The rods surrounded an irregular area with a diameter of approximately 4 m. Concentrations of flint created a wall effect, which respected the outlines of the rods. In the central part of the construction a concentration of burnt flint was observed, indicating the remains of a hearth. The structure has been interpreted as a hut dating to the Middle Mesolithic.

Outline comparisons of the hut from Rönneholm 6 and the huts of Context 5 show that the

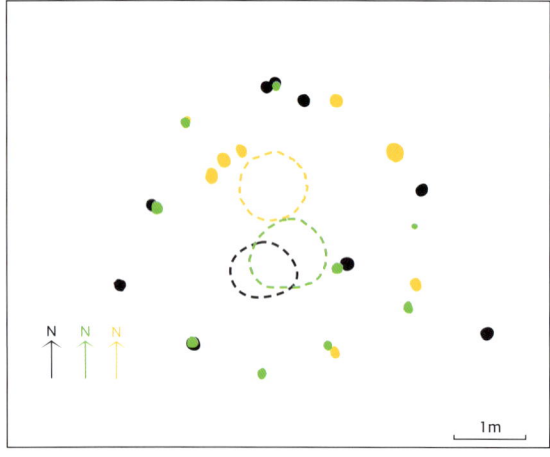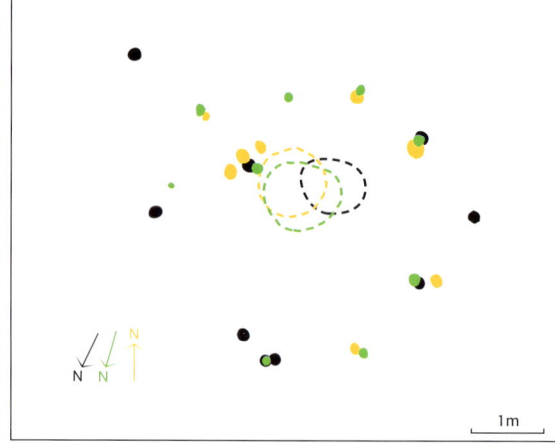

■ Northern hut Årup
■ Southern hut Årup
■ Rönneholm 6

Figure 106. Outline comparisons of the huts of Context 5 and the hut from Rönneholm 6. 1: Outline comparison of the huts when overlapped. 2: Outline comparison of the huts with the northern hut of Context 5 and the Rönneholm hut turned clockwise 180°.

structures share striking similarities (fig. 106). The huts are almost identical in size with the rods and postholes partly overlapping. Curiously enough, the Rönneholm hut also seems to have one rod retracted in the same way as in the huts of Context 5. Moreover, the presumed hearth is located close to the retracted rod just as in the Årup huts. Only one rod seems to be somewhat displaced in relation to the Årup huts, but one has to consider that some posts may have been removed while others have appeared without any spatial connection with earlier constructions.

The Rönneholm hut and the Årup huts give the best evidence yet of dwellings from the Middle Mesolithic and the Kongemose culture. The huts strengthen each other in a way that gives rise to interesting questions about Middle Mesolithic dwelling structures and organisation as well as regional settlement patterns. Are we, for example, dealing with a Middle Mesolithic standardised way of building huts with an idealised size and construction? The different expressions and constituents of the Kongemose culture, like the standardised flint objects, the accuracy, and the artistic idiom, very clearly indicate a society with explicitly defined rules. The culture seems to have functioned well, with careful planning, and was most likely adapted in every way to the conditions of the surrounding environment (Karsten 2004:113). If any culture had thought of standardising their way of building huts, the Kongemose culture is easily the best candidate.

Not surprisingly, the find material associated with Context 5 is totally dominated by flint. However, a very limited amount of worked stone and quartz was also retrieved. Of this, it is worth noticing a small fragmented pierced shale pendant with carvings found on an undisturbed Mesolithic level inside the southern hut (fig. 107).

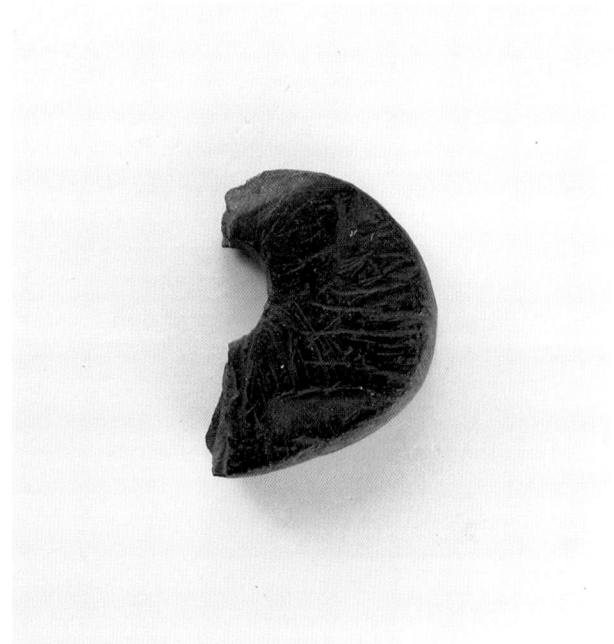

3 cm

Figure 107. The shale pendant from the southern hut (viewed from two sides). The object in question has carvings on both sides. The surface is filled with short strokes, converging and parallel lines, and quickly executed patterns of squares and crosses. The carvings do not seem to have a thought-out pattern, with the exception of four more distinct vertical lines on one side of the object. However, due to its raw material and finely worked hole the artefact is unique in southern Scandinavia, although a few similar pieces have been found on Mesolithic sites. An ornamented sandstone, approximately 3 cm in diameter, with five vertical lines is known from the Maglemose site at Ålyst on Bornholm (Casati & Sørensen 2003:6, photo 2). Moreover, parallels to the carvings on the shale pendant could be found on flint with carvings on the crust. This artefact category, which seems to be closely associated with find spots from the Maglemose and Kongemose cultures, shows elements of decoration that is very often made in a haphazard way which according to Karsten and Knarrström (2003:118) could be summed up in the word haste. This cortex art is an obvious contrast to the way that contemporary bone and antler objects were decorated, which is characterised by carefulness and stringency. However, the shale pendant of Context 5 indicates other activities than practical and economic ones on the Årup site during the early Atlantic period. Photo by Staffan Hyll.

The flint assemblage is dominated by Kristianstad flint, although a relatively high element of Senonian flint is present. Senonian flint dominates the formal artefacts and the blades, which may indicate that imported flint was used for specialised tool manufacturing, probably due to its higher quality. The assemblage, which is Mesolithic in character can on technological and morphological grounds very well be seen as contemporaneous with the dating of the huts. Long symmetrical blades and blade fragments of primarily high-quality Senonian flint, handle cores, symmetrical microblades, and microblade fragments support such an interpretation.

Different types of lancet-shaped and triangular microliths totally dominate the microlith inventory. These types of microliths are generally regarded as Early Mesolithic key artefacts, even though triangles could occur during the early part of the Kongemose culture as well (Vang Petersen 1993:85; Sørensen 1996:58). In most cases early Kongemose materials are characterised and dominated by the presence of various types of trapezoid microliths – or Blak microliths if you will – used primarily as transverse arrowheads (Karsten & Knarrström 2003:59ff). These types of microliths are totally absent at Årup, although it cannot be ruled out that some of the blade fragments lacking retouch were in fact used as transverse arrowheads (cf. Karsten & Knarrström 2003:66).

However, the presence of lanceolates can of course easily be explained by repeated habitation during the Early Mesolithic. Charcoal samples taken from features in the area had produced datings indicating earlier activities. An alternative explanation, though, could be that we are in fact dealing with a local tradition of microlith manufacturing, which could be explained in functional terms, and where the lanceolates for some reason have been regarded as superior to the transverse microliths. This assumption is further strengthened by the fact that the microliths of Context 5 are dominated by Senonian flint, which seems to be of chronological significance at Årup, where imported flints tend to increase in number during the late Early Mesolithic and Middle Mesolithic periods (cf. Context 4).

Moreover, the flint material comprises several blade fragments with heavy retouching along the edges and two "pointed scrapers". These artefact categories are also present in Context 6 and may indicate a relationship between the two contexts (see next section).

In conclusion, Context 5 is interpreted as a settlement unit consisting of two huts with integrated activity areas. The huts were of identical size, layout, and shape and were most likely in use simultaneously, although it cannot be ruled out that the huts represent the replacement and improvement of a dwelling that had fallen into disrepair. The huts could very well have been of a mobile tepee type construction, erected with eight to ten posts and covered with a tent, probably made of hide which is easy to transport. Speaking against this is that such structures most often do not leave any traces of the erected posts. For that reason, a perhaps even more plausible interpretation is a rounded cupola-like structure built up with bent rods that were dug and fixed into the ground. This type of construction is known from several ethnographic examples, for example, in America and Australia (e.g. Jelinek 1978:71ff). Experiments have shown that this type of structure is both simple to build as well as excellent in its shape, as it creates more internal space than a tepee type construction (Sjöström 2000:22; Sjöström personal communication). The internal space of the huts in Context 5 roughly encompasses an area of 12 m^2, which would have made it comfortable for a family of four to six people.

The context could very well be seen as a small independent settlement unit, used during a short period. However, it cannot be ruled out that adjoining settlement remains are concealed just outside the investigation area that can be linked to Context 5. The dating and find material also indicate that the huts could be contemporaneous with Context 6 (see next section), which in that case means that we are dealing with a much larger settlement complex with several units of huts and workshops (see landscape reconstruction in fig. 24). With such an interpretation, Context 5 could represent a somewhat longer period of habitation by single families, perhaps up to a month's stay. The reader should have a look at Context 6 to investigate this conceivable relationship further.

Figure 108. A selection of flint and stone artefacts from Context 5. Photo by Staffan Hyll.

3 cm

 Context 6

A slotted bone point Manufacturing site

Also on the highest point of the eastern slope, just a short distance south of Context 5, Mesolithic flint material was found spread over an area comprising roughly 70 m². It has to be pointed out that the area between Context 5 and 6 was investigated by both test pitting and machine stripping. Apart from a few sporadic features and stray finds dating to the Bronze Age, the area contained no find material whatsoever. Whether the contexts are contemporaneous or not, this shows that they are definitely separated from each other, and have to be considered as two different activity areas.

The cultural deposit dating to the Bronze Age that was overlying the Mesolithic level in Context 5 gradually narrowed and thinned out to the south. The remaining part of it covering Context 6 was only a few centimetres thick and was easily removed by machine stripping. Apart from a few small Bronze Age pits, containing mixed up material, these later activities had not affected the Mesolithic level in this particular part, nor had bioturbating activities to any appreciable extent.

Despite the very dry and dusty conditions that prevailed during fieldwork, it was still possible to register a few sporadic features in connection with the finds on the Mesolithic level. The most striking feature was an approximately 3 by 3.5 m large colouring located in the western part of the context, interpreted as a floor layer. The layer consisted of blackish-grey fine-grained sand, approximately 0.1 m thick at its deepest point, containing numerous finds. Within the feature two sooty concentrations were registered, containing fire-cracked stones and flint material, some of it burnt. Outside the feature were two postholes, consisting of blackish-grey sand, with depths of 0.14 and 0.18 and a diameter of 0.26 m. Besides this, nothing was found which

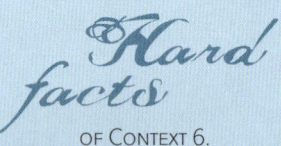

Hard facts OF CONTEXT 6.

In total 2,291 pieces or 2,956 g of flint are associated with the context. Of these, 693 pieces or 609 g are burnt. The assemblage is dominated by 1,226 pieces or 1,810 g of Kristianstad flint, while 1,065 pieces or 1,146 g were of Senonian flint. Two pieces of stone were found. Divided into categories, the assemblage comprises 1,146 flakes, 574 splinters, 139 blades and blade fragments, 252 microblades, 7 cores, 3 microblade cores, 10 handle cores, 6 rejuvenation flakes, 22 formal scrapers, 1 formal knife, 1 formal borer, 4 formal burins, 6 microliths, 1 transverse arrowhead, 3 microburins, 1 strike-a-light, 1 worked piece of flint, 116 other flints, and 2 hammerstones.

could help determine any details of the construction. Our interpretation is that the colouring and the adjoining postholes were parts of a small hut or a wind shelter with a somewhat sunken floor.

In the eastern part of the context six postholes and a furrow and a pit containing two and one posthole respectively were observed. A hearth containing burnt flint, soot, and charcoal was also registered. The postholes were of the same character as in the western part, varying in depth between 0.14 and 0.17 m and in diameter between 0.25 and 0.30 m. Two of them contained small blades, microblades, and flakes. Curiously enough, five of the postholes seemed to form a crescent-shaped structure approximately 3 m wide with the hearth centrally placed. In addition, the furrow and the sixth posthole seemed to form an adjoining structure. No floor layer was observed whatsoever, but it was

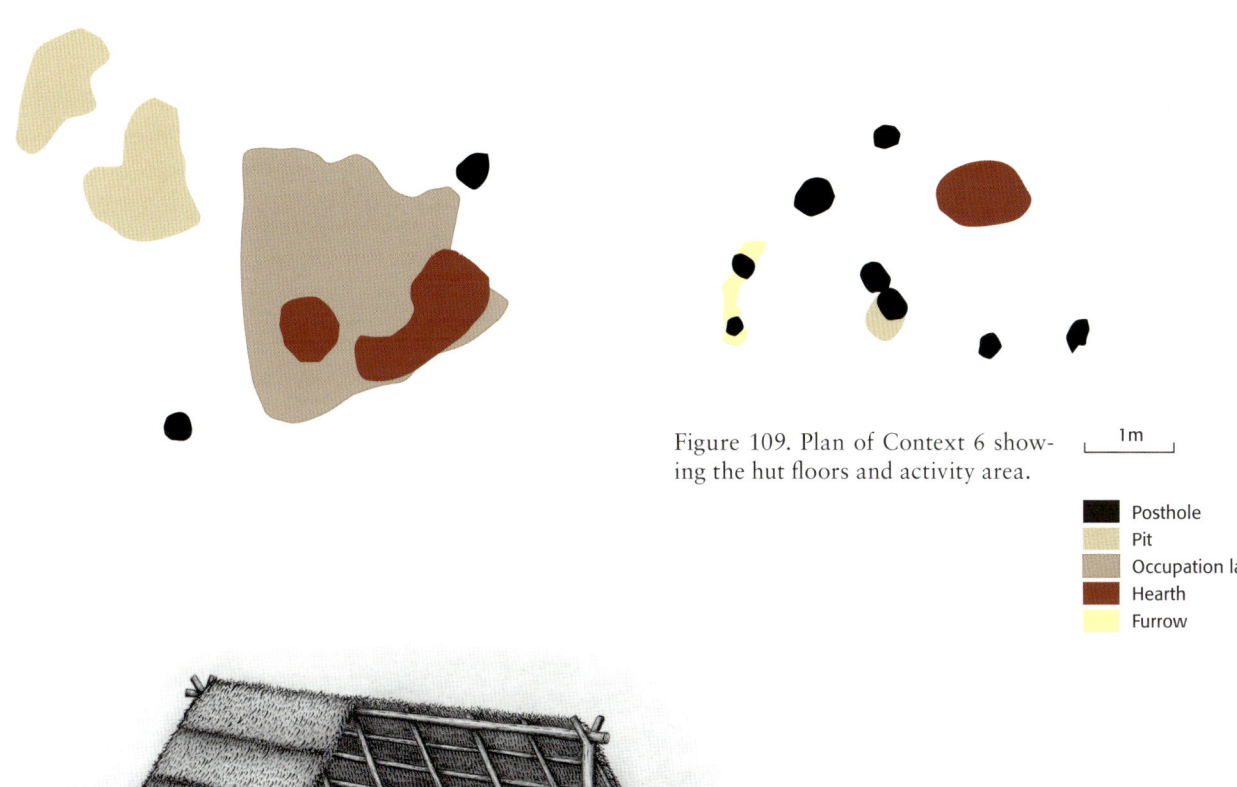

Figure 109. Plan of Context 6 showing the hut floors and activity area.

1m

■ Posthole
▨ Pit
▨ Occupation layer
▨ Hearth
▨ Furrow

Figure 110. Suggested reconstructions of the workshops in Context 6. Drawings by Björn Nilsson.

obvious that concentrations of flint were located close to the hearth. The postholes are not of much help for working out the structural details. However, in terms of construction the north-east side lacked any features and therefore seems to have been open. Taken toget her, a reasonable interpretation would be that we are in fact dealing with a second small hut or wind shelter in the area.

Unfortunately, the floor layer in the western part of the context contained no material suitable for radiocarbon dating. However, a charcoal sample from the northerly of the two adjoining postholes, identified as being of pine (*Pinus silvestris*), produced an age of 7390 ± 50 ^{14}C-years BP in the interval 6390–6100 cal. BC with 2 sigma, indicating a date to the early Atlantic chronozone and the early part of the Middle Mesolithic. A charcoal sample also identified as being of pine, taken from the posthole in the pit in the eastern structure, produced an age of 7370 ± 50 ^{14}C-years BP in the interval 6380–6090 cal. BC with 2 sigma. Judging by these results the two structures can be considered as being contemporaneous. Moreover, it is worth noticing that the datings overlap with the dating of the huts in Context 5. Is this a coincidence or should Context 5 and 6 be seen as contexts of the same age, of the same habitation, of the same people?

The find assemblage associated with the context is totally dominated by flint. Only a few stone artefacts were retrieved, consisting of two intact hammerstones and a piece of a fragmented hammerstone of quartzite with knapping marks and peculiar faceted sides. The facets have obviously been formed in connection with knapping of some kind, but in which way exactly and for what purpose is unclear (fig. 111:1). Before the Årup excavation this type of faceted hammerstones was known only from the eponymous site of Kongemosen on Zealand and from the Askehoved site in the Roskilde fjord. The type is not known from any other Kongemose sites, but similar pieces made of softer material are known from a few Maglemose contexts (Sørensen 1996:67).

The flint assemblage is dominated by Kristianstad flint, even though Senonian flint dominates the formal artefact categories. The assemblage shows a relatively high artefact diversity, although many of the formal artefact categories are only represented in very small numbers, such as one borer, one fragmented knife, and some microburins. A few microliths exists – not surprisingly – in the form of lanceolates (cf. Context 5).

One of the most prominent features of the context are the microblade cores and handle cores together with a significant number of whole and fragmented microblades. A conspicuous fact is that these artefact categories are almost exclusively made from high-quality Senonian flint, probably reflecting a specialised technology with high demands on the raw material. Still, a few examples of cores and microblades of Kristianstad flint are represented in the material, indeed showing that the microblade technique was applicable to raw materials other than Senonian flint. The technique was introduced in the late Maglemose culture and continued for some time into the Ertebølle culture (Karsten & Knarrström 2003:142; Karsten 2004:100). The main purpose of microblade technology is the manufacture of flint-edged tools, such as slotted bone points and slotted bone daggers (Karsten 2004:100ff).

Regarding the microblade cores and handle cores, an interesting observation is that they to a great extent are totally exhausted or even reworked into new artefacts, a phenomenon signifying economical handling of desirable raw materials not readily available (cf. Knarrström 1997). The majority of the handle cores have one front, though there are examples with two fronts (cf. Larsson 1982b:34).

The classical handle core typology is above all based on the manufacturing technique reflected in the platforms; cores with a negative platform and cores with a positive platform have been distinguished (Vang Petersen 1979:15). This morphology has been used to separate earlier (negative) from later (positive) material. There are, however, several problems in applying this distinction. The most important objection is that negative platforms can be a result of refreshing positive handle cores (Karsten & Knarrström 2003:48). This may be especially important to call attention to in areas where high-quality raw material is not readily available and in consequence of this is maximally exhausted. Criticism has also been levelled against the chronological significance, since, according to Sørensen (1996:59), both types of platforms often appear together in closed contexts.

Besides the presumed significance of the platforms there also seems to be a chronological significance in the height of the fronts, where earlier examples (late Maglemose and early Kongemose) are higher, on average 50–30 mm, and later examples (late Kongemose and early Ertebølle) lower, on average 20–10 mm (Vang Petersen 1993:58; Karsten & Knarrström 2001:305f, 2003:221). The handle cores from Context 6 are totally dominated by negative platforms. The height of the fronts of the most intact examples is on average 30 mm. Morphologically these attributes indicate an earlier chronology of the cores, which could very well be in accordance with the datings of the huts.

Besides the microblade cores, handle cores, and microblades, one of the most frequent find categories are broken blades originating from long symmetrical high-quality blades of Senonian flint. Intact blades and blade fragments with preserved proximal ends found at the site display typical morphological attributes, such as relatively small pointed-oval platforms with a slight overhang, a "lip", on the ventral side, denoting an indirect technique (Crabtree 1972:74; Andrefsky 1998:xxiv, 18). This means that they were manufactured with an antler puncher struck with a club of wood or antler, a technique primarily associated with the Kongemose culture, where the use of punches was the very foundation for the rich production of perfectly shaped symmetrical blades (Karsten & Knarrström 2003:38). Curiously enough, no blade cores corresponding to the blades were found on the site. A possible explanation for this is that the cores were totally exhausted or reworked for other purposes. Another plausible explanation is that the blades were imported to the site in a prepared state, a phenomenon that has been observed on other Middle Mesolithic sites (e.g. Sjöström 2000:20).

However, even though most formal tools were made from blades during the Kongemose culture, all the blades just broken in half remains to be explained. Visible macro use-wear on the edges and on the breakage points indicates that the fragments were used. In order to find out their function ten fragments were selected for traces of use-wear. Unfortunately, the surfaces of eight of the bade fragments analysed had been subjected to mechanical alteration by sand blasting, thus rendering identification of use-wear impossible. However, two blade fragments display traces of use-wear. One of them shows use-wear on the edges indicative of having been employed to work wood. The other has use-wear oriented to the edge on a break, on the ventral side of the fracture, indicative of working of hard organic material, probably bone or antler, in a scraping manner. The edge on a break had been used like the edge of a burin, probably to plane bone or antler. This type of tool has been identified as one of the most common artefact categories in Kongemose contexts, interpreted as having functioned as planes for the manufacture of different types of bone points (Knarrström 2001:46ff;

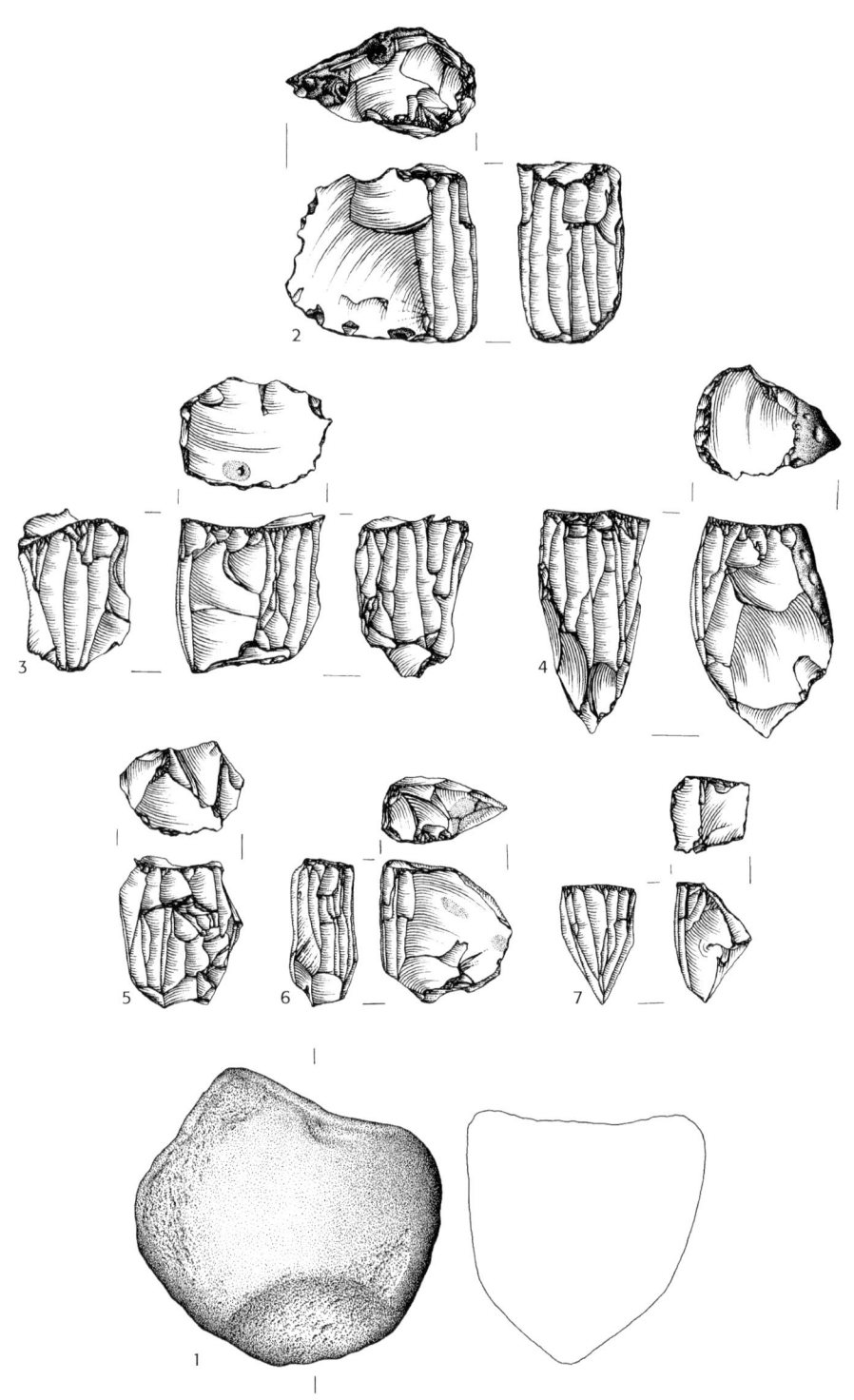

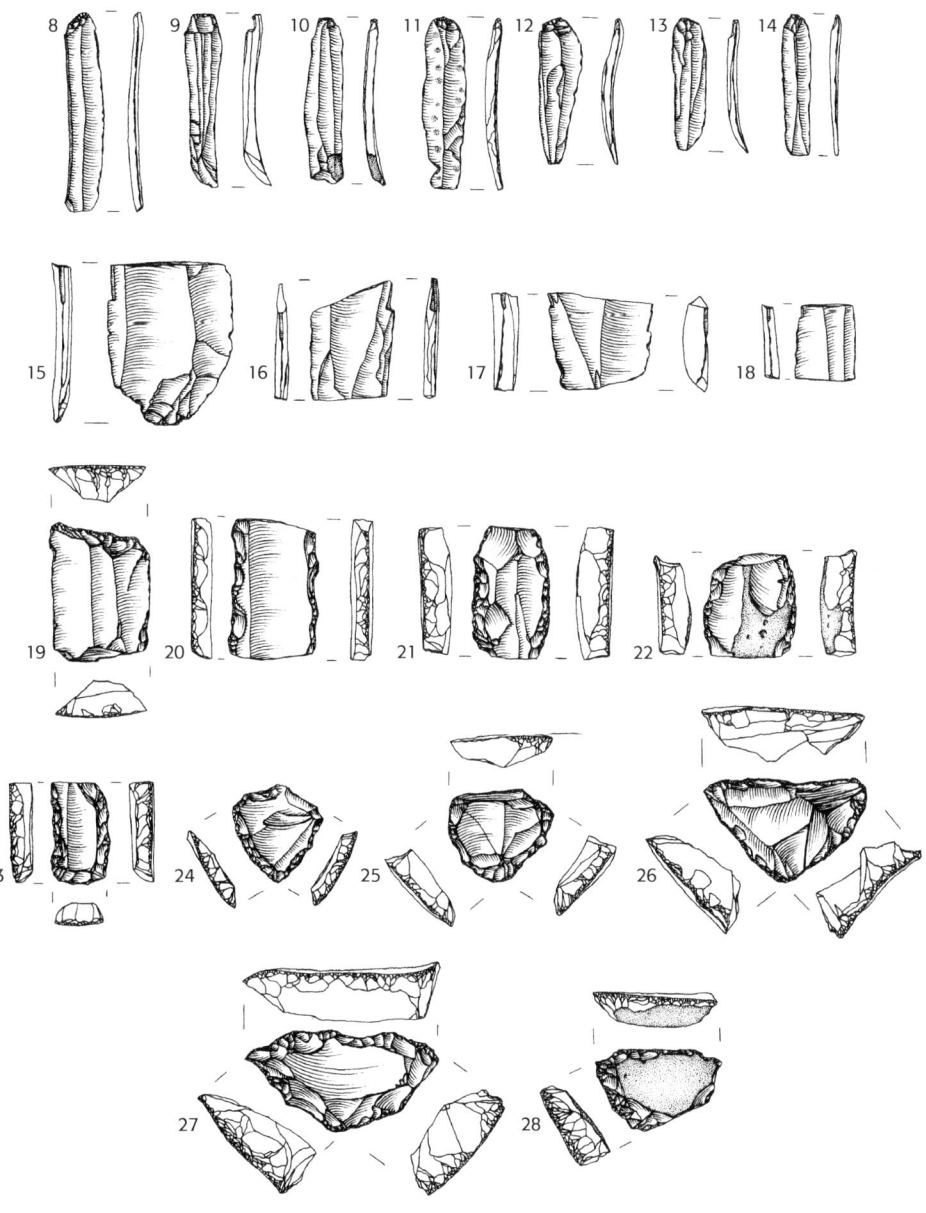

Figure 111. A selection of artefacts from Context 6. 1: Stone with faceted sides. 2–7: Handle cores and microblade cores. 8–14: Microblades. 15–18: Burins. 19–23: Scrapers. 24–28: Pointed tools. Drawings by Björn Nilsson.

Karsten & Knarrström 2003:64, 68, fig. 44). As a curiosity, four blade fragments displayed very fine and small scars oriented to one or two of the edges on a break indicative of the removal of burin spalls (fig. 111:15–18). The blade fragments were interpreted as tools used to make small cuts or carvings in bone or antler.

Moreover, worth special mention are a lot of blade fragments and truncated blades with heavy retouching and macro use-wear along the edges, interpreted as scrapers (fig. 111:19–23). In total ten pieces were analysed for traces of use-wear. Five of these had been subjected to mechanical alteration by sand blasting, four display use-wear not possible to assign to either material or function and one displays use-wear indicative of working of bone.

Beside this, an extraordinary artefact category has been identified in the find assemblage, consisting of what can best be described as pointed tools (fig. 111:24–28). These are made from either small flakes or blade fragments and have two or three sides retouched in a way making most of them somewhat triangular in shape with one or more pointed edges at the ends. The morphology has so far not been identified in other south Scandinavian Mesolithic contexts, making them quite unique in this perspective. Of four pieces analysed for traces of use-wear, one displays no wear whatsoever and two had been subjected to mechanical alteration by sand blasting, making it impossible to classify them. However, one of the pieces displays a generic polish confined to the ventral side of the pointed edge and to the higher parts of the microtopography. Moreover, the polish shows a direction perpendicular to the pointed edge, indicating use in a scraping or carving manner. The material could not be identified but an educated guess would be some kind of hard organic material, probably wood or bone. In conclusion, we are most probably dealing with some kind of local morphology of scrapers most likely used as carving tools in connection with working of wood or bone. As has been mentioned earlier, this type of scraper was found in Context 5 as well, which could be seen as a link that further strengthens the relationship between the two contexts.

It may be concluded from this run-through that the use-wear analysis, due to mechanical alteration of the tools by sand blasting, cannot be considered successful. However, the few positive results could very well serve as guidance for the function of the categories analysed. Our interpretation is that we most likely are dealing with some kind of specialised working of hard organic material in the area, probably wood and bone.

The flint was clearly concentrated in the two identified structures (fig. 112). The major part of the find material was found in and around the floor layer in the western part of the context. Artefacts predominating in this area, beside flakes and blades, were microblades and formal scrapers as well as fragmented and truncated blades with macro use-wear and retouch. In addition, the four burins were retrieved from this area. It is worth noticing that a concentration of microblades and the formal scrapers seemed to follow the western limit of the floor layer. Moreover, a concentration of microblades was found in the south-western part of the feature. Other formal artefact categories recovered from the floor layer and close by were a few microliths and microburins as well as handle cores, a microblade core, a fragmented blade knife, and a hammerstone.

The highest incidence of burnt flint was concentrated in the centre of the floor layer, with an elongated spatial distribution oriented diagonally through the feature and with two dumps at each end of the structure. What this actually represents is hard to tell, but it could very well be seen as a result of a hearth that has been cleared of flint.

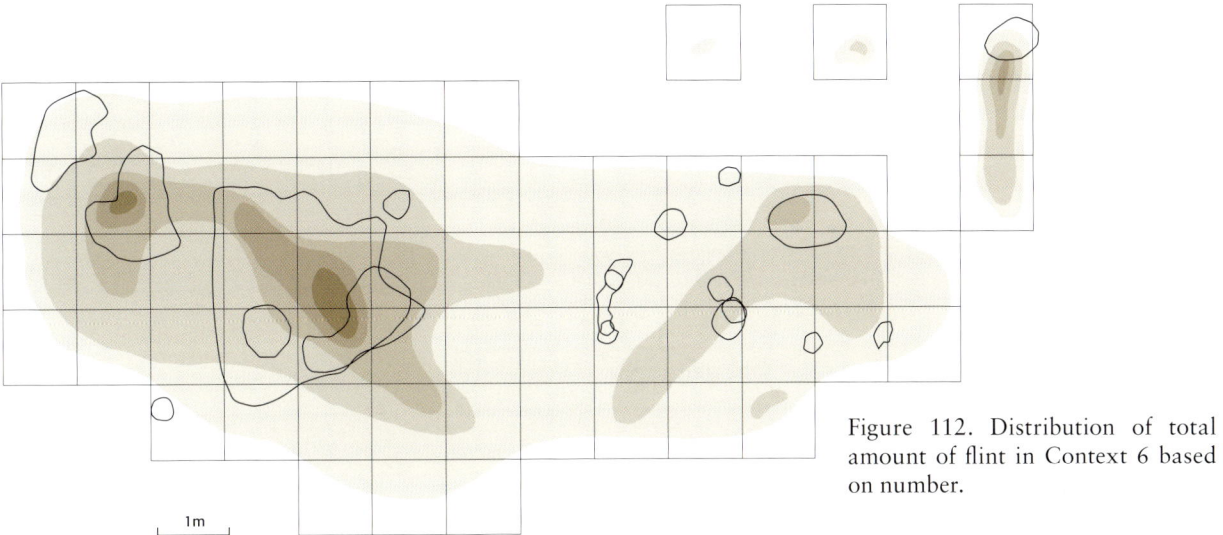

Figure 112. Distribution of total amount of flint in Context 6 based on number.

Find intensity based on number

■ 1 - 14
■ 15 - 35
■ 36 - 73
■ 74 - 132
■ 133 - 186

1 m

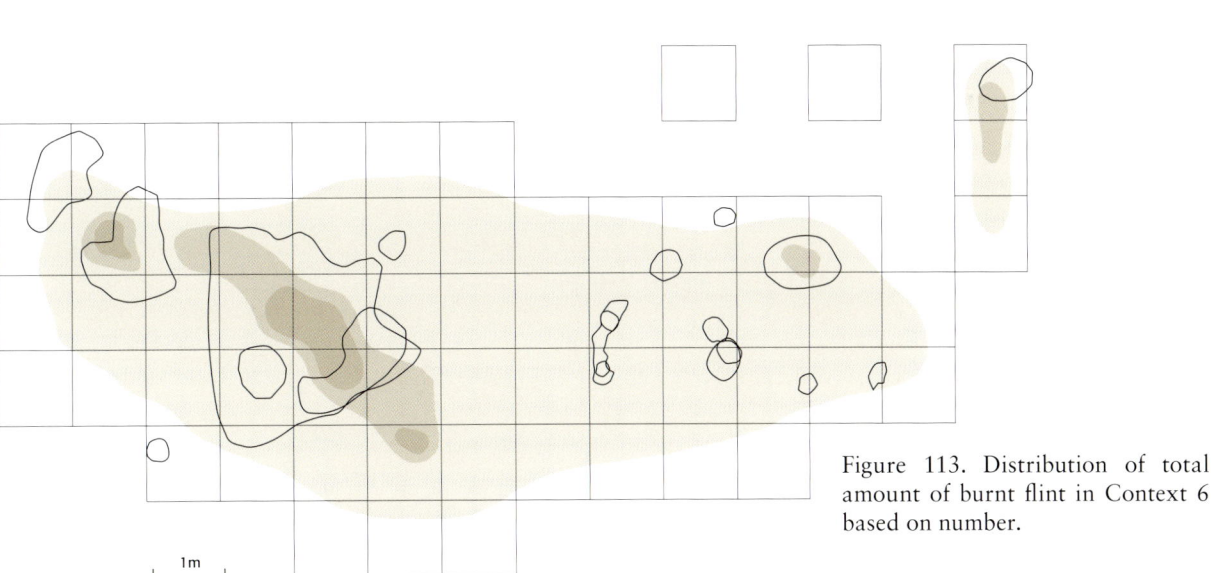

Figure 113. Distribution of total amount of burnt flint in Context 6 based on number.

Find intensity based on number

■ 1 - 14
■ 15 - 35
■ 36 - 65

1 m

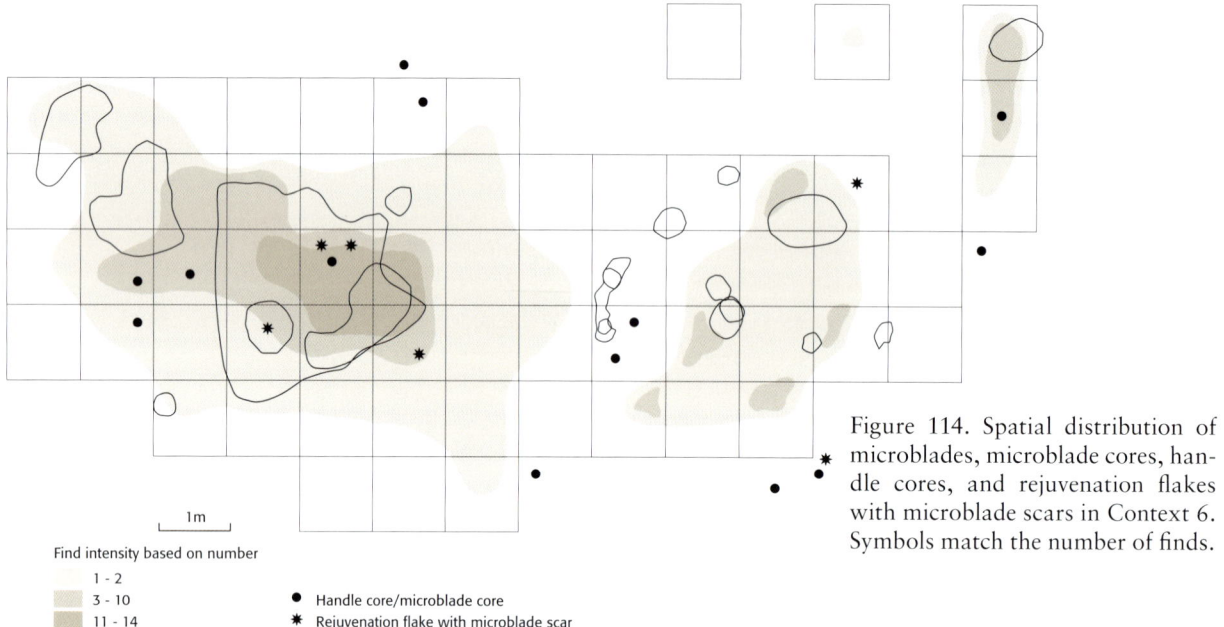

Figure 114. Spatial distribution of microblades, microblade cores, handle cores, and rejuvenation flakes with microblade scars in Context 6. Symbols match the number of finds.

1m

Find intensity based on number

1 - 2
3 - 10
11 - 14

● Handle core/microblade core
✳ Rejuvenation flake with microblade scar

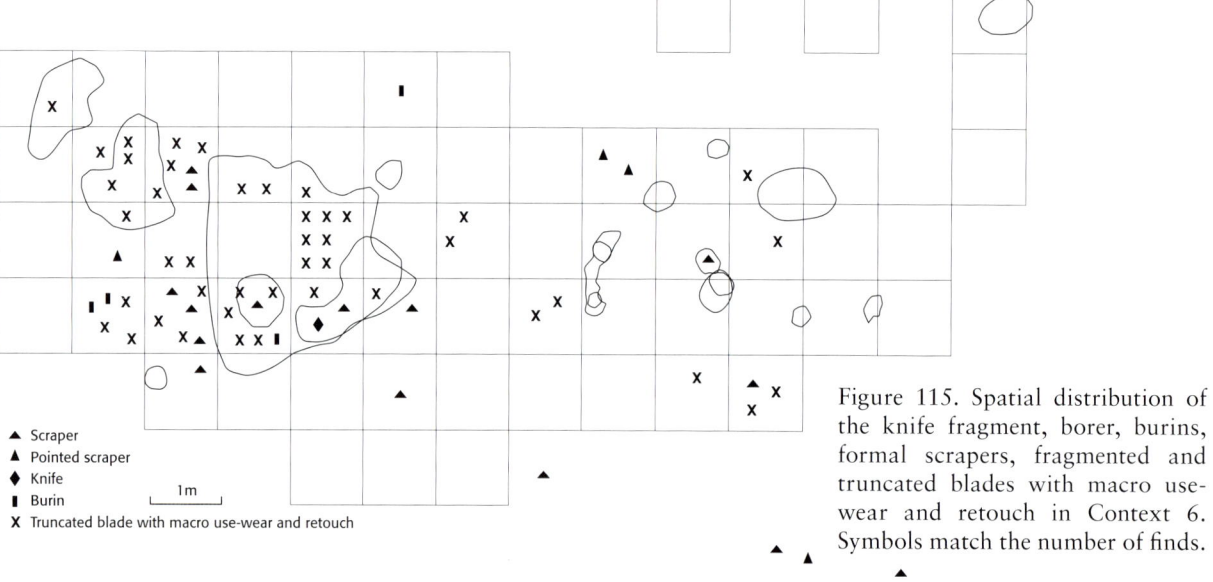

Figure 115. Spatial distribution of the knife fragment, borer, burins, formal scrapers, fragmented and truncated blades with macro use-wear and retouch in Context 6. Symbols match the number of finds.

▲ Scraper
▲ Pointed scraper
◆ Knife
▮ Burin
X Truncated blade with macro use-wear and retouch

1m

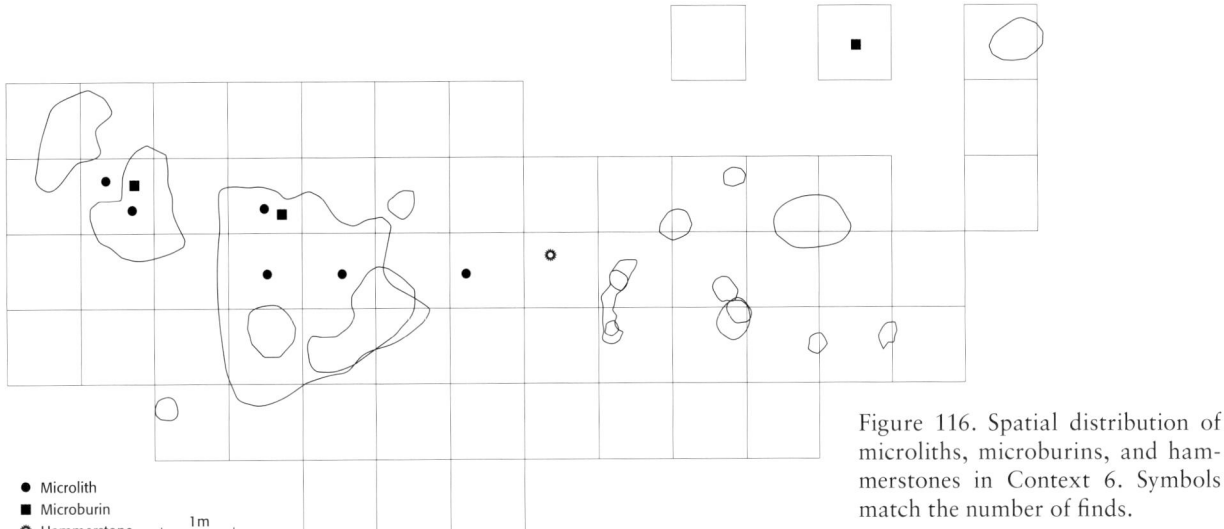

Figure 116. Spatial distribution of microliths, microburins, and hammerstones in Context 6. Symbols match the number of finds.

● Microlith
■ Microburin
○ Hammerstone

1 m

In and around the eastern construction several microblades and a few formal scrapers were found. A concentration of burnt flint was located at the hearth. Moreover, it is worth noting a small collection of handle cores found south of the construction together with several microblades.

The results of the use-wear and spatial analysis clearly define two activity zones in the context. In the western part, formal tools and artefact categories indicate activities connected with wood and bone working as well as handling of microblades. In the eastern part, the find material is indicative of microblade production.

In conclusion, Context 6 is seen as a small settlement unit consisting of two huts with integrated activity areas. The context does not comprise any regular tool production, ordinary household activities, or traces of habitation. The number of tool and artefact categories associated with the context indicates quite specialised activities performed on the

site. Our interpretation is that Context 6 represents a specialised site for manufacturing flint-edged tools such as slotted bone points and slotted bone daggers. The microblade production, the working of bone and wood can be translated into the production of flint edges, bone points, and wooden points or shafts. The structures identified at each end of the context could therefore be seen as workshops rather than regular dwellings.

The technological as well as morphological profile of the context suggests a dating to the early Middle Mesolithic and the Kongemose culture. This is further supported by the radiocarbon datings from the structures, which also confirm the relation between the material and the workshops as being contemporaneous. Moreover, as mentioned above, the datings of Context 6 overlap with the datings of the huts in Context 5. This, in combination with close points of similarities between the technological and morphological attributes of the

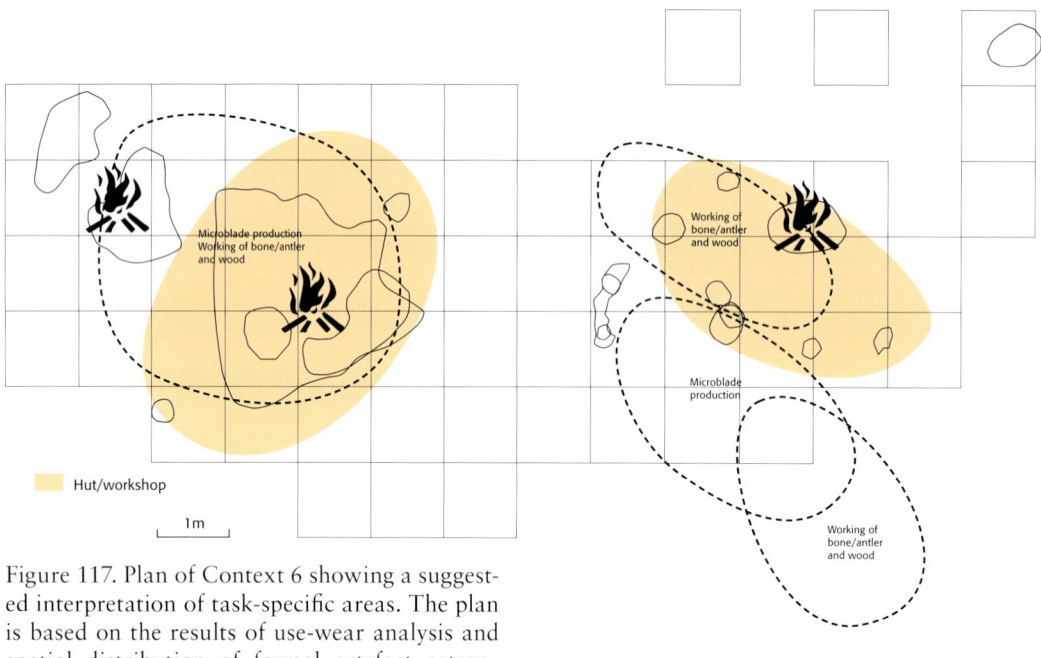

Figure 117. Plan of Context 6 showing a suggested interpretation of task-specific areas. The plan is based on the results of use-wear analysis and spatial distribution of formal artefact categories.

flints, points towards the inference that the two contexts should be seen as the unit of ordinary habitation and the workshop of the same settlement, in use contemporaneously.

All in all, Context 6 reflects one of the most special forms of objects associated with the Kongemose culture, the slotted bone points and daggers, without having a single find of them. The tradition of flint-edged tools – introduced in the late Maglemose culture, characterising the Kongemose culture – seems to have been deeply rooted in north-eastern Scania. The tradition expresses its influence in the region through the example of the slotted bone point from the Barum grave as well as the many slotted bone points and the remarkable slotted bone dagger from Lake Råbelövssjön (see *A slotted bone dagger from Kongemose?*, page 158–160).

A SPLASH OF ERTEBØLLE

During the last day of excavation, on the fringe of Context 6, a hoard consisting of 14 whole and fragmented unburnt microblades was found in a sooty area (posthole) of a small pit. They are all made from Kristianstad flint measuring on average 20 mm. A charcoal sample from the pit identified as lime (*Tilia sp.*) produced a date of 6370 ± 40 ^{14}C-years BP in the interval 5460–5290 cal. BC with 2 sigma. This put the hoard in the early late Mesolithic and the early Ertebølle culture.

Just a short distance from the hoard a burnt handle core of Kristianstad flint was found. The core differs morphologically from the examples in Context

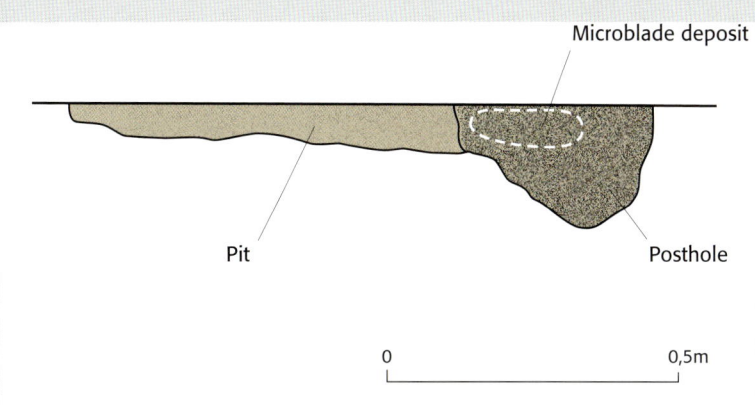

Figure 118. The section of the small pit with the hoard of microliths marked.

6 as it has a positive platform as well as a lower front (20 mm), which can be taken as an indication of it being of a later date (cf. discussion Context 6). Moreover, a really ugly transverse arrowhead made from a natural

cracked piece of flint was found close to the hoard.

Taken together, there is no doubt about it – a splash of Ertebølle had fallen onto Årup as well!

Figure 119. The transverse arrowhead, handle core, and microblades. Photo by Staffan Hyll.

A slotted bone dagger from Kongemose?

By Per Karsten

Finds of exotic animal tooth beads, amber, stone adzes, and flint axes in different Mesolithic contexts and areas have since long attracted scholarly interest. Above all, such finds can shed light on problems concerning prehistoric trade and exchange networks (Larsson 1988b). The slotted bone dagger from Lake Råbelövssjön seems to offer an interesting example of long-distance contact during the Middle Mesolithic. It was found in the late nineteenth century during drainage work in the southern outlet of the lake together with slotted bone points and several other bone artefacts. The distance from Årup is 14 km to the west as the crow flies.

The dagger is undoubtedly a strange bird. It is the only certainly known Swedish find of this typical Danish artefact of which there are about 25 known examples mainly from Zealand (see Voss 1961:153 ff). According to Ulla-Karin Larsson (1973) a couple of fragmented daggers have also been found at the settlements in Ageröd Bog, and Lars Larsson mentions a find from the cemetery of Skateholm II (1988a:121 ff). But these small medial fragments cannot be used for identifying daggers, because of the obvious difficulties in distinguishing them from slotted bone points. Only intact examples can be used. Anyhow, using the term dagger seems to be perfectly logical because the artefact has two functional sections: a practical handle at the base and a razor-sharp edge towards the tip. In contrast the slotted bone points instead functioned as tips in wooden arrows or spears.

The dagger was most probably manufactured from an elk tibia. As can be seen in figure 121, the 25-cm long dagger is not in perfect condition. All the microblades once inserted are gone.

In the earliest published drawing one can hardly see any decoration at all (Montelius 1917, fig. 59), but a new drawing in a seminar paper (Larsson 1973) showed distinctive patterns in the form of Z-shaped signs arranged in eleven small groups along the side of the dagger. However, a re-examination displays a somewhat different picture, as can be seen in figure 120. The Z-shaped signs are in fact rhomboids, some full and some half, of the same design as we know from Kongemose sites in southern Scandinavia. The rhomboid was undoubtedly *the* key symbol in the portable art of Kongemose Culture (Karsten & Knarrström 2003:104 ff).

Comparing the decoration on the dagger with known South Scandinavian examples the closest parallels are to be found in the Åmosen area in Zealand, Denmark. Two sites in particular come to mind: the eponymous site of Kongemosen and the settlement Magleø, situated close by. A slotted bone point and an antler axe from Kongemosen deserve special mention (Jørgensen 1956, fig. 7 & 8). On both of these objects there is specific rhomboid-like decoration in small groups or lines, very similar to our dagger. Moreover, the peculiar shape of the tip on the Råbelöv object is remarkably similar to the tip of the slotted bone point from

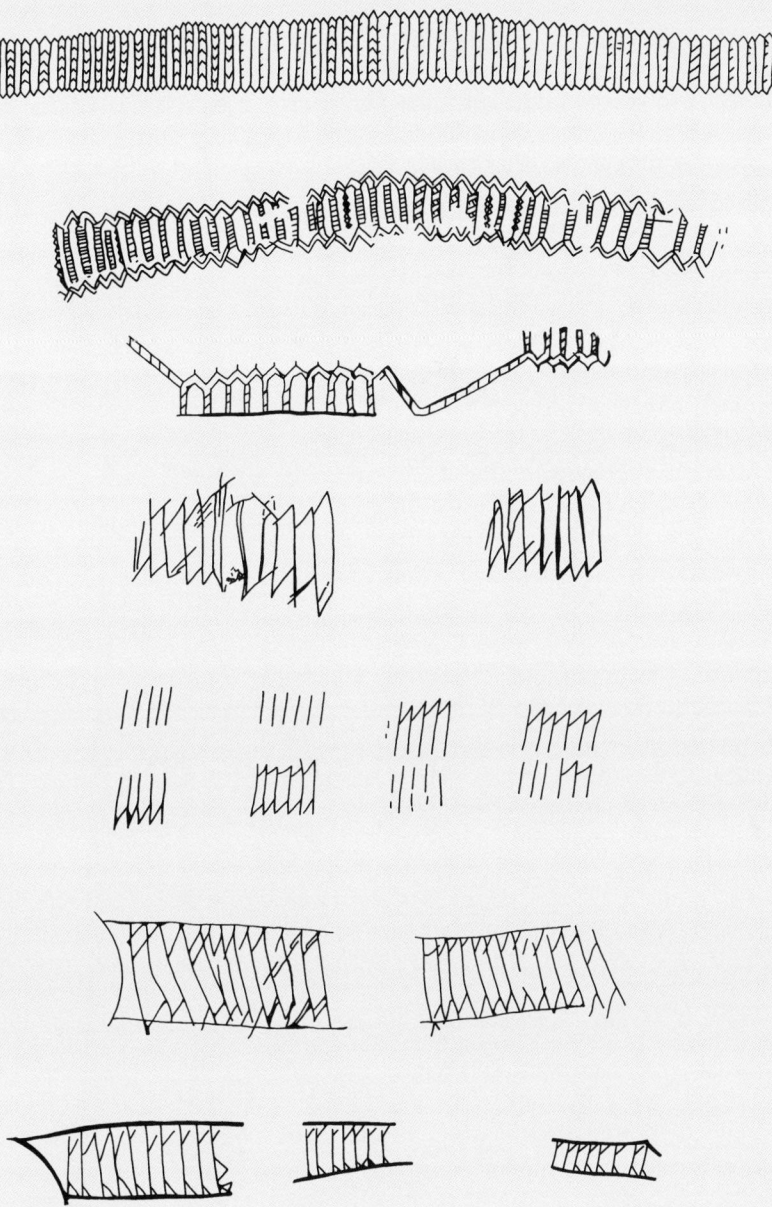

Figure 120. South Scandinavian rhombic figures. From top to bottom: Tågerup, Sjöholmen, Kongemose, Magleø, Lake Råbelövssjön, Kongemose, and Ageröd (redrawn by
Björn Nilsson from Jørgensen 1956, figs. 7, 7a, 8, 8a; Karsten et al. 1998; Larsson
1978b, fig. 3 & 30; Mathiassen 1943 fig. 50).

Kongemosen (compare also with the Mullerup dagger in Johansson 2000, fig. 132). In the varied and somewhat hastily performed decoration found on an antler axe from Magleø, there are also several rows of rhomboid-like patterns of the same type (Mathiassen 1943, fig. 50).

In conclusion, the Råbelöv dagger lacks Swedish counterparts. The tool type, decoration, and tip shape clearly demonstrate a Danish origin. Most probably it was manufactured by a skilled craftsman who lived on the shores of the great Åmosen lake, western Zealand, sometime during the early Kongemose culture, around 6300 BC. As a prestigious gift it was exchanged by and between the clans – from the Åmosen area, via the people of the lagoons around the Öresund strait, then eastwards into the interior of Scania to the lake Ringsjön clan. But it still had another 50 km to go. As the dagger went from hand to hand astonishing stories of its origin and fate flourished. Each time the dagger changed ownership new adventures were added. Finally the dagger reached its final destination, southern Lake Råbelövssjön, 200 km north-east from its Danish birthplace. Right there, just before the dagger broke the water surface to embark on its journey to the powers of the lake, the spectators, at last, heard the end of the story.

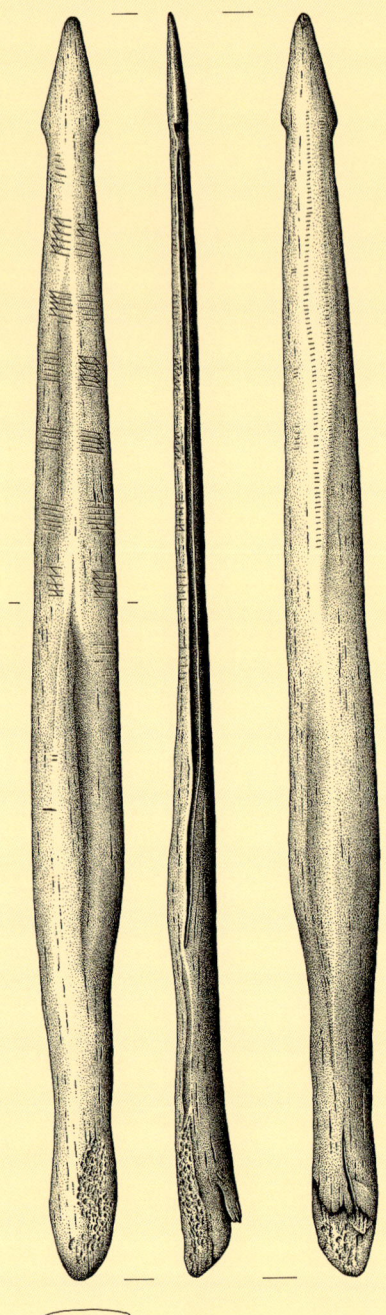

Figure 121. The slotted bone dagger from Lake Råbelövssjön. Drawing by Björn Nilsson.

Contexts 7 & 8
RITUAL ÅRUP

Not only did Årup provide us with a splendid insight into the ordinary household activities of everyday life. In addition, we were allowed a glimpse of the usually more obscure and elusive realms of human life – the rituals.

In Denmark and outside Scandinavia it seems to be difficult to find acceptance for Stone Age depositions as offerings, and rather than ritual acts the finds are regarded and explained in functional terms, such as caches for later use (Bradley 1987, 1990; Schilling 2001; cf. Karsten 1994:24; Larsson 2000a:93).

Evidenced by the archaeological record, two separate areas at the Årup site displayed signs interpreted as indicative of ritual behaviour. Both areas had close proximity to water in common, one being situated to the east by the River Skräbeån and the other to the west by a presumed wetland since drained. The eastern context, Context 7, comprised a large posthole situated on a slight elevation and close to this, beneath the fossil riverbank down by the Skräbeån, three pieces of flint. The western context, Context 8, consisted of an area with fine-grained white sand where high concentrations of burnt flint were found. We are obviously dealing with two contexts that have close relationship to water and fire respectively.

Ritual acts connected to water and fire have received only limited attention in Mesolithic research. However, Scandinavian archaeologists have long accepted later depositions in wetland as offerings. It seems to have been more problematic and more difficult to relate to sacral destruction by burning. The act as such is accepted but it has not received the same attention as offerings in wetlands. Lars Larsson has discussed this topic and believes that these attitudes might mirror our own relation to water and fire, where water is seen as

something that is creative, in contrast to fire which is more destructive (2000a:93f). However, in prehistory both elements most likely were filled with much more spiritual and positive power than today, as they were obvious prerequisites of daily life.

A TOTEM POLE AND VOTIVE OFFERINGS OF FLINT

In the eastern part of the area of investigation, a substantial pit cut by a large posthole was found down by the fossil riverbank, situated between Contexts 2 and 3 on a slight elevation at a level of 5.2 m above present sea level. It was quite clear that a sturdy post of some kind had stood on the spot in the past.

The pit was 0.42 m deep and 1.11 m in diameter, with a filling consisting of sand, light grey in colour with an element of charcoal. The posthole was 0.36 m deep and 0.22 m in diameter, the filling consisted of sooty dark grey sand. Two stones present on either side of the post-pipe had presumably acted as wedges stabilising the post. Possibly, a blackish-grey feature in connection with the post-pipe also constituted the remnants of a wooden wedge. Neither the pit nor the posthole contained any finds.

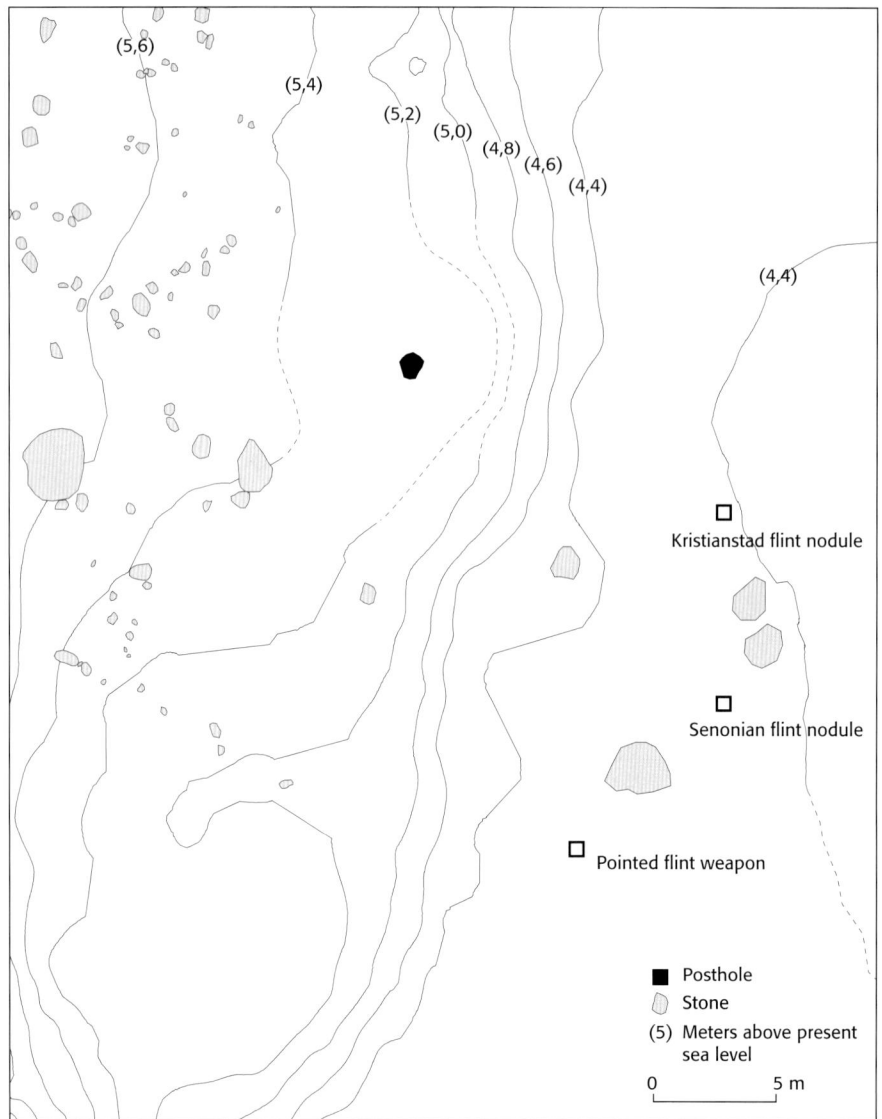

(5,6)

(5,4)

(5,2)

(5,0)

(4,8)

(4,6)

(4,4)

(4,4)

☐ Kristianstad flint nodule

☐ Senonian flint nodule

☐ Pointed flint weapon

■ Posthole

 Stone

(5) Meters above present
    sea level

0   5 m

Figure 122. Plan of Context 7 showing the position of the totem pole and the votive offerings.

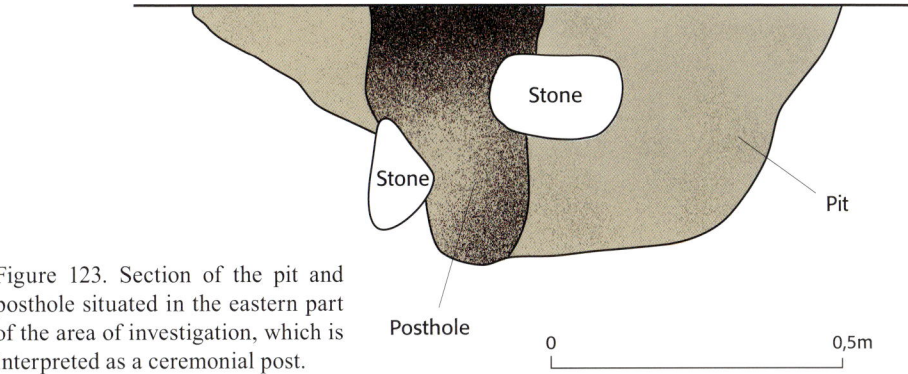

Figure 123. Section of the pit and posthole situated in the eastern part of the area of investigation, which is interpreted as a ceremonial post.

Stone

Stone

Pit

Posthole

0   0,5m

A sample of charcoal taken from the pit close to the post-pipe identified as being of pine (*Pinus silvestris*), was radiocarbon-dated to 7975 ± 70 ^{14}C-years BP in the interval 7070–6650 cal. BC with 2 sigma. This suggested that the post had been erected on the site sometime during the early Atlantic, in the time-span including the lifetime of the Barum woman.

Contrary to the initial assumptions, the posthole turned out not to be contemporary with either of the two huts situated close by, i.e. Contexts 2 and 3. Instead, the radiocarbon date was more in line with the later datings derived from the highest point of the investigation area. Even though the dates from Contexts 5 and 6 show that these are clearly younger than the posthole, there were charcoal samples taken from features near by – presumably belonging to settlement remains just outside the area of investigation – which produced datings that overlapped in time with the posthole.

In attempting to explain why a solitary post of sturdy dimensions was erected by the riverside some 9,000 years ago, one has to weigh up various reasonable explanations. Telling against the post being a purely practical construction of some sort, such as for instance a stand or platform for drying or storage purposes, was the fact that the post was somewhat displaced in relation to the known contemporary dwellings on the site. Then again, the post could be interpreted as the securing part of a stationary fishing device lying in the shallow water close to the shore, or for that matter an anchor post for tying canoes. However, both the post and pit certainly seem to be rather oversized and somewhat displaced for such purposes.

Perhaps a more likely interpretation is that the post should be seen as signifying something, a symbolic or ceremonial post oriented towards the river. The position of the post close to the water, some distance away from the contemporary dwellings, suggests that it could very well be a territorial marker of some sort.

Given the strategic setting of the site, situated by a waterway uniting the coast with the inland and optimally placed within easy reach of several natural resource areas, signs of territorial awareness should not come as a surprise. Groups of people were no doubt attracted to the area and its resources. Dependence on natural resources in an area can create a strong sense of identity with that land, especially in the presence of other competing groups of people.

Signs of territorial behaviour have frequently been seen as indicating greater complexity among hunter-gatherers. Territoriality having been taken as a response to constraints in mobility, the idea being that restrictions in various forms, natural or social, lead to different responses in order to solve the problems of reduced mobility (cf. Carneiro 1970; Price & Brown 1985:8; Larsson 1984a:34f). Social territories delimited by the presence of neighbouring groups are characterised by signalling of identity and defending of borders (Wobst 1976).

In the light of this it is quite reasonable to assume that the dwellers at Årup during the early Atlantic had reason to materially establish the right to the area and its resources. A clearly visible symbol of some kind placed by the riverside would inform neighbouring groups and passers-by in a direct way regarding which group of people, clan, or family inhabited the area. Hence, the mysterious pit and posthole by the riverside could indeed be interpreted as the physical remains of a material manifestation like a totem pole.

The phenomenon of totem poles, known from the north-west Pacific coast of America and Canada, has been the object of extensive research over the years (e.g. Barbeau 1990; Codere 1966). Although there is a complex religious aspect to totem poles, they also express the identity of the people, such as rank, social position, kinship, group belonging, and unity as well as prestige and pride. Characteristics like these would have been easily recognisable and understood by groups of people in the area around Årup.

Finds of large postholes that have been suggested to be of a symbolic or ceremonial nature akin to totem poles are not unheard of from Mesolithic contexts. From the famous site of Stonehenge in England, where three substantial pits containing postholes aligned in a row were discovered, the postholes all provided Mesolithic dates and have been interpreted as totem-pole-like structures (Allen 1995:55f). Another example comes from the

Late Mesolithic cemetery of Skateholm I in southern Scania. A cremation grave (Grave 20) in the shape of a large metre-deep posthole was interpreted as a possible totem pole (Larsson 1988a:118; cf. Larsson 2003:xxix). The circumstances concerning a grave (Grave 1) at the Tågerup site in north-western Scania indicate something similar, where a post marked the position of a woman's buried remains. A deposition of the majority of a burnt offering or the remains of a meal was placed beside the post (Karsten & Knarrström 2003:79).

We will never be able to verify whether totem poles did in fact exist on Mesolithic sites or not, unless we find one preserved in a bog or a marsh or deep under the sea. However, in our opinion it is more likely than unlikely that totem poles were in fact in use during the Mesolithic. We could not find any better interpretation. In today's world we have flags, national emblems, political emblems, etc. The symbols bound up in these emblems are very roughly equivalent to a totem pole. Human beings have always needed to express their identity.

That the inhabitants' perception of flint extended beyond the purely practical and functional realm was illustrated by the separate finds of two flint nodules and a small pointed flint weapon. The artefacts were found beneath the fossil riverbank down by the Skräbeån approximately 4 m above present sea level. A very small number of finds were discovered in this area, which made the artefacts stand out as very special in the context.

To begin with the nodules, both are of high-quality flint, one of Senonian flint and the other of Kristianstad flint (fig. 123). Curiously enough, the nodules display four negative flake scars each, giving the impression that they had been checked for quality before being deposited in the water. In the case of the nodule of Senonian flint, the quality test may very well have been performed in the area of origin in south-western Scania or Zealand. Perhaps this was done in order to make certain that the flint was of such a high standard that the nodule was worth transporting to the north-east, or for that matter that it was worthy of offering.

Given that Senonian flint does not occur naturally in north-eastern Scania and thus had to be imported to the region, it is quite remarkable that such high-quality flint should end up deposited in intact condition. On the contrary, one would have expected to find that Senonian flint was maximally used and for that reason ought to be found in a far more fragmented state. This is also what one would expect regarding high-quality Kristianstad flint. It might also be important to mention that no other nodules of such high quality and in intact condition were found on the site.

The exclusive nature of Senonian flint in the context of north-eastern Scania unites the two critical factors of high quality and limited supply; to some extent this could be said to be true of good quality Kristianstad flint as well. Presumably, Senonian flint was in high demand and regarded as desirable by people in the region. The relative scarcity of high quality flint most probably made the artefacts extra valuable. This was no doubt also the prime reason why these were chosen as votive offerings.

Regarding the pointed flint weapon, this is also made of high-quality Kristianstad flint. It is a slender, well-made and completely intact specimen, finely worked from three sides and triangular in cross section. It is thickest in the middle with a sharply pointed butt and point and slightly curved in the longitudinal direction (cf. Mathiassen 1948: 20).

Small pointed flint weapons have been described as usually being 10–15 cm in length and have been suggested to have functioned as axes or spear points, depending on whether they are two-sided or three-sided (Mathiassen 1948:20). As yet there exists no way of metrically distinguishing

between small pointed flint weapons and pointed axes (cf. Vang Petersen 1993:98; Karsten & Knarrström 2003:127f). Regarding large pointed flint weapons these have been defined simply by stating that they should be more than 25 cm in length (Mathiassen 1948:20; Sørensen 1996:61) and a characteristic often seen is that they are made from Danian flint or moraine flint of poor quality (Karsten & Knarrström 2003:95).

Pointed flint weapons are generally ascribed to the late Maglemose or early Kongemose Culture and have been interpreted as a weapon or a sign of rank (Vang Petersen 1993:98). Furthermore, pointed flint weapons have been associated with ritual activities (for a discussion, see Karsten & Knarrström 2003:94). The artefact type is not numerous and only 45 specimens from 26 locations are known from Zealand, Jutland and Scania including the one from Årup (Sørensen 1996:61; Karsten & Knarrström 2003:94, 128).

The Årup specimen was analysed for traces of use-wear in order to find out whether it had been used or shafted in any particular manner. Lo and behold, to our great surprise it displays very distinctive polish confined to the protruding surfaces of the butt half of the implement (fig. 124).

The polish clearly indicates that the pointed flint weapon had indeed been shafted either directly in a shaft or handle of antler, bone, or wood or indirectly in a socket in turn fixed to a shaft. Since no further traces of use-wear or other damage were observable on the point end of the artefact, it was apparently shafted but unused when deposited.

If we are to suggest a plausible reconstruction of what the pointed flint weapon may have looked like originally in a shafted condition, the shape of the object itself provides us with some clues as to the nature of this. There are essentially three aspects in the shape of the object with a bearing on

Figure 124. Votive deposits of high-quality Senonian and Kristianstad flint nodules, found separately beneath the fossil riverbank. The flint nodules each display four negative flake scars. Photo by Staffan Hyll.

3 cm

the shafting: the triangular cross-section, the curved longitudinal shape, and a pronounced shoulder constituting the thickest part of the object and separating the point end from the butt end.

The triangular shape of the object restricts the possible ways of mounting. Preferably, a flat surface of the object needs to be orientated downwards in the shaft hole in order to make the shafting stable. The curving of the object also limits the possible positions of the point if we presuppose that the point was aligned straight in the longitudinal direction. The shoulder present on the object shows in a direct way how the butt end was secured in the shaft, with the shoulder acting as a stop.

In the reconstruction (fig. 125), we have combined different elements from existing finds of South Scandinavian Late Palaeolithic and Mesolithic shafts. The shaft was most likely made of wood, bone or antler and could very well have been finely decorated. A few examples of decorated shafts from Mesolithic contexts give a glimpse of how important status symbols and votive ceremonial artefacts sometimes were decorated (e.g. Andersen 2001: 88ff; Karsten 2001:134; Karsten & Knarrström 2003:103). In the reconstruction we have chosen a longer shaft made of antler with the pointed flint weapon inserted like an axe. The decorations are of Early Mesolithic character as known from south Scandinavian sites. The reconstruction gives an impression of a fearsome weapon, capable of any kind of deliberate or brutal killing.

Figure 125. To the left, the pointed flint weapon found beneath the fossil riverbank and to the right a suggested reconstruction. Drawings by Björn Nilsson.

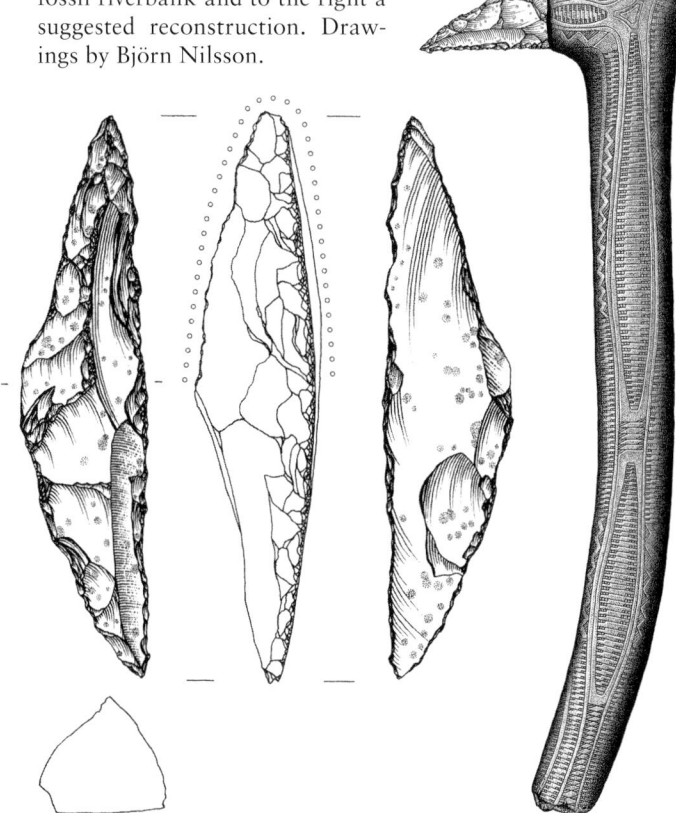

When were the artefacts deposited in the water? Votive offerings in wetlands are a well-known phenomenon throughout the Mesolithic with a great variability. Preboreal finds are known from Lundby Mose on Zealand, where some concentrations of elk bones have been found in a kettle hole, interpreted as results of rituals that were part of hunting magic or subsequent feasting (Møller Hansen 2003). From the early Boreal we know, for example, two hoard finds of almost complete skeletons of elk, with six and two individuals respectively, the first found in Skottemarke bog on Lolland and the latter in Favrbo on Zealand (Möhl 1978; Sørensen 1978). From the late Boreal and the Atlantic periods, we know of several votive offerings, both single finds and hoards, consisting of bone points, flint blades, axe shafts and different kind of tools made of bone and antler (e.g. Welinder 1977; Larsson 1978a; Trönndahl 1993; Karsten 1994:166ff, 2001:123ff; Karsten & Knarrström 2003:91ff).

To answer the question of when the three artefacts from Årup were deposited in the wetland adjacent to the totem pole, the pointed flint weapon indirectly dates the finds to the early Atlantic and the late Maglemose culture. Moreover, since both nodules had been struck with four blows each and were found only 7.6 m apart, and since all three artefacts in addition were found on the same level, these facts might be seen as indicating a reasonably synchronous event.

Moreover, the finds from the wetland at Årup should possibly be seen as related to activities connected with the totem pole, as they were situated roughly 14 m south-west of this. The totem pole, the flint nodules, and the pointed flint weapon in combination with the lagoon-like environment constitute the essence of a ritual context, dated to the early Atlantic and the late Maglemose culture.

In the western part of the area of investigation at a level of roughly 7 m above present sea level, a clearly defined concentration of flint comprising roughly 60 m² was discovered. The flint assemblage was lying in white and very fine-grained sand stretching along the north-eastern side of a drained wetland (cf. Context 4). Three features were present within the area, one small pit and two small sooty concentrations.

The flint assemblage is characterised by high concentrations of burnt Kristianstad flint, found in four distinct concentrations within the area (fig. 128). Based on number, 66% of the total amount of flint is burnt. Most of the material is so fragmented that it is almost impossible to distinguish whether the pieces derive from formal tools or just from waste material. However, only a very limited number of formal tools have been identified.

The unburnt flint was concentrated in an area comprising roughly 6 m² in the north-western part of the context, giving the impression of the material having been dumped at the place. A plausible interpretation could be that it was brought together with the intention to burn it.

The flint assemblage displays characteristic Mesolithic morphological and technological attributes. The finds of burnt artefacts, such as a fragmented core axe, some lanceolates, a blade core, and small irregular blades and microblades, in combination with unburnt lanceolates, a small tanged point, blades, and microblades, is in good agreement with an Early Mesolithic chronology. The fact that the material is totally dominated by Kristianstad flint further strengthens this assumption (cf. discussion Context 4).

Moreover, worth special mention are four flint tools of Kristianstad flint with rounded edges and ends (fig. 131:1–4), two of which had been subjected to fire, found in the large central concentration

Hard facts

OF CONTEXT 8.

In total 2,334 pieces or 2,882 g of flint are associated with the context. Of these, 1,540 pieces or 1,544 g are burnt. The assemblage is dominated by 2,242 pieces or 2,761 g of Kristianstad flint, while 92 pieces or 121 g are of Senonian flint. Divided into categories, the assemblage comprises 827 flakes, 467 splinters, 108 blades and blade fragments, 22 microblades, 3 cores, 4 rejuvenation flakes, 1 formal scraper, 1 core axe, 6 microliths, 1 tanged point, 3 microburins, 4 strike-a-lights, and 887 other flints.

of burnt flint. The remaining two were found outside the concentrations of burnt flint, one of them in the small pit, and had not been exposed to fire. The two unburnt examples were analysed for traces of use-wear, which displayed characteristic signs of having been used as strike-a-lights. Apart from the fact that they displayed heavy rounding of the edges and ends where massive parallel scratching could be observed, they also displayed heavy macro use-wear in the form of crush marks and retouches (cf. Johansen & Stapert 2000:52; Knarrström 2001:52). Strike-a-lights made of flint have been in use throughout prehistory and history until the present (Vang Petersen 1993:140). A general view is that Stone Age man started fires by using flint, sulphur pyrite, and tinder (Johansson 1993:42ff).

Strike-a-lights are known from Late Palaeolithic and Mesolithic contexts as well as Neolithic contexts with a high degree of morphological variation (Johansen & Stapert 2000:51; Knarrström 2001:51f). If not made from discarded formal tools, which can be easily dated, it is often very

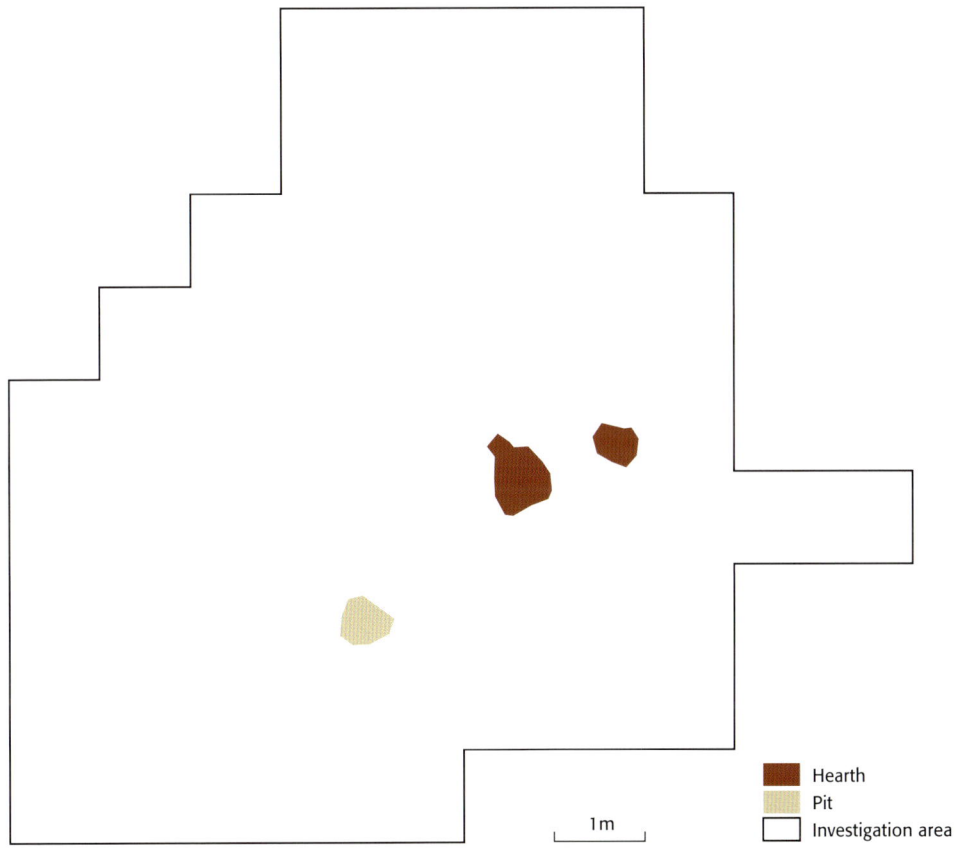

Hearth
Pit
Investigation area

1m

Figure 126. Plan of Context 8.

hard to date them solely based on morphological grounds. Thus, the find circumstances play a central role in the dating.

The four strike-a-lights of Context 8 can certainly be linked to the act of burning, which resulted in the high concentrations of burnt flint in the area. In connection with the other formal artefact categories found in Context 8, the strike-a-lights could be dated to the Early Mesolithic. Early Mesolithic strike-a-lights are known from several sites,

for example Star Carr, where both rounded flint tools, interpreted as strike-a-lights, and pieces of pyrite and tinder have been found (Clark 1954).

What is being expressed at Context 8 differs from finds of burnt single artefacts and small concentrations of burnt flint, which is evident at settlement sites with everyday activities. Context 8 was a delimited area lacking settlement debris. The three features present within the area all indicate activities connected with the act of burning.

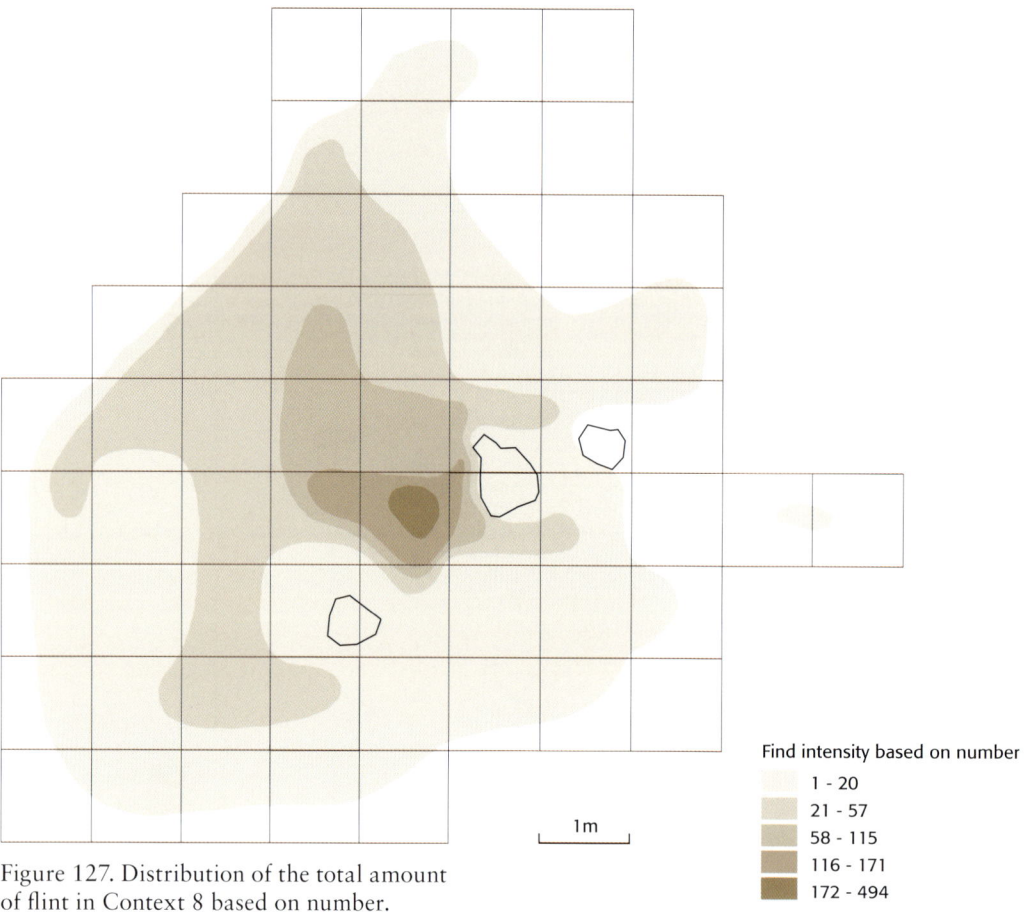

Find intensity based on number

  1 - 20
 21 - 57
 58 - 115
116 - 171
172 - 494

1 m

Figure 127. Distribution of the total amount
of flint in Context 8 based on number.

The sooty concentrations have been interpreted as
the remains of two small fireplaces where the flint
material was most likely burnt. Curiously enough,
the features contained very few finds. The smaller
sooty concentration did not have a single find, and
the larger one only a few burnt splinters. A pre-
sumable interpretation would be that the fireplaces for some reason were cleaned after the burning and that the flint was spread and dumped in
small concentrations all over the area. The small

pit contained no other finds than four small splinters and one of the unburnt strike-a-lights. The
meaning of this can hardly be explained, but may
well be linked to the act of burning. Unfortunately, no material suitable for radiocarbon dating was
found in any of the features whatsoever.

In conclusion, Context 8 is interpreted as a delimited area showing evidence of an intentional destruction of flint by fire, giving a snapshot of a special ritual behaviour during the Early Mesolithic.

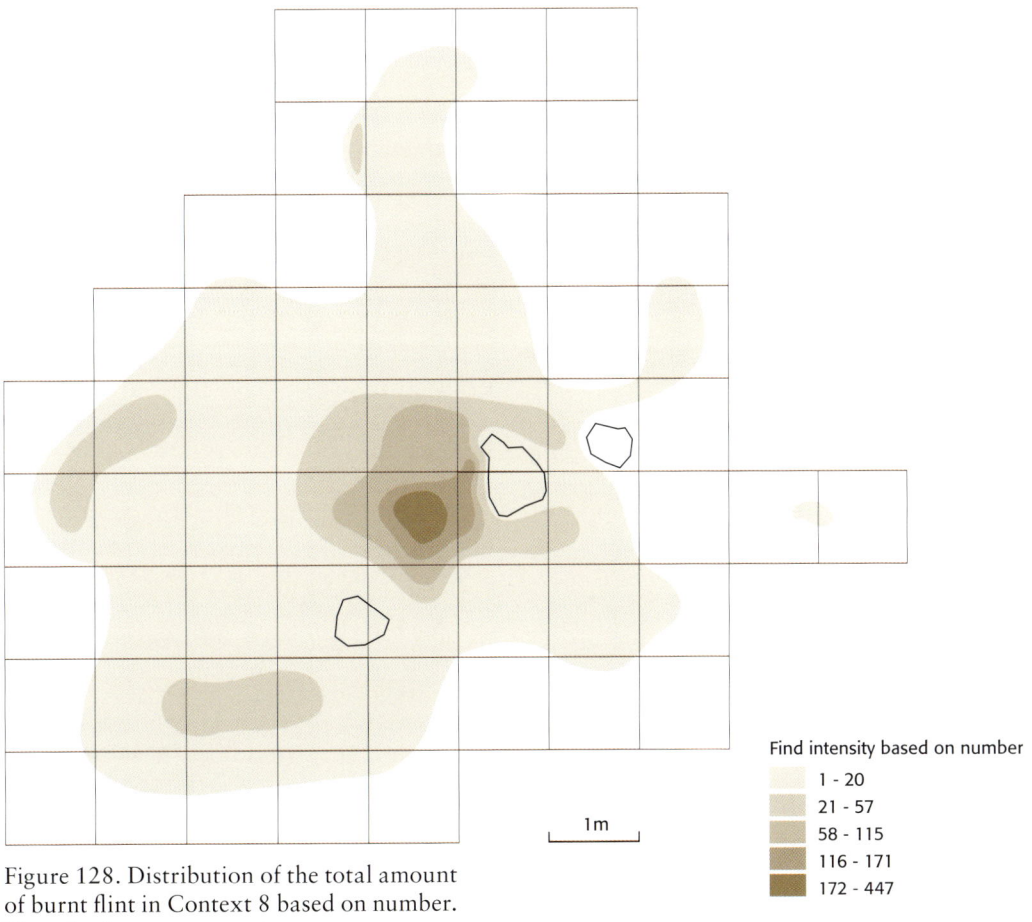

Figure 128. Distribution of the total amount
of burnt flint in Context 8 based on number.
Note the four concentrations.

Find intensity based on number

- 1 - 20
- 21 - 57
- 58 - 115
- 116 - 171
- 172 - 447

1m

Most likely the context represents ritual burning
during a short-term interval and the finds probably reflect the remains of just one firing, which indicate that the activities should be regarded as
completed depositions of the material (cf. Larsson
2000b:609). It might also be important that the
context is located at the highest point of the area,
clearly visible to the surroundings.

However, Context 8 should not be seen as remains of ritual activities without any connection

to other aspects of social life. Fire played an important role for prehistoric people and in a variety
of ritual acts. The burning of flint would have had
a direct visual as well as auditory impact. During
the burning the flint undergoes remarkable and
rapid changes, with a clattering sound, continuous
rapid movements of fragmentation, and an obvious change of colour. Lars Larsson wants to see
similarities between the process of cremation of a
human body and the intentional burning of flint;

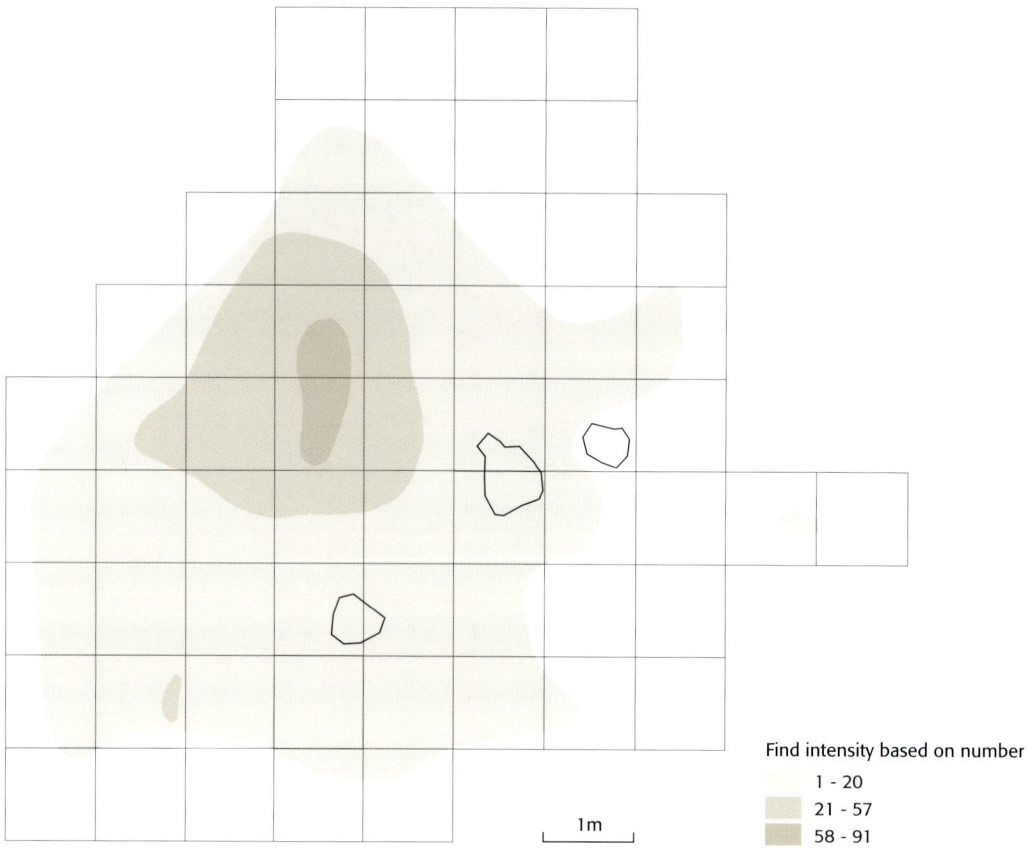

Find intensity based on number

1 - 20
21 - 57
58 - 91

1m

Figure 129. Distribution of the total amount of unburnt flint in Context 8 based on number.

the cremation of flint objects (2000a:101). Such an act could possibly be seen as connected to some kind of *rite de passage* (van Gennep 1909, 1977).

Moreover, it is very likely that Context 8 is related to Early Mesolithic settlement remains nearby. As have been mentioned earlier, the area of white fine-grained sand extending along the eastern side of the drained wetland indicates Early Mesolithic activities, which could very well be related to Context 8. Furthermore, Context 9 (see

next section) displays characteristics similar to the assemblages. It is also plausible that the context is connected to activities hidden to us due to restrictions of the area of investigation.

Destruction of tools by fire is relatively frequent at settlement sites throughout the Stone Age. Ritually significant burning, though, seems to be less common during the Early Stone Age periods. From the Mesolithic only a few examples of ritual destruction of flint by fire are known

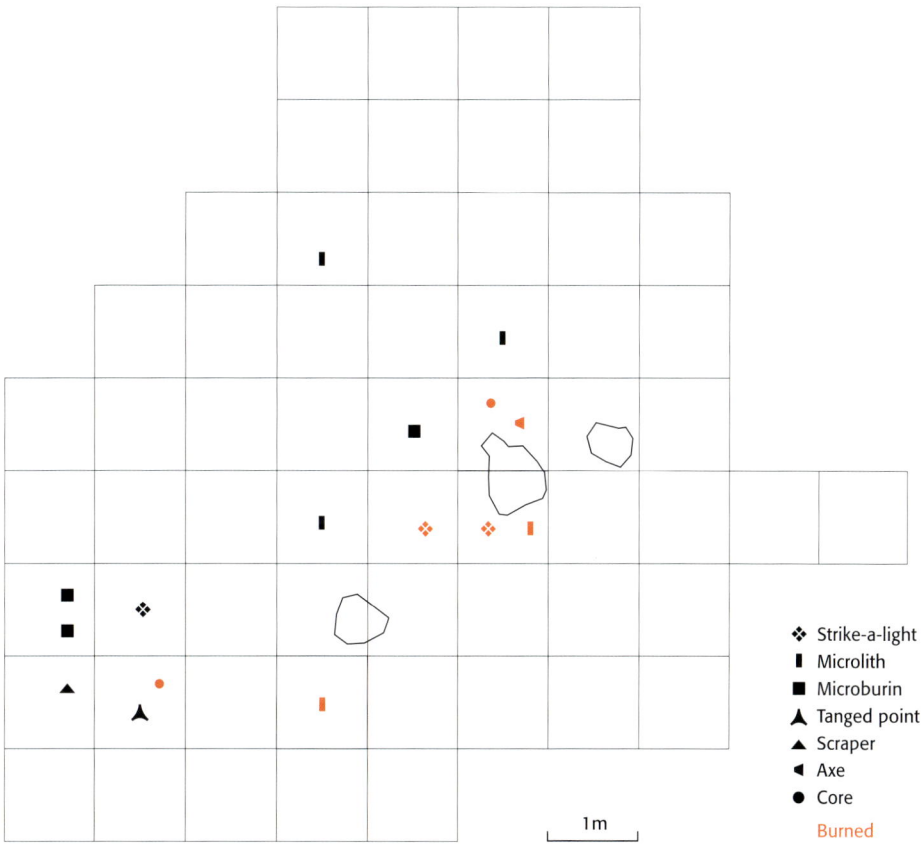

Figure 130. Distribution of formal artefact categories in Context 8 based on number.

Strike-a-light
Microlith
Microburin
Tanged point
Scraper
Axe
Core
Burned

1 m

and it seems that mostly single artefacts were involved in the act (e.g. Karsten & Knarrström 2003:95). During the Neolithic, ritual burning of flint tools, especially axes, is more common (Karsten 1994). Massive destruction of large numbers of artefacts does exist but seems to be rare. Only two sites are known, Svartskylle and Kverrestad in south-eastern Scania, dated to the Early and Middle Neolithic periods respectively (Larsson 2000a, b).

As no contemporary and explicit parallels to Context 8 are known, the question is whether Context 8 constitutes evidence of special ritual behaviour at the Årup site or if similar sites have not yet been recognised elsewhere. We are quite certain that ritual burning was much more common than we usually suspect. Thus, it is our belief that parallels to Context 8 will be discovered in the future, or maybe they already have been, but are still not recognised or interpreted as the remains of ritual burning.

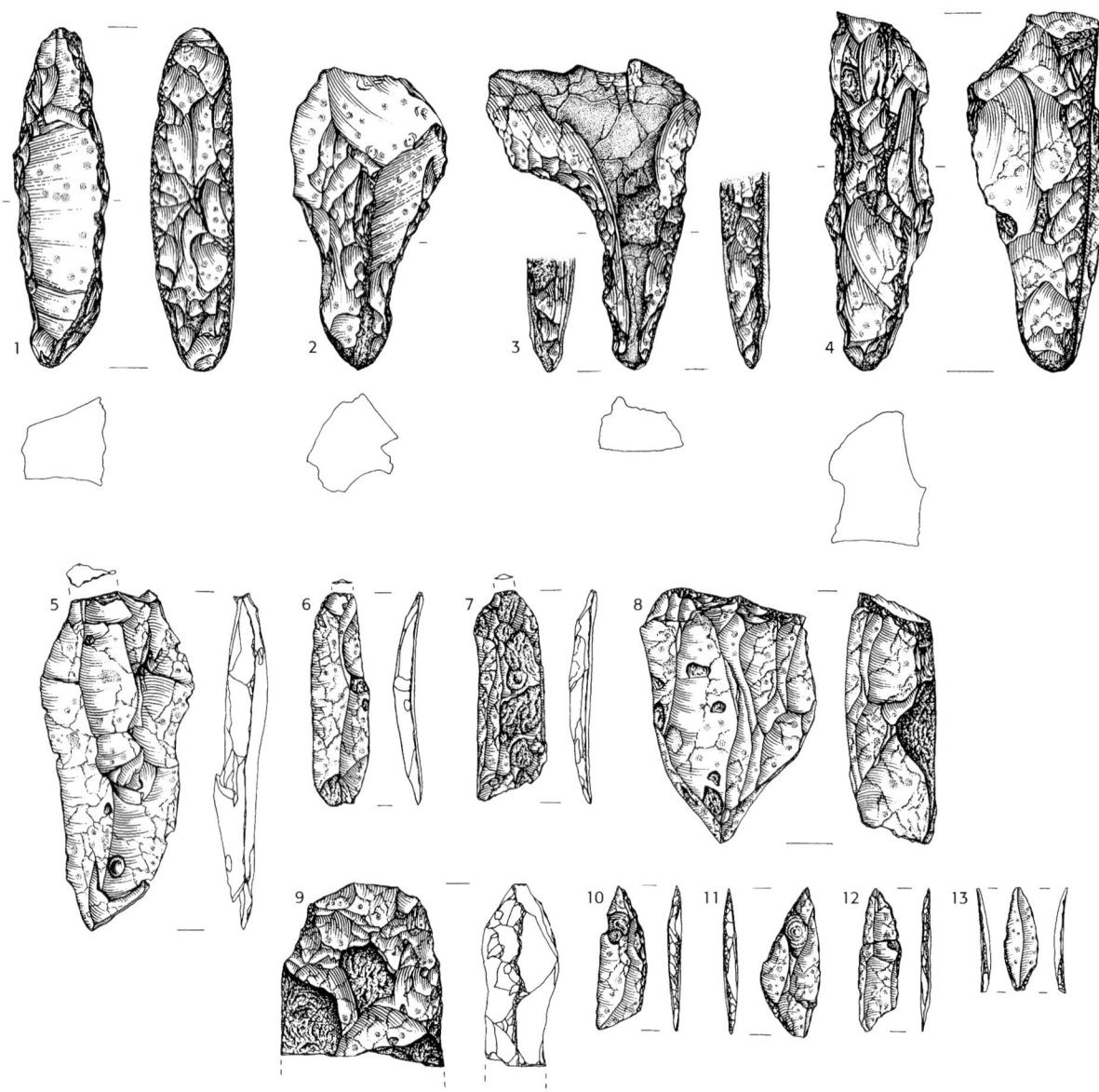

Figure 131. A selection of artefacts from Context 8. 1–4: Strike-a-lights. 5–7: Blades. 8: Core. 9: Fragmented core axe. 10–12: Microliths. 13: Tanged point. Drawings by Björn Nilsson. Photo on next page by Staffan Hyll.

The conclusion to be drawn from this run-through of ritual acts at Årup is that the specific acts involving flint are related to both water and fire. Even if there are common denominators of the ritual contexts, as for example the location by former wetlands, there seems to be a very marked difference in the attitude towards burning of flint compared with offerings in water in prehistory (Larsson 2000a). According to Lars Larsson, the destruction of artefacts by burning is easily visible at the point when the practical function of the tool ceases to exist. The opposite result goes for the artefacts placed in wetlands which allow preservation for future use. Larsson points out: "Fire is the destroyer, water the preserver" (2000a:100). Thus, the act of ritual destruction of flint by fire should be regarded as completed depositions, while the wetland offerings as long-lasting unfinished projects.

Context 9

TO BE CONTINUED...?

As has been mentioned earlier, the primary strength of contract archaeology is the large areas that are often the subject of archaeological investigation, facilitating the exploration of entire structures. At the same time, contract archaeology is subjected to restrictions and the archaeologists have no chance of influencing the choice of location or for that matter the object of investigation. These choices are governed by society's demand for development. The essence of this is that the construction of a motorway only allows us a brief glimpse of prehistory through the "infrastructural wound". What we see is only a minute fraction of the great prehistoric jigsaw puzzle, sometimes with its pieces cut off by the restrictions. When

Hard facts

OF CONTEXT 9.

In total 1,648 pieces or 1,531 g of flint are associated with the context. Of these, 195 pieces or 141 g are burnt. The assemblage is dominated by 1,461 pieces or 1,305 g of Kristianstad flint, while 167 pieces or 199 g are of Senonian flint and 20 pieces or 27 g of Danian flint. Divided into categories, the assemblage comprises 721 flakes, 757 splinters, 52 blades and blade fragments, 53 microblades, 3 cores, 2 rejuvenation flakes, 5 formal scrapers, 7 microliths, 8 microburins, and 39 other flints.

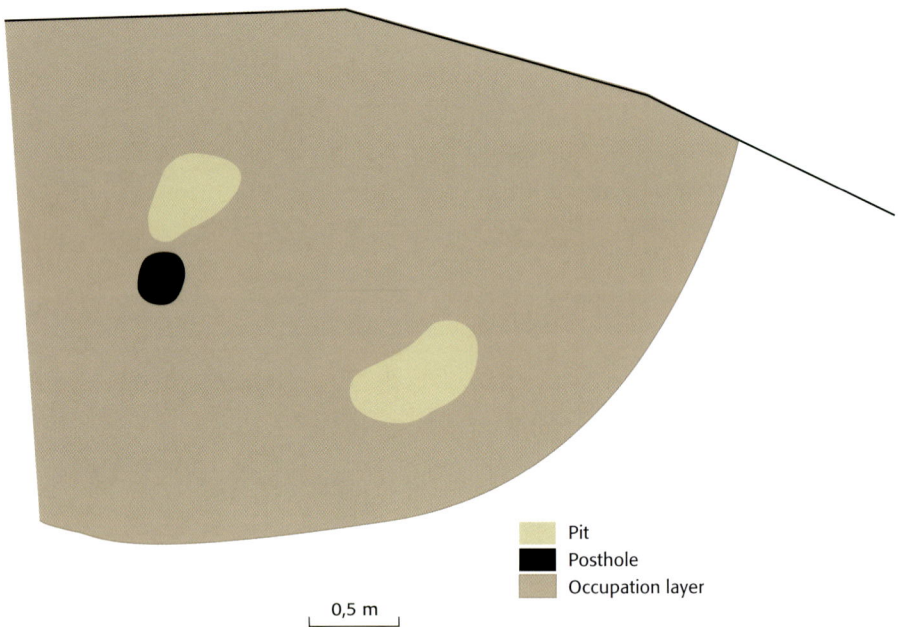

Pit
Posthole
Occupation layer

0,5 m

Figure 132. Plan of context 9.

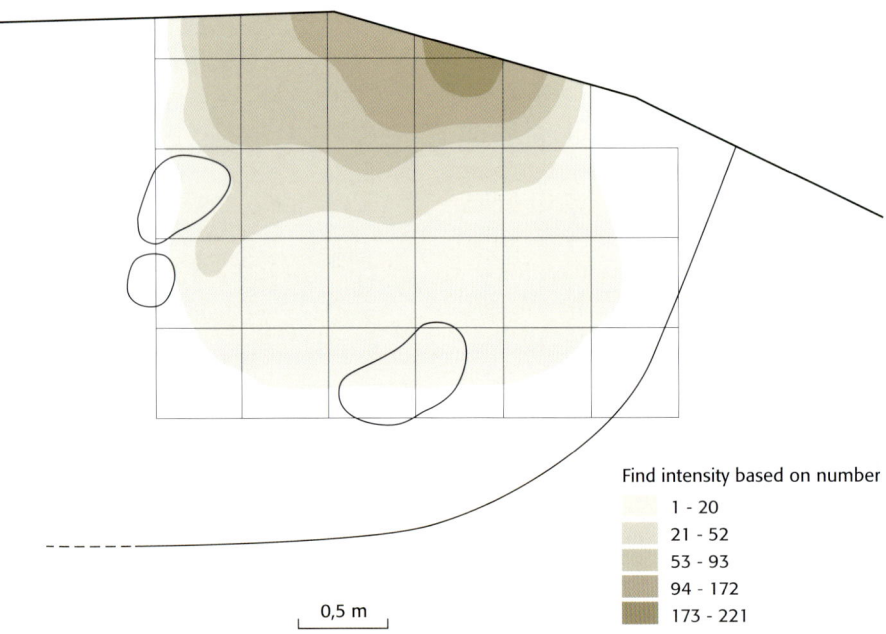

Find intensity based on number

1 - 20
21 - 52
53 - 93
94 - 172
173 - 221

0,5 m

Figure 133. Distribution of flint in Context 9 based on number.

Figure 134. A selection of scrapers, cores, microliths and blades from Context 9. Photo by Staffan Hyll.

this happens we can only imagine what is hidden under the surface just outside the area of investigation. "Context cut off" is a common occurrence in contract archaeology, where the restrictions are to be followed. It happens in small as well as large-scale excavations, and Årup was no exception. Context 9 is the example.

This context was observed as a cultural deposit consisting of greyish-brown fine-grained sand, peeping out of the north-eastern profile wall, continuing out of the area of investigation. Due to the restrictions, only a limited peripheral part could be investigated properly.

The context covered roughly 6 m² and was characterised by high concentrations of knapped flint. A simple refitting of some blades and flakes, together with high concentrations of splinters, clearly indicates contemporaneity in the assemblage as well as knapping on site.

Small blades, microblades, and flakes, predominantly irregular in shape, indicating direct hard hammer percussion technology, dominate the material. The finds of small conical irregular cores, simple lanceolates, of which one displays the classical shape of a Vig microlith with a microburin facet at the point end, small flake and blade scrapers, date the material to the Early Mesolithic. This is further corroborated by the fact that the material is totally dominated by Kristianstad flint (cf. discussion Context 4). It might also be important that the context was located on a lower point, approximately 5 m above present sea level, of the eastern slope down towards the River Skräbeån. According to the dated contexts at Årup, this seems to be of chronological significance, indicating an older age of the settlement remains.

Three features were present within the area consisting of two small pits and a posthole. The pits contained a few blades, flakes and splinters of the same character as the surrounding material, which linked them very well to Early Mesolithic activities.

What exactly Context 9 represents is hard to tell, but a reasonable assumption is that it follows the pattern of well-delimited contexts of a specialised nature, which seems to be a characteristic of the Årup site.

We will not try to force an interpretation of Context 9, instead that task will be willingly handed over to anyone who is privileged enough to excavate at Årup in the future.

Context 9 underlines the potential of the Årup site for future investigations. What lies hidden beneath the surface outside the area of investigation, we can only imagine. However, we are quite certain that the Årup site and its surroundings comprise one of the richest Early Mesolithic settlement complexes in South Scandinavia. In the landscape along the reaches of the River Skräbeån, from Lake Ivösjön in the north to the sea in the south, settlement remains are no doubt lying like a string of pearls waiting to be excavated.

Epilogue

By Björn Nilsson, Conleth Hanlon & Per Lagerås

Concluding remarks
– a few selected topics

The studies and analyses presented in this book are a contribution to the knowledge of the earliest inhabitants in north-eastern Scania. The outcome of our work should not be seen as conclusions comprising final answers and solutions. However, the Årup excavation has yielded a great many valuable insights, which hopefully will inspire and be combined with further studies in the area. Some of these insights are commented on below.

To begin with some palaeoenvironmental conclusions, it can be established that the stratigraphy at Årup could be linked to the environmental history of the region as a whole. Combinations of local on-site analyses with regional palaeoenvironmental information have a great scientific and pedagogic value, and the Årup site turned out to be very suitable for such an approach. The long record of Quaternary research in the region – in particular on shoreline displacement – together with the preserved organogenic sequence on the site, enabled us to put the archaeological remains at Årup in a larger palaeoenvironmental context.

The Late Palaeolithic and the Early Mesolithic together was a period of great environmental change. In a series of regressions and transgressions, the shorelines of the Baltic moved rapidly back and forth several times and turned coastal areas to inland and vice versa. These changes, in combination with the climatic warming and the transition from tundra to woodland, make up a very complex and interesting environmental history. Therefore, to understand the environmental setting of the Stone Age sites at Årup and elsewhere in the region, careful palaeoenvironmental studies and independent chronologies are needed.

The results of the analyses clearly show that the transition from open tundra to closed woodlands during the Early Mesolithic was one of the most important environmental changes during the last 100,000 years, and it was certainly of utmost importance to humans. As a consequence of this change, the Ice Age way of life – based on hunting large herbivores in an open landscape – came to an end, and was gradually replaced by a more varied and complex economy adapted to woodlands. In a local perspective, the Littorina transgression and the formation of a lagoon close to the Årup Site offered a good basis for this new economy.

The archaeology at Årup yielded evidence of repeated occupation at the site from the Late Palaeolithic to the Late Mesolithic, spanning more than 5,000 years. The find material, which consists exclusively of lithics, could be directly linked to several individual contexts and displays distinct technological and morphological traits indicative of different chronological periods. Most of the contexts were well delimited with spaces completely devoid of features or finds in between. This, in combination with a rather meagre quantity of flint, indicates that we are dealing predominantly with short-term occupations. The exception to this was constituted by the Middle Mesolithic dwelling contexts which displayed a more complex picture with more features and partial overlapping of flint assemblages, attributes indicating a greater time depth and repeated habitation. In short, it has been possible to illuminate differences existing in the settlement pattern over time at Årup.

There are certainly chronological changes in technology as well as morphology at the site, from the characteristic technology and archaic features of the Late Palaeolithic flints to the specialised production of high-quality microblades and blades in the late Early and Middle Mesolithic. However, it has to be mentioned that the dramatic change occurs in the late Early Mesolithic with the introduction of the specialised blade and microblade production. Before that, only small changes can be traced in the material, indicating a moderately unilinear technological tradition from the Late Palaeolithic into the Early Mesolithic (cf. Andersson & Knarrström 1999:107).

Presumably intimately associated with the technological development are changes in the preferences of raw material, which also seem to be of chronological significance. While the earlier contexts belonging to the Late Palaeolithic and the early part of the Early Mesolithic are totally dominated by Kristianstad flint, the later contexts belonging to the late Early and Middle Mesolithic contain a much larger amount of Senonian flint. It seems quite reasonable to assume that the new specialised blade and microblade technology raised the standards of the raw material.

Interestingly enough, this technological revolution seems to correlate with the introduction of a more varied and complex economy adapted to woodlands, including a gradually more permanent settlement structure. Contacts and cultural exchange with south-western Scania are suggested to have intensified in connection with this new economy.

Beside these observations, one of the most important outcomes of the Årup excavation is the substantial contribution to the knowledge of Mesolithic dwelling structures. Finds of indisputable Mesolithic huts and houses are very rare indeed. In relation to the large number of excavations of Mesolithic remains, the amount of traces of buildings discovered does not correspond in any way to the fieldwork efforts or to the Mesolithic population structure.

Before the Årup excavation only about 15 secure Mesolithic hut and house structures were known in South Scandinavia. This could be explained by the way of life during the Mesolithic. High mobility combined with huts of light construction left no or very few traces, which could be hard to identify as remains of dwelling structures. Another explanation could be that the methods carried out within the traditional Stone Age archaeology have been defective for investigating traces of settlement (Karsten & Knarrström 2003:150).

From the Late Mesolithic, huts are known from e.g. Bredasten (Larsson 1986), Bökeberg II and III (Karsten 1986, 2001; Karsten & Regnell 1995), Møllegabet II (Skaarup & Grøn 2004), Skateholm (Larsson 1985), and Tågerup in Scania (Cronberg 2001; Karsten & Knarrström 2003) as well as Lollikhuse (Sørensen 1993) and Nivaa on Zealand (Jensen 1998).

Concerning the Middle Mesolithic, there is not a single certain example of a dwelling structure in the whole of southern Scandinavia, with the exception of the Rönneholm hut (Sjöström 2000) and a possible structure from Saxtorp (Larsson 1975; questioned by Karsten & Knarrström 2003:37).

Early Mesolithic huts are known from Ageröd (Larsson 1975) and Bare Mosse in Scania (Welinder 1971), Ulkestrup Lyng, Lundby II (Henriksen 1980), and Baremose on Zealand (Andersen et al. 1982; Degn Johansen 1990) as well as Duvensee in Schleswig-Holstein (Bokelman 1981). Moreover, two huts have recently been discovered and excavated at Ålyst on Bornholm (Casati et al. 2002; Sørensen 2002, 2003; Casati & Sørensen 2003; see also *Short note* on page 126).

The construction and planning of Mesolithic dwelling structures display a variation of round to round-oval forms as well as rectangular huts or houses. The constructions vary in size between approximately 2 and 14 m in length and 2.5 and 6 m in width. Some are countersunk constructions, some have platforms of bark/wood, and others have postholes, trenches and hearths or both postholes and floor layers as well as stone constructions (Biwall et al. 1997:266).

This general picture of Mesolithic hut contexts, with a high degree of variability, does not differ to any appreciable extent from the known Late Palaeolithic huts (e.g. Rust 1972; Tromnau 1975; Jelinek 1978). The most striking difference in a diachronic perspective, from the Late Palaeolithic to the Late Mesolithic, is the size of the huts. Generally speaking, irrespective of form, the size tends to increase during the Late Mesolithic.

There may be several explanations regarding why the huts look so different. According to Binford (1990:119ff) the degree of mobility and type of hut are intimately associated. A group of hunters/gatherers which moved often probably had light huts, easy to move and set up again. Such camps rarely leave any traces other than distributions of finds (cf. Karsten & Knarrström 2003:37). As a general rule, huts of a mobile society differ from those of a more permanent society. Moreover, designs and sizes probably varied depending on season (Karsten & Knarrström 2003:151).

Then, of course, the purpose and function of a hut influences a design as well; a dwelling and a workshop probably followed different plans.

The morphology and size of the huts from Årup are in accordance with the general picture outlined above, with a high degree of variability. The forms vary with an oval to round morphology and with sizes of 6 by 2.5 m (Context 2), 4.5 by 2.5 (Context 3), 9 by 4 m (Context 4), 4 m in diameter (Context 5), and 3 by 3 m and 3 by 2 m (Context 6).

In conclusion, the most striking feature is the variation in size and appearance, although a rounded morphology seems to be a common denominator and could be considered as significant during the Late Palaeolithic as well as the Early and Middle Mesolithic periods. Even if there might have been a notion of standardisation with idealised sizes and constructions during some periods, we are of the opinion that the traditional search for period-indicating remains to establish chronotypological systems seems to be rather pointless. So is the statement, that there always has to be a system in the morphology of the hut and house constructions, a kind of "type huts" or "type houses" (Jensen 1998: 21). Instead, the key is the concept of *variation*.

WHY ÅRUP?

Traces of repeated occupation spanning more than 5,000 years, from the Late Palaeolithic to the Late Mesolithic, illustrate that Årup must have constituted a most favourable location. Still, one may ask oneself what factors contributed to the repeated settling of Årup. What was the appeal? It is a justifiable question because we know that the shifting character of the landscape during the Late Palaeolithic and Mesolithic entailed fluctuations in the environment and wildlife, thus continuously changing the prerequisites for subsistence in the area.

Contrary to our initial assumptions, occupation at Årup over time does not seem to have been dependent on the immediate proximity to the coast. In conclusion, according to the local shoreline data, Årup was apparently attractive for settling even when the coast was situated quite some distance away.

One appeal for the repeated settling was without doubt the strategic location in the light of transportation and communication. In fact, River Skräbeån formed one of very few water passages leading inland in the region during the Mesolithic; by way of the Bay of Möllefjorden, River Skräbeån and Lake Ivösjön it was possible to reach far into the interior. Watercourses have always attracted human activity and River Skräbeån most probably worked as natural through route where contacts and exchange of ideas took place.

Furthermore, it is obvious to think of access to rich natural resources as a strong contributory factor in the establishment at Årup. Considering the setting of Årup on what periodically constituted an isthmus separating Lake Ivösjön from the Baltic Sea, this narrow stretch of land would have acted as a natural corridor leading passing game in a WSW–ENE direction. It is a well-established fact that animals tend to use certain fixed routes in the landscape when moving between habitats on a daily or seasonal basis (cf. Vang Petersen & Johansen 1993, 1996). Such pathways would also have followed along the banks of the Skräbeån as well as crossing the river at suitable fords where excellent hunting opportunities would have been at hand. It is quite reasonable to assume that the concentration of Late Palaeolithic and Early Mesolithic settlement remains indicating short-term occupation and activities intimately associated with hunting might reflect the site's strategic position in relation to a big game migration route during these periods.

During the early Middle Mesolithic, proximity to the coast characterised the environment. At this point in time, judging by the archaeological evidence, a more permanent settlement was established at the site with a more varied and complex economy adapted to a living in woodlands. The location, situated by an outlet in the inner part of a cove or lagoon, was well chosen. Here they could take advantage of the resources offered by the relatively new-formed marine environment and at the same time make use of the River Skräbeån leading inland for tens of kilometres, to familiar hunting grounds and probably also ancient settlement areas.

In a south Scandinavian perspective, it should also be mentioned that it is precisely in the Kongemose culture that we can detect the earliest traces of stationary fishing devices and traps, that from now on supplemented and to some extent replaced fishing with bow and arrow, spears or leister prongs (Andersen 2001:55; cf. Larsson 1982b:97; Karsten & Knarrström 2003).

Moreover, it is quite reasonable to assume that Årup during the early Middle Mesolithic was a site within a linear settlement pattern. This type of settlement pattern is characterised by establishment along coastlines with protective and productive coves, in areas with access to watercourses or lakes functioning as habitats for water-fowl and fish as well as a source of freshwater (Yesner 1980:729f).

Reasons given for the location of Mesolithic settlements along coastlines are that these biotopes are characterised by ecological stability, high biodiversity, high bio-productivity and that maritime resources tend to vary seasonally rather than spatially (Yesner 1980:728f; Andersen 1995:42; Paludan-Müller 1978).

In the case of Årup, seasonal catching of migratory species such as salmon (*Salmo salar*), sea trout (*Salmo trutta trutta*), common whitefish (*Coregonus lavaretus*), and eel (*Anguilla anguilla*) would have been highly sought after resource. These species are available in today's River Skräbeån which is famous for the seasonal sport fishing of a form of common whitefish, known in Swedish as *älvsik* [elvsi:k], in December of each year. Even though the environmental conditions have changed through time, several of these tasty species of fish that frequent River Skräbeån today may have done so also during the Mesolithic. In common for these migratory species, the eel excepted, is that they swim up rivers in great numbers to spawn. The salmon does so from April until September, the sea trout in late autumn until December, and the whitefish in autumn until early winter. The eel differs in that it swims up rivers in the summer as yellow eels and out of rivers in autumn as silver eels to spawn in the Sargasso Sea (Pethon & Svedberg 1996).

In conclusion, there are several conceivable reasons for settlement at Årup.

Figure 135. "In the wake of a woman". Photo by Thomas Hansson.

A FIELD TRIP

It is quite reasonable to assume that the last of the probably numerous dwelling sites the Barum woman occupied during her lifetime was situated close to her final resting place. Considering the area in question, the setting on an isthmus separating Lake Ivösjön from Lake Oppmannasjön seemed a very favourable one in terms of communication and subsistence through collecting, hunting and fishing. Since the site was located only 9 km from Årup as the crow flies and the two sites were connected by water, this gave rise to questions regarding movement and settlement patterns as well as contacts in the area. At the time of the Barum woman, as indeed today also, the River Skräbeån constituted one of very few negotiable waterways leading to and from the coast in the area. In the autumn of 2003, the authors together with colleagues of the Årup Project made a field trip to the area of Lake Ivösjön and Lake Oppmannasjön.

The incentive was primarily to explore possible transportation routes by water, but it was also felt that an excursion *per se* would generate new ideas and questions concerning the Mesolithic in the region. The aim was twofold. Firstly, by using boats, the object was to investigate the eastern side of the isthmus separating the two lakes in order to pinpoint a feasible passage between these. Secondly, it was of interest to experience a crossing of Lake Ivösjön from the outlet in the south-eastern part in a west-north-westerly direction towards the isthmus and the Barum grave.

The present water levels of Lake Oppmannasjön and Lake Ivösjön are situated at 5.9 and 5.8 m respectively above sea level. These levels are by no means natural, but are the results of repeated acts of lowering the water level of the lakes in order to gain arable land. Lake Ivösjön was lowered in 1873 when a canal was constructed 300 m south of the old outlet by the town of Bromölla, resulting in a water level of 5.7 m above present sea level. The original level of the lake was 7.1–7.5 m above

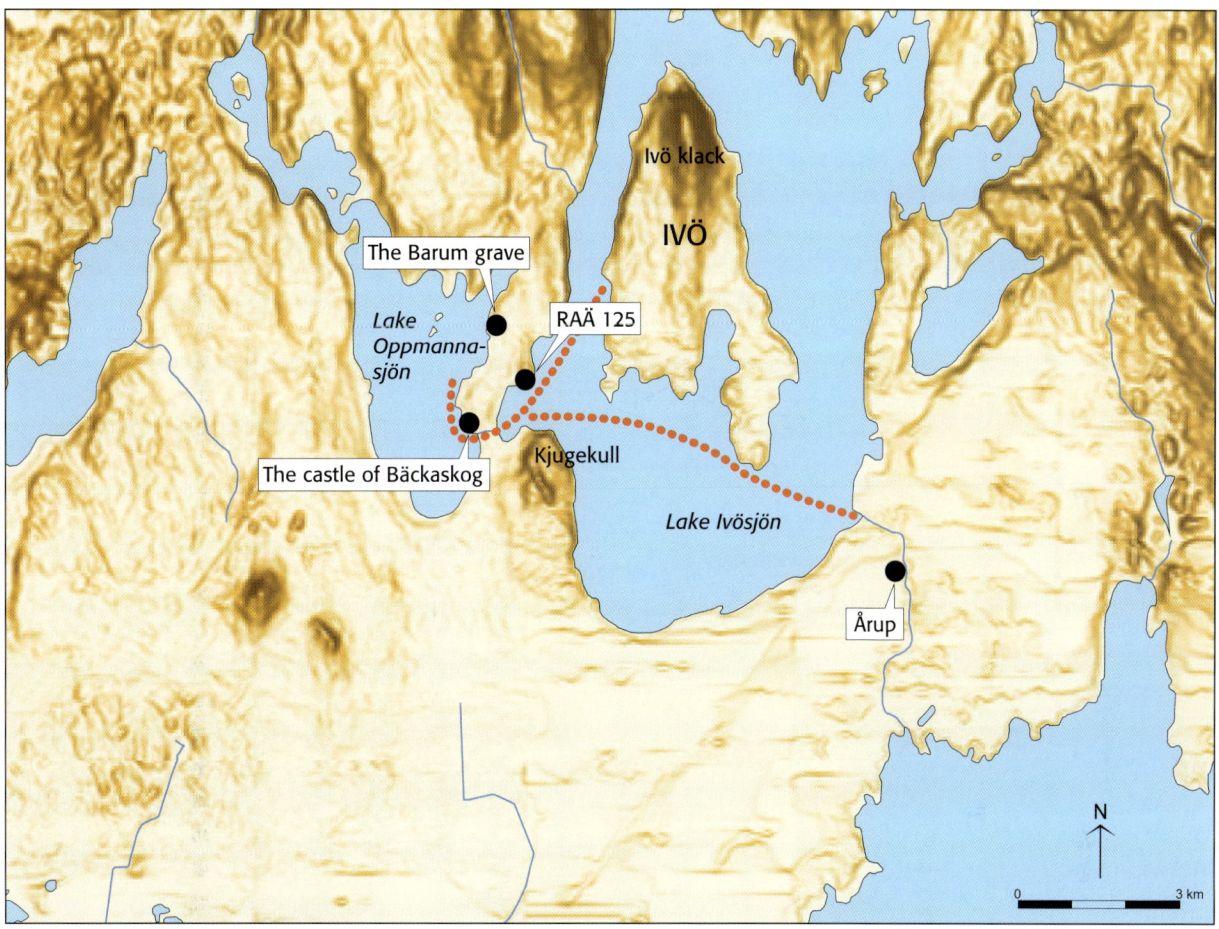

Figure 136. Map of the area showing the field trip route and marking sites mentioned in the text.

present sea level (De Geer 1889:3f). Lake Oppmannasjön was lowered in 1886 to the same level as Lake Ivösjön, i.e. 5.7 m, by the construction of a canal 100 m south of the castle of Bäckaskog across a bog at the narrowest part of the isthmus separating the two lakes. Before the lowering of Lake Oppmannasjön the water level was situated at 8 m above present sea level, suggested by the incidence of marked beach terraces indicating a

previously higher water level (De Geer 1889:4f). According to De Geer, the outlet was previously located beneath the southern part of the castle of Bäckaskog. This is also the case according to the Scanian Reconnaissance Map of 1812–20 and the Topographical Map of 1869. Whether this outlet was natural or constructed is difficult to decide, though. A circumstance indicating that the outlet was in fact natural is that the castle of Bäckaskog started

Figure 137. Ivöklack hill viewed from the south. Photo by
Thomas Hansson.

as a monastery founded in the early thirteenth
century by the Premonstratensian order. By erect-
ing the monastery in such a way that the stream
was incorporated into the establishment, this
could be used for fishing, irrigation, and milling
purposes (Olsson 1922:154ff; Åström 1948:32ff;
Kjellberg 1966:45f; Rosander 1994:84, 86f). The

oldest depiction of the castle of Bäckaskog dates
from 1680, on which a partly natural, partly chan-
nelled stream can be seen leading water through
the estate and beneath some of the buildings of the
castle (Burman 1756). The stream was rich in fish;
especially the eel fishing in the stream that ran
from Lake Oppmannasjön to Lake Ivösjön was

Figure 138. The island of Ivö viewed from the isthmus separating Lake Oppmannasjön and Lake Ivösjön. Photo by Thomas Hansson.

very successful. Carl von Linné, on visiting Bäckaskog in 1749, describes how eel was caught by leading water from the stream to a pond from which the water in turn was led to an eel-trap (Linné 1751).

The present width of the isthmus is only 350 m at the narrowest part and the elevation of the isthmus is 10 m above present sea level at the highest point. The fixed point situated closest to the narrowest part of the isthmus is constituted by the base of the southern tower of the castle of Bäckaskog with a level of 8.75 m above present sea level (ATA 651/83). It seems very likely that the narrowest and surely the lowest part of the isthmus was inundated in prehistory, at least periodically, facilitating easy transport between the lakes. Thus, the location of the canal at the narrowest and boggy part of the isthmus suggests that this area would have been the most suitable part to cross during the Mesolithic.

During the field trip, on a stop to have lunch, a Mesolithic site was discovered on a sandy promontory in the northern part of the cove leading to the presumed passage between the two lakes. Finds of flakes, blades, microblades, and a handle core at the edge of the water strengthen the idea of a transportation route leading to and from the southern outlet of Lake Ivösjön to Lake Oppmannasjön. The site was registered as RAÄ 125, and was taken as another wash in the wake of the Barum woman. Interestingly enough, the sandy promontory was quite conspicuous and could be seen from quite some distance when approached by boat from the east-south-east. Moreover, the two prominent heights of Ivöklack to the north and Kjugekull slightly to the south stood out in the landscape at 133.5 m and 65.6 m respectively above present sea level, framing the cove and guiding the way to Lake Oppmannasjön and the final resting place of the Barum woman – at least until the summer of 1939.

The woman from Barum is long dead and gone. Her memory is locked and she herself keeps the key to it. What she left to posterity are the brittle physical remains of her body and the last gifts, presumably given by loving children and relatives. By studying these remains, fragmented pictures of the woman and her way of living our understanding of the Mesolithic can be deepened. The more rounded picture, the portrait of a human being, has to be created in our own minds. Only by imagination could we bring life back to her and give her a voice to convey her story.

By maintaining the relationship and keeping on following in the wake of the woman from Barum, her ancestors and surviving relatives in Mesolithic times, the mapping of the rather sparsely known Mesolithic sites in the area will surely grow to yield one of the richest Mesolithic environments in southern Scandinavia. Finally, some day, we will probably also be lucky to find the last site the Barum woman occupied during her lifetime.

Aaris-Sørensen, K. (ed.). 1984. Uroksen fra Prejlerup. Et arkæozoologisk fund. Copenhagen.

Agrell, H. 1980. Inlandsdyner på Kristianstadsslätten. *Svensk geografisk årsbok* 56, 23–27.

Ahlén, A. 1879. Kristianstads Högre Allmänna Läroverks Historiska Museum. Kort Beskrifning. Kristianstad.

Åkerlund, A. 1996. *Human responses to shore displacement: living by the sea in eastern middle Sweden during the Stone Age*. Riksantikvarieämbetet. Avdelningen för arkeologiska undersökningar. Skrifter 16. Stockholm.

Albrethsen, S.E. & Brinch Petersen, E. 1977. Excavation of a Mesolithic Cemetery at Vedbæk, Denmark. *Acta Archaeologica* 47, 1–48.

Allen, M. J. 1995. Before Stonehenge. In: Cleal, R., Walker, K. & Montague, R. *Stonehenge in its Landscape. Twentieth-century excavations*. London, 41–62.

Althin, C.-A. 1954. *The Chronology of the Stone Age Settlement of Scania, Sweden. I. The Mesolithic Settlement*. Acta Archaeologica Lundensia, Series in 4°, No. 1. Lund.

Anderberg, A.-L. & Berggren, G. 1994. *Atlas of seeds and small fruits of Northwest-European plant species. Part 4: Resedaceae–Umbelliferae*. Naturhistoriska riksmuseet, Stockholm.

Andersen, S.H. 1981. *Danmarkshistorien. Jægerstenalderen*. Copenhagen.

– 1995. Coastal adaptation and marine exploitation in Late Mesolithic Denmark – with special emphasis on the Limfjord region. In: Fischer, A. (ed.). *Man & Sea in the Mesolithic. Coastal settlement above and below present sea level*. Oxbow Monograph 53. Oxford, 41–66.

– 2001. *Oldtiden i Danmark. Jægerstenalderen*. Copenhagen.

Andersen, K., Jørgensen, S. & Richter, J. 1982. Maglemose hytterne ved Ulkestrup Lyng. *Nordiske Fortidsminder*, Bind 7. Copenhagen.

Andersson, M. & Knarrström, B. 1999. *Senpaleolitikum i Skåne. En studie av materiell kultur och ekonomi hos Sveriges första fångstfolk*. Riksantikvarieämbetet. Avdelningen för arkeologiska undersökningar. Skrifter 26. Stockholm.

Andersson, S., Wigforss, J. & Nancke-Krogh, S. (eds.). 1988. *Fångstfolk för 8000 år sedan. Om en grupp stenåldersboplatser i Göteborg*. Arkeologi i Västsverige 3. Göteborgs arkeologiska museum. Göteborg.

Andrefsky, W. 1998. *Lithics. Macroscopic approaches to analysis*. Cambridge.

Andrén, T., Björck, J. & Johnsen, S. 1999. Correlation of Swedish glacial varves with the Greenland (GRIP) oxygene isotope record. *Journal of Quaternary Science* 14, 361–371.

Arwidsson, G. 1979. Stenåldersmannen från Stora Bjärs i Stenkyrka. *Arkeologi på Gotland*.

Åström, L.E. 1948. *Skånska slott och herrgårdar*. Forum. Stockholm.

References

Barbeau, M. 1990. *Totem Poles According to Location.* Canadian Museum of Civilization. Quebec.

Bartholin, T. & Berglund, B. E. 1992. The prehistoric landscape in the Köpinge area. A reconstruction based on charcoal analysis. In: Larsson, L., Stjernquist, B., Callmer, J., (eds.). *The archaeology of the cultural landscape. Field work and research in a south Swedish rural region.* Almqvist & Wiksell International, Stockholm, 345–358.

Bartholin, T., Berglund, B. E. & Malmer, N. 1981. Vegetation and environment in the Gårdlösa area during the Iron Age. In: Stjernquist, B. (ed.). *Gårdlösa. An Iron Age community in its natural and social setting.* I. Gleerup, Lund, 45–53.

Battarbee, R. W. 1986. Diatom analysis. In: Berglund, B. E. (ed.). *Handbook of Holocene palaeoecology and palaeohydrology.* Wiley, Chichester, 527–570.

Becker, C.J. 1945. En 8000-årig Stenalderboplads i Holmegaards Mose. *Nationalmuseets Arbejdsmark* 1945. Copenhagen, 61–72.

Berggren, G. 1981. *Atlas of seeds and small fruits of Northwest-European plant species. Part 3. Salicaceae–Cruciferae.* Naturhistoriska riksmuseet, Stockholm.

Berglund, B. E. 1964. The Postglacial shore displacement in eastern Blekinge, southeast Sweden. *Sveriges Geologiska Undersökning,* Serie C 599, 1–47.

– 1966a. *Late-Quaternary vegetation in eastern Blekinge, south-eastern Sweden. A pollen-analytical study. 1. Late-glacial time.* Almqvist & Wiksell, Stockholm.

– 1966b. *Late-Quaternary vegetation in eastern Blekinge, south-eastern Sweden: a pollen-analytical study. 2. Post-glacial time.* Almqvist & Wiksell, Stockholm.

– 1971. Littorina transgressions in Blekinge, south Sweden. A preliminary survey. *Geologiska Föreningens i Stockholm Förhandlingar* 93, 625–652.

– (ed.). 1986. *Handbook of Holocene palaeoecology and palaeohydrology.* Wiley, Chichester.

– (ed.). 1991. *The cultural landscape during 6000 years in southern Sweden. The Ystad project.* Ecological Bulletins 41. Copenhagen.

Berglund, B. E. & Björck, S. 1994. Late Weichselian and Holocene shore displacement in Blekinge, SE Sweden. *Acta Universitatis Nicolai Copernici Geographica* 27, 75–95.

Berglund, B. E. & Ralska-Jasiewiczowa, M. 1986. Pollen analysis and pollen diagrams. In: Berglund, B. E. (ed.) *Handbook of Holocene palaeoecology and palaeohydrology.* Wiley, Chichester, 455–484

Berglund, B. E. & Welinder, S. 1972. Stratigrafin vid Siretorp. *Fornvännen* 1972(2), 75–92.

Berglund, B. E., Sandgren, P., Barnekow, L., Hannon, G., Jiang, H, Skog, G., Yu, S. Y. 2005. Early Holocene history of the Baltic Sea, as reflected in coastal sediments in Blekinge, southeastern Sweden. *Quaternary International,* 109, 111–139.

Binford, L.R. 1980. Willow Smoke and Dogs' Tails. Hunter-Gatherer Settlement Systems and Archaeological Site Formation. *American Antiquity,* Vol. 45, No. 1, 1980, 4–20.

– 1990. Mobility, Housing and Environment. A Comparative Study. *Journal of Anthropological Research* 46, 119–152.

Biwall, A., Hernek, R., Kihlstedt, B., Larsson, M. & Åhlin, I. Torstensdotter. 1997. Stenålderns hyddor och hus i Syd- och Mellansverige. In: Larsson, M. & Olsson, E. (eds.). *Regionalt och interregionalt. Stenåldersundersökningar i Syd- och Mellansverige.* Riksantikvarieämbetet. Avdelningen för arkeologiska undersökningar. Skrifter 23. Stockholm, 265–300.

Björck, S. 1979. *Late Weichselian stratigraphy of Blekinge, SE Sweden, and water level changes in the Baltic Ice Lake.* Lundqua Thesis 7. Department of Quaternary Geology, Lund University.

– 1981. A stratigraphic study of Late Weichselian deglaciation, shore displacement and vegetation history in south-eastern Sweden. *Fossils and Strata* 14, 1–93.

– 1995. A review of the history of the Baltic Sea, 13.0–8.0 ka BP. *Quaternary International* 27, 19–40.

Björck, S., Ekström, J., Iregren, E., Larsson, L. & Liljegren, R. 1996a. Reindeer, and palaeoecological and palaeogeographic changes in South Scandinavia during late-glacial and early post-glacial times. In: *Proceedings from the 6th Nordic conference on the application of scientific methods in archaeology, Esbjerg 1993.* Esbjerg Museum, Arkæologiske Rapporter 1, 195–214.

Björck, S., Kromer, B., Johnsen, S., Bennike, O., Hammarlund, D., Lemdahl, G., Possnert, G., Rasmussen, T. L., Wohlfarth, B., Hammer, C. U., Spurk, M. 1996b. Synchronized terrestrial atmospheric deglacial records around the North Atlantic. *Science* 274, 1155–1160.

Björkman, L. 1996. *The Late Holocene history of beech Fagus sylvatica and Norway spruce Picea abies at stand-scale in southern Sweden.* Lundqua Thesis 39. Department of Quaternary Geology, Lund University.

Bokelman, K., Averdiek, F.-R. & Willkom, H. 1981. Duvensee. Wohnplatz 8. Neue Aspekte zur Sammelwirtschaft im frühen Mesolithikum. *Offa* 38, 21–40.

Bradley, R. 1987. Stages in the Chronological Development of Hoards and Votive Deposits. *PPS* (Proceedings of the Prehistoric Society) 53, 351-362.

– 1990. *The Passage of Arms. An archaeological analysis of prehistoric hoards and votive deposits.* Cambrige.

Broecker, W. S., Kennett, J. P., Flower, B. P., Teller, J. T., Trumbore, S., Bonani, G., Wolfli, W. 1989. Routing of meltwater from the Laurentide Ice Sheet during the Younger Dryas cold episode. *Nature* 341, 318–321.

Burenhult, G. 1982. *Arkeologi i Sverige 1. Fångsfolk och herdar.* Wiken.

– (ed.). 1999. *Arkeologi i Norden 1.* Stockholm.

von Burman, G. 1756. *Prospecter af åtskillige märkvärdige byggnader, säterier och herre-gårdar uti Skåne, som i fordna tider hafva til större delen varit befästade med vallar, vattugrafvar och vind-bryggor, och blifvit år 1680 aftagne, ritade och samlade : af ingenieur capitain Burman men nu til det almännas tjenst, förnyade och med kongl: maij:ts allernådigste privilegio på trycket utgifne år 1756 af Abraham Fischer.* Stockholm.

Pleistocene – Holocene Transition (ca. 11 000–9 000 B.C.) in Northern Central Europe. Internationale Archäologie – Arbeitsgemeinschaft, Tagung, Symposium, Kongress 5, 113–132.

Casati, C. & Sørensen, L. 2003. *Ålyst – et boplats kompleks fra Maglemosekulturen på Bornholm. Foreløbige resultater baseret på okonventionelle udgravningsmetoder.* Unpublished paper. Institut for Arkæologi og Etnologi, Københavns Universitet.

Christensen, C. 1998. Miljøet omkring Spodsbjergbopladsen. In: Hugo H. Sørensen (ed.). *Spodsberg – en yngre stenalders boplads på Langeland.* Rudkøbing, 7–27.

Clark, J. G. D. 1954. *Excavations at Star Carr. An Early Mesolithic site at Seamer near Scarborough.* Cambridge.

Codere, H. (ed.). 1966. Kwakiutl ethnography. *Classics in anthropology.* University of Chicago Press. Chicago.

Crabtree, D. E. 1972. *An Introduction to Flintworking.* Occasional Papers no. 28. Idaho State University Museum. Pocatello.

Cronberg, C. 2001. Husesyn. En studie av fem senmesolitiska huslämningar från Tågerup. In: Karsten, P. & Knarrström, B. (eds.). *Tågerup specialstudier.* Skånska Spår. Arkeologi längs Västkustbanan. Riksantikvarieämbetet, Stockholm, 82–155.

Carneiro, R.L. 1970. A theory of the origin of the state. *Science* 169, 733–738. Washington.

Casati, C., Sørensen, L. & Vennersdorf. 2002. Current research of the Early Mesolithic on Bornholm, Denmark. In: Terberger, T. & Eriksen, B.V. (eds.). *Hunters in a changing world. Environment and Archaeology of the*

Degn Johansson, A. 1990. *Baremose-gruppen. Preboreale bopladsfund i Sydsjælland.* Aarhus.

– 2000. *Ældre Stenalder i Norden.* Farum.

De Geer, G. 1889. Beskrifning till kartbladet Bäckaskog. *Sveriges Geologiska Undersökning.* Ser. Aa. N:o 103. Stockholm.

Digerfeldt, G. 1988. Reconstruction and regional correlation of Holocene lake-level fluctuations in Lake Bysjön, South Sweden. *Boreas* 17, 165–182.

Dürre, W. 1971. *Fundplätze der Ahrensburger Kultur im Kreise Soltau.* Materialhefte zur Ur- und Frühgeschichte Niedersachsens, Heft 4. Hildesheim.

Edgren, T. 1997. Om fågelpilen. In: Åkerlund, A., Bergh, S., Nordbladh, J. & Taffinder, J. (eds.). Till Gunborg. Arkeologiska samtal. *Stockholm Archaeological Reports* Nr 33. Stockholm, 23–38.

Ekman, M. 1996. A consistent map of the postglacial uplift of Fennoscandia. *Terra Nova* 8, 158–165.

Ekström, J. 1993. *The Late Quaternary history of the urus* (Bos primigenius *Bojanus 1827*) *in Sweden*. Lundqua Thesis 29. Department of Quaternary Geology, Lund University.

Ellis, C.J. 1997. Factors Influencing the Use of Stone Projectile Tips. An Ethnographic Perspective. In: Knecht, H. (ed.). *Projectile Technology. Interdisciplinary Contributions to Archaeology*. New York, 37–74.

Eriksen, B.V. 2000. Grundlæggende flintteknologi. In: Eriksen, B.V. (ed.). *Flintstudier. En håndbog i systematiske analyser af flintinventarer.* Aarhus Universitetsforlag, 37–50.

Fairbanks, R.G. 1989. A 17,000-year glacio-eustatic sea-level record. Influence of glacial melting rates on the Younger Dryas event and deep-ocean circulation. *Nature* 342, 637–642.

Fischer, A. 1978. På sporet af overgangen mellem palæoliticum og mesoliticum i Sydskandinavien. *Hikuin* 4/1978, 27–50.

– 1988. A Late Palaeolithic Flint Workshop at Egtved, East Jutland – a Glimpse of the Federmesser Culture in Denmark. *Journal of Danish Archaeology* 7, 7–23.

– 1990. A Late Palaeolithic "School" of Flintknapping at Trollesgave, Denmark. *Acta Archaeologica* 60. 1989. Copenhagen, 33–49.

– 1993. Senpaleolitikum. In: Hvass, S. & Storgaard, B. (ed.). 1993. *Da Klinger i Muld. 25 års arkæologi i Danmark*. Aarhus, 51–57.

– 1994. Dating the early trapeze horizon. Radiocarbon dates from submerged settlements in Musholm Bay and Kalø Vig, Denmark. *Mesolithic Miscellany* 15:1, 1–7.

Fischer, A. & Malm, T. 1997. The settlement in the submerged forest in Musholm Bay. In: Pedersen, L., Fischer, A., & Aaby, B. (eds.). *The Danish Storebælt since the Ice Age – man, sea and forest*. The Storebælt Publications. Copenhagen, 78–86.

Fischer, A. & Tauber, H. 1986. New C-14 Datings of the Late Palaeolithic Cultures from Northwestern Europe. *Journal of Danish Archaeology* 5, 7–13.

Forsström, P. 1996. Från stock till stockbåt. Ett försök med mesolitiska redskap. Unpublished seminar paper, Lunds Universitet. Lund.

Fugl Petersen, B. 1994. Rundebakke. En senpalæolitisk boplads på Knudshoved Odde, Sydsjælland. *Aarbøger* 1992, 7–46.

Gaillard, M-J., Hannon, G. E., Håkansson, H., Olsson, S., Possnert, G. & Sandgren, P. 1996. New data on the Holocene forest and land-use history of Scania based on AMS ^{14}C dates of terrestrial plant macroremains, and biostratigraphical, chemical, and mineral magnetic analyses of lake sediments. *GFF* 118A, 65–66.

Gaillard, M-J. & Lemdahl, G. 1993. *Biostratigrafiska undersökningar av flintgruvorna vid Ängdala, Skåne – miljö- och klimattolkningar*. Unpublished.

Gedda, B. Hav och land. Nivåförändringar i Östersjön. In: Carlie, A. (ed.). *Berättelser från Vætland. En arkeologisk resa längs E22 i Skåne*. Riksantikvarieämbetet. Stockholm, 23–25.

Gejvall, N-G. 1970. The fisherman from Barum – mother of several children! Palaeo-anatomic finds in the skeleton from Bäckaskog. *Fornvännen* 65, 281–289.

Gennep van, A. 1909. *Les rites de passage: étude systématique des rites*. Paris.

– 1960. *The Rites of Passage*. Chicago.

Göransson, H. 1991. *Vegetation and man around Lake Bjärsjöholmssjön during prehistoric time*. Lundqua Report 31. Department of Quaternary Geology, Lund University.

Grøn, O. 2003. Mesolithic dwelling places in South Scandinavia: their definition and social interpretation. *Antiquity*, Vol. 77, No. 298. December 2003.

Handbok överlevnad. 1999. Chefen för Armén. Uppsala.

Hansen, F. 1941. Fiskaren från Barum – från äldre stenåldern. In: *Handlingar angående Villands härad.* Villands härads Hembygdsförening. Kristianstad, 13–19.

Hansen, L.1987. Submarina gyttjor, torv och stubbar. *Skånes Natur* 4:87, 265–282.

Hartz, N. & Winge, H. 1906. Om Uroxen fra Vig, saaret og dræbt med Flintvaaben. *Aarbøger for Nordisk Oldkyndighet og Historie* 1906, 225–237.

Hedberg, H. D. 1976. *International stratigraphic guide. A guide to stratigraphic classification, terminology, and procedure.* Wiley, Chichester.

Hellberg, K. 1971. *Inlandsisens recession och den senglaciala strandförskjutningen i västra Blekinge och nordöstra Skåne.* Rapporter och notiser 9. Naturgeografiska institutionen, Lunds universitet.

Henriksen, B. 1980. *Lundbyholmen.* Nordiske Fortidsminder 6. Copenhagen.

Hodder, I. 1986. *Reading the past. Current approaches to interpretation in archaeology.* Cambridge.

Högberg, A., Mardell, L., Rudebeck, E., Sarnäs, P., Sheker, L. & Ödman, C. 2000. *Nomenklatur och sorteringsschema för flintregistrering. Utarbetad inom ramen för projektet Öresundsförbindelsen.* Stadsantikvariska avdelningen, Kultur Malmö. Malmö.

Iversen, J. 1973. *The development of Denmark's nature since the last glacial.* Geological Survey of Denmark, V Series 7C.

Jacomet, S. 1987. *Prähistorische Getreidefunde. Ein Anleitung zur Bestimmung prähistorischer Gersten- und Weizen-Funde.* Botanisches Institut der Universität Basel.

Jelinek, J. 1978. *Den stora boken om människans forntid.* Stockholm.

Jensen, O. Lass. 1998. En stenalderboplads i Nivåfjorden. Udgravningen af bopladsen Nivå 10 fra yngre Kongemose- og ældre Ertebøllekultur. *Hørsholm Egns Museum Årbog* 1997, 7–24.

Johansen, L. 1997. The Late Palaeolithic in Denmark. In: Bodu, P., Christensen, M. & Valentin, B. (eds.). *L'Europe septentrionale au Tardiglaciaire. Proceedings of a congress held in Nemours (Fr.), May 1997.*

Johansen, L. & Stapert, D. 2000. Two 'Epi-Ahrensburgian' Sites in the Northern Netherlands: Oudehaske (Friesland) and Gramsbergen (Overijssel). In: Palaeohistoria. *Acta et Communicationes Instituti Archaeologici Universitatis Groninganae,* 39/40, 1997/1998. Offprint. Rotterdam, 1–88.

Johansson, T. 1993. *Forntida teknik.* Västerås.

Juel Jensen, H. 1988. A functional analysis of flake axes from Skateholm I. In: Larsson, L. (ed.). *The Skateholm Project I. Man and Environment.* Acta Regiae Societatis Humaniorum Litterarum Lundensis LXXIX. Skrifter utgivna av Kungl. Humanistiska Vetenskapssamfundet i Lund: XXIX. Lund, 175–178.

Jørgensen, S. 1956. Kongemosen. Endnu en Aamose-Boplads fra Ældre Stenalder. *Kuml* 1956, 23–40.

Jöris, O. & Thissen, J. 1995. Übach–Palenberg. In: Schirmer, W. (ed.). Quaternary field trips in Central Europe 2. *INQUA* 1995. Munich, 957–961.

Karsten, P. 1986. Jägarstenålder kring Yddingen. *Limhamniana* 1986, 65–89.

- 1994. *Att kasta yxan i sjön. En studie över rituell tradition och förändring utifrån skånska neolitiska offerfynd.* Acta Archaeologica Lundensia, Series in 8°, No. 23. Lund.
- 2001. *Dansarna från Bökeberg. Om jakt, ritualer och inlandsbosättning vid jägarstenålderns slut.* Riksantikvarieämbetet. Avdelningen för arkeologiska undersökningar. Skrifter 37. Stockholm.
- 2004. Peak and transformation of a Mesolithic society 7500–4800 BC. In: Andersson, M., Karsten, P., Knarrström, B. & Svensson, M. *Stone Age Scania. Significant places dug and read by contract archaeology.* Riksantikvarieämbetet. Skrifter 52. Stockholm, 71–94.

Karsten, P. & Knarrström, B. 2001. Kvantitet och kvalitet. Typbestämningar av flintredskap från Tågerup. In: Karsten, P. & Knarrström, B. (eds). *Tågerup specialstudier.* Skånska Spår. Arkeologi längs Västkustbanan. Stockholm, 302–325.

- 2003. *The Tågerup Excavations.* Skånska Spår. Arkeologi längs Västkustbanan. Riksantikvarieämbetet. Stockholm.

Karsten, P., Knarrström, B. & Regnell, M. 1998. Forntida tecken – ett unikt ornerat yxskaft från Kongemosekultur. *Ale* 1998:3, 17–29.

Karsten, P. & Regnell, M. 1995. Bökeberg III – Intryck och avtryck från en senmesolitisk inlandsboplats. *Limhamniana* 1995, 72–83.

Kindgren, H. 1996. Reindeer or seals? Some Late Palaeolithic sites in central Bohuslän. In: Larsson, L. (ed). *The Earliest Settlement of Scandinavia – and its relationship with neighbouring areas.* Acta Archaeologica Lundensia, Series in 8°, No. 24. Lund, 191–205.

Kjällquist, M. 2001. Gåvor eller avfall? En studie av sex mesolitiska gravar från Tågerup. In: Karsten, P. & Knarrström, B. (eds). *Tågerup specialstudier.* Skånska Spår – arkeologi längs Västkustbanan. Stockholm, 32–69.

Kjellberg, S. T. 1966. *Slott och herresäten i Sverige.* Skåne. Malmö.

Knarrström, B. 1997. Neolitisk flintteknologi i ett skånskt randområde. In: Karsten, P. (ed.). *Carpe Scaniam. Axplock ur Skånes förflutna.* Riksantikvarieämbetet. Arkeologiska undersökningar. Skrifter 22. Stockholm, 7–25.

- Vikingatida flintverktyg. Utdrag ur avhandlingsarbete kring metalltida flintutnyttjande i västra Skåne. *Bulletin för arkeologisk forskning i Sydsverige* 1/1999, 21–40.

- 2000a. *Flinta i sydvästra Skåne. En diakron studie av råmaterial, produktion och funktion med fokus på boplatsteknologi och metalltida flintutnyttjande.* Acta Archaeologica Lundensia, Series in 8°, No. 33. Lund.
- 2000b. Materialstudier av Skånes äldsta stenålder. Om tiden efter Bromme och tidigmesolitisk expansion i norra Skåne. In: Ersgård, L. (ed.). *Människors platser – tretton arkeologiska studier från UV.* Riksantikvarieämbetet. Avdelningen för arkeologiska undersökningar. Skrifter No 31. Stockholm.
- 2001. *Flint – a Scanian Hardware.* Skånska Spår. Arkeologi längs Västkustbanan. Riksantikvarieämbetet. Stockholm.
- 2004. The introduction of culture 12000–7500 BC. In: Andersson, M., Karsten, P., Knarrström, B. & Svensson, M. *Stone Age Scania. Significant places dug and read by contract archaeology.* Riksantikvarieämbetet. Skrifter No 52. Stockholm, 21–42.

Knarrström, B. & Wrentner, R. 1996. Diagnostik av plattformar. *Bulletin för arkeologisk forskning i Sydsverige.* Nr. 2–3 1996, 80–87.

Knutsson, H. 1982. Skivyxor. Experimentell analys av en redskapstyp från den senatlantiska bosättningen vid Soldattorpet. Unpublished seminar paper. Arkeologiska institutionen, Uppsala Universitet.

Körber-Grohne, U. 1991. Bestimmungsschlüssel für subfossile Gramineen-Früchte. *Probleme der Küstenforschung im Südlichen Nordseegebiet* 18, 169–234.

Krammer, K. & Lange-Bertalot, H. 1986. Bacillariophyceae 1. Teil Naviculaceae. In: Ettl, H. G. J., Heynig, H., Mollenhauser, D. (ed.). *Süsswasserflora von Mitteleuropa 2/1.* Stuttgart.

- 1988. Bacillariophyceae 2. Teil Bacillariaceae, Epithemiaceae, Surirellaceae. In: Ettl, H. G. J., Heynig, H., Mollenhauser, D. (ed.). *Süsswasserflora von Mitteleuropa 2/2.* Stuttgart.
- 1991a. Bacillariophyceae 3. Teil Centrales, Fragilariaceae, Eunotiaceae. In: Ettl, H. G. J., Heynig, H., Mollenhauser, D. (ed.). *Süsswasserflora von Mitteleuropa 2/3.* Stuttgart.
- 1991b. Bacillariophyceae 4. Teil Achnanthaceae. Kritische Ergänzungen zu Navicula (Lineolate) und Gomphonema. In: Ettl, H. G. J., Heynig, H., Mollenhauser, D. (ed.). *Süsswasserflora von Mitteleuropa 2/4.* Stuttgart.

Lagerås, P. 1996. Long-term history of land-use and vegetation at Femtingagölen – a small lake in the Småland Uplands, southern Sweden. *Vegetation History and Archaeobotany* 5, 215–228.

– 2002. Skog, slåtter och stenröjning: paleoekologiska undersökningar i trakten av Stoby i norra Scania. In: Carlie, A. (ed.). *Skånska regioner – Tusen år av kultur och samhälle i förändring*. Arkeologiska undersökningar, Skrifter 31. Riksantikvarieämbetet. Stockholm, 363–411.

– 2003. Vindpinad slätt. In: Carlie, A. (ed.). *Berättelser från Vætland. En arkeologisk resa längs E22 i Scania*. Riksantikvarieämbetet. Stockholm, 42–45.

Lagerås, P. & Bartholin, T. 2003. Fire and stone clearance in Iron Age agriculture. New insights inferred from the analysis of terrestrial macroscopic charcoal in clearance cairns in Hamneda, southern Sweden. *Vegetation History and Archaeobotany* 12, 83–92.

Lambeck, K., Smither, C., Ekman, M., 1998. Test of glacial rebound models for Fennoscandinavia based on instrumented sea- and lake-level records. *Geophysical Journal Int.* 135, 375–387.

Larsson, L. 1975. A Contribution to the Knowledge of Mesolithic Huts in Southern Scandinavia. *MLUHM* 1973–1974, 5–28.

– 1978a. *Ageröd I:B – Ageröd I:D. A Study of Early Atlantic Settlement in Scania*. Acta Archaeologica Lundensia, Series in 4°, No. 12. Lund.

– 1978b. Mesolithic Antler and Bone Artefacts from Central Scania. *MLUHM* 1977–1978, 28–67.

– 1982a. De äldsta gutarna. *Gotländskt arkiv* 1982.

– 1982b. *Segebro. En tidigatlantisk boplats vid Sege ås mynning*. Malmöfynd 4. Malmö.

– 1984a. The Skateholm Project. A Late Mesolithic Settlement and Cemetery Complex at a Southern Swedish Bay. *MLUHM* 1983–1984, 5–38.

– 1984b. Skateholmsprojektet. På spåren efter gravsedsförändringar, ceremoniplatser och tama rävar. *Limhamniana* 1984, 49–84.

– 1985. Of House and Hearth. The Excavation, Interpretation and Reconstruction of a Late Mesolithic House. *Archaeology and Environment* 4. Umeå.

– 1988a. *Ett fångstsamhälle för 7000 år sedan*. Kristianstad.

– 1988b. Aspects of Exchange in Mesolithic Societies. In: Hårdh, B., Larsson, L., Olausson, D. & Petré, R. (eds.). *Trade and Exchange in Prehistory. Studies in honour of Berta Stjernquist*. Acta Archaeologica Lundensia, Series in 8°, No. 16. Lund, 25–32.

– 1994a. The Earliest Settlement in Southern Sweden. Late Palaeolithic Settlement Remains at Finjasjön, in the North of Scania. *Current Swedish Archaeology* 2, 159–177.

– 1994b. De äldsta boplatslämningarna i Sydsverige. Fynd och boplatser kring Finjasjön, norra Skåne. *Ale* 1/1994, 2–16.

– 1996. The Colonization of South Sweden during the Deglaciation. In: Larsson, L. (ed.). 1996. *The Earliest Settlement of Scandinavia and its relationship with neighbouring areas*. Acta Archaeologica Lundensia, Series in 8°, No. 24. Lund, 141–155.

– 2000a. Axes and Fire – Contacts with the Gods. In: Olausson, D & Vandkilde, H. (ed.). *Form, Function & Context. Material culture studies in Scandinavian archaeology*. Lund, 93–103.

– 2000b. The passage of axes. Fire transformation of flint objects in the Neolithic of southern Sweden. *Antiquity*, Vol. 74, No. 285, 602–610.

– 2001. De senaste kvartsseklets stenåldersarkeologi i Skåne. In: Bergenståhle, I. & Hellerström, S. (eds.). *Stenåldersforskning i fokus. Inblickar och utblickar i sydskandinavisk stenåldersarkeologi*. Riksantikvarieämbetet Arkeologiska undersökningar. Skrifter 39. Stockholm, 17–46.

– 2003. The Mesolithic of Sweden in retrospective and progressive perspectives. In: Larsson, L., Kindgren, H., Knutsson, K., Loeffler, D. & Åkerlund, A. (eds.). *Mesolithic on the Move. Papers presented at the sixth International Conference on the Mesolithic in Europe, Stockholm 2000*. Oxbow, Oxford, XXII–XXXII.

Larsson, L., Liljegren, R., Magnell, O. & Ekström, J. 2002. Archaeo-faunal aspects of bog finds from Hässleberga, southern Scania, Sweden. In: Eriksen, B. V. & Bratlund, B. (eds.). *Recent studies in the Final Palaeolithic of the European plain*. Proceedings of a U.I.S.P.P Symposium, Stockholm, 14–17 October 1999. Jutland Archaeological Society. Højbjerg, 61–74.

Larsson, M. 1986. Bredasten. An Early Ertebölle Site with a Dwelling Structure in South Scania. *MLUHM* 1985–1986, 25–51.

Larsson, U.-K. 1973. *De svenska fynden av flinteggade benspetsar*. Unpublished Seminar Paper. Arkeologiska institutionen, Lunds universitet.

Lidén, O. 1942. *De flinteggade benspetsarnas nordiska kulturfas. Studier i anslutning till nya sydsvenska fynd*. Skrifter utgivna av kungl. Humanistiska vetenskapssamfundet i Lund. XXXIII. Lund.

– 1948. *Aktuella sydsvenska stenåldersproblem. Jonstorp, Sjöholmen och Barumsgraven*. Lund.

Liljegren, R. 1982. *Paleoekologi och strandförskjutning i en Littorinavik i mellersta Blekinge. Palaeoecology and shore displacement in a Littorina bay at Spjälkö*. Lundqua Thesis 11. Department of Quaternary Geology, Lund University.

Liljegren, R. & Lagerås, P. 1993. *Från mammutstäpp till kohage. Djurens historia i Sverige*. Lund.

Liljegren, R., & Ekström, J. 1996. The terrestrial Late Glacial fauna in South Sweden. In: Larsson, L. (ed.). *The earliest settlement of Scandinavia and its relationship with neighbouring areas*. Acta Archaeologica Lundensia, Series in 8°, No. 24. Lund, 135–139.

Linné, Carl von. 1751. *Carl von Linnés Skånska resa 1749*. Faksimiledition efter 1751 års originalupplaga, 2:a tryckningen. Utgivare: John Kroon. 1956. Malmö.

Lundqvist J, & Wohlfahrt B. 2001. Timing and east-west correlation of south Swedish ice marginal lines during the Late Weichselian. *Quaternary Science Reviews* 20, 1127–1148.

Mathiassen, T. 1937. Gudenaa-Kulturen. En Mesolitisk Inlandsbebyggelse i Jylland. *Aarbøger for Nordisk Oldkyndighed og Historie* 1937, 1–186.

– 1943. *Stenaldersbopladser i Aamosen*. Nordiske Fortidsminder 3. Copenhagen.

– 1948. *Danske Oldsager*, bd. I. Copenhagen.

Meeks, N. D., Sieveking, de, G., Tite, M. S. & Cook, J. 1982. Gloss and Use-wear Traces on Flint Sickles and Similar Phenomena. *Journal of Archaeological Science* 9, 317–340.

Milne, G. A., Davis, J. L, Mitrovica, J. X., Schernek, H-G., Johansson, J. M, Vermer, M., Koivula, H., 2001. Space-Geodetic Constraints on Glacial Isostatic Adjustment in Fennoscandia. *Science* 291, 2381–2385.

Mogren, M. 2003. Coalitions-allén och den engelska parken vid Årup. In: Carlie, A. (ed.). 2003. *Berättelser från Vætland. En arkeologisk resa längs E22 i Skåne*. Riksantikvarieämbetet. Stockholm, 46–49.

Möhl, U. 1978. Elsdyrskeletterne fra Skottemarke og Favbro. Skik og brug ved borealtidens jagter. *Aarbøger for Nordisk Oldkyndighed og Historie* 1978, 5–32.

Møller Hansen, K. 2003. Pre-Boreal elk bones from Lundby Mose. In: Larsson, L., Kindgren, H., Knutsson, K., Loeffler, D. & Åkerlund, A. (eds.). *Mesolithic on the Move. Papers presented at the sixth International Conference on the Mesolithic in Europe, Stockholm 2000*. Oxford, 521–526.

Montelius, O. 1917. *Minnen från vår forntid*. Stockholm.

Moore, P. D., Webb, J. A. & Collinson, M. E. 1991. *Pollen analysis*. 2nd edition. Oxford.

Madsen, B. 1983. New Evidence of Late Palaeolithic Settlement in East Jutland. *Journal of Danish Archaeology* 2, 12–31.

– 1992. Hamburgkulturens flintteknologi i Jels. In: Holm, J. & Rieck, F. *Istidsjægare ved Jelssøerne. Hamburgkulturen i Danmark*. Skrifter fra Museumsrådet for Sønderjyllands amt 5. Haderslev, 93–131.

– 1996. Late Palaeolithic Cultures of South Scandinavia – Tools Traditions and Technology. In: Larsson, L. (ed.). 1996. *The Earliest Settlement of Scandinavia and its relationship with neighbouring areas*. Acta Archaeologica Lundensia, Series in 8°, No. 24. Lund, 61–73.

Malmer, M. P. 1969. Die Mikrolithen in dem Pfeil-Fund von Loshult. *MLUHM* 1966–1968, 249–255.

Nelson, M.C. 1997. Projectile Points: Form, Function, and Design. In: Knecht, H. (ed.). *Projectile Technology. Interdisciplinary Contributions to Archaeology*. New York, 371–384.

Newcomer, M.H. & Sieveking, G. de G. 1980. Experimental Flake Scatter-Patterns. A New Interpretative Technique. *Journal of Field Archaeology* 7.

Nilsson, B. 2005. Årup – bidrag till kännedomen om det senpaleolitiska Skåne. Unpublished seminar paper,

Institutionen för arkeologi och samiska studier, Umeå universitet.

Nilsson, S. 1838–1843. *Skandinaviska Nordens Ur-invånare. Ett försök i komparativa Ethnografien och ett bidrag till menniskoslägtets utvecklingshistoria. Första delen, innehållande beskrifning öfver de vilda urfolkens redskap, hus, grifter och lefnadssätt m.m. samt utkast till beskrifning öfver en i forntiden hit inflyttad kimbrisk koloni.* Lund.

Nilsson, T. 1935. Die pollenanalytische Zonengliederung dcr spät und postglazialen Bildungen Schonens. *Geologiska Föreningens i Stockholm Förhandlingar* 57.

– 1964. Standardpollendiagramme und ¹⁴C-datierungen aus der Ageröds Mosse im mittleren Schonen. *Lunds Universitets Årsskrift*, N.F. 2, 1–52.

– 1968. Pollenanalytische Daterung der Pfeilfunde aus Loshult im Nördlichten Schonen. *Geologiska Föreningens i Stockholm Förhandlingar* 90.

Noe-Nygaard, N. 1987. Taphonomy in Archaeology with Special Emphasis on Man as a Biasing Factor. *Journal of Danish Archaeology* 6, 7–52

Nordqvist, B. 1997. Västkusten. Regionalitet under mesolitikum. In: Larsson, M. & Olsson, E. (eds.). *Regionalt och interregionalt. Stenåldersundersökningar i Syd- och Mellansverige.* Riksantikvarieämbetet. Skrifter 23. Stockholm, 32–55.

– 2000. *Coastal Adaptions in the Mesolithic. A study of coastal sites with organic remains from the Boreal and Atlantic periods in Western Sweden.* GOTARC Series B. Gothenburg Archaeological Theses 13. Gothenburg.

Odell, G.1981. The Morphological Express at Function Junction: Searching for Meaning in Lithic Tool Types. *Journal of Anthropological Research* 37, 319–342.

Olsson, I. U. 1986. Radiometric dating. In: Berglund, B. E. (ed.). *Handbook of Holocene palaeoecology and palaeohydrology.* Wiley, Chichester, 273–312.

Olsson, I. U. & Possnert, G. 1992. The interpretation of ¹⁴C measurements on pre-Holocene samples. *Sveriges Geologiska Undersökning* Ca 81, 201–208.

Olsson, P.A. 1922. Skånska Herreborgar. *Ur synpunkten av de fortifikatoriska anordningarnas betydelse för arkitekturen.* Lund.

Paddayya, K. 1971. The Late Palaeolithic of the Netherlands – a review. *Helinium* 11, 257–270.

Paludan-Müller, C. 1978. High Atlantic Food Gathering in Northwestern Zealand, Ecological Conditions and Spatial Representation. In: Kristiansen, K. & Paludan-Müller, C. (eds.). *New Directions in Scandinavian Archaeology.* Studies in Scandinavian Prehistory and Early History. 1. Copenhagen, 120–157.

Persson, A. 1992. Den europeiska kärrsköldpaddan Emys orbicularis (Linnaeus 1758) och dess forntida förekomst i Sverige. *Snoken* 22(4), 12–23.

Persson, M. 1995. Beskrivning till jordartskartan Karlshamn SO. *Sveriges Geologiska Undersökning*, Series Ae 116. Uppsala.

Petersson, M. 1951. Mikrolithen als Pfeilspitzen. Ein Fund aus dem Lilla Loshult-Moor Ksp. Loshult, Skåne. *MLUHM* 1951, 123–137.

Pethon, P. & Svedberg, U. 1996. *Fiskar i färg.* Norstedts.

Price, D.T. & Brown, J.A. 1985. Aspects of hunter-gatherer complexity. In: Price, D.T. & Brown, J.A (eds.). *Prehistoric hunter-gatherers – the emergence of cultural complexity.* New York, Academic Press, 3–20.

Rackham, O. 1994. *The illustrated history of the countryside.* London.

Regnéll, J. 1989. *Vegetation and land use during 6000 years: palaeoecology of the cultural landscape at two lake sites in southern Scania, Sweden.* Lundqua Thesis 27. Department of Quaternary Geology, Lund University.

Regnell, M. 1998. *Archaeobotanical finds from the Stone Age of the Nordic countries: A catalogue of plant remains from archaeological contexts.* Lundqua Report 36. Department of Quaternary Geology, Lund University.

Ringberg, B. 1991a. Beskrivning till jordartskartan Kristianstad SO. *Sveriges Geologiska Undersökning* Ae 88. Uppsala.

Ringberg, B. 1991b. Beskrivning till jordartskartan Karlshamn SV. *Sveriges Geologiska Undersökning* Ae 106. Uppsala.

Rosander, L. 1994. Bäckaskog – biskopar, grevar, kungar. In: Lång, H. (ed.). *Skånska hus och herresäten.* Höganäs, 84–91.

Rust, A. 1943. *Die alt- und mittelsteinzeitlichen Funde von Stellmoor.* Neumünster.

– 1958. *Die jungpaläolitischen Zeltanlagen von Ahrensburg.* Offa Bucher. Band 15.

– 1972. *Vor 20 000 Jahren. Reintierjäger der Eiszeit.* Neumünster.

Salomonsson, B. 1965. Linnebjär. A Mesolithic Site in South-West Scania. *MLUHM* 1964–1965, 5–31.

Sandegren, R. 1939. Torvgeologisk och pollenanalytisk undersökning av torvmarken N intill boplatskomplexet vid Siretorp. In: Bagge, A. & Kjellmark K. *Stenåldersboplatserna vid Siretorp i Blekinge.* Kungl. Vitterhets Historie och Antikvitets Akademin, Stockholm, 251–256.

Schilling, H. 2001. Veje til en mesolitisk kulturhistorie. In: Jensen, O. Lass, Sørensen, S. & Møller Hansen, K. (eds.). *Danmarks Jægerstenalder – Beretning fra symposiet "Status og perspektiver inden for dansk mesolitikum" afholt i Vordingborg, september 1998.* Hørsholms Egns Museum. Hørsholm, 201–207.

Schweingruber, F. H. 1976. *Prähistorisches Holz – Die Bedeutung von Holzfunden aus Mitteleuropa für die Lösung archäologischer und vegetationskundlicher Probleme.* Bern.

– 1978. *Mikroskopische Holzanatomie – Formenspektern mitteleuropäischer Stamm- und Zwerghölzer zur Bestimmung von rezentem und subfossilem Material.* Bern.

Sjöström, A. 2000. Ringsjöbornas vardag för 8000 år sedan. *Frostabygden 2000.* Frosta Härads Hembygdsförening, 17–24.

Skaarup, J. & Grøn, O. 2004. Møllegabet II. A submerged Mesolithic settlement in southern Denmark. *BAR IS* 1328.

Sørensen, I. 1978. Dateringen af eldyrsknoglerne fra Skottemarke og Farvbro. *Aarbøger for Nordisk Oldkyndighed og Historie* 1978, 33–44.

Sørensen, L. 2002. *Beretning om udgravningen af en Maglemose boplads ved Ålyst i Klemensker sogn, Bornholm. 29/7 til 1/11 2002.* Photocopy. Bornholms Museum.

Sørensen, L. 2003. *Coastal Research Potential in the Early Mesolithic on Bornholm.* Kontaktseminar 2003. Kontaktstencil 44. Photocopy. Københavns Universitet.

Sørensen, M. 2001. *Det operative skema i Maglemosekulturen. En diakron flintteknologisk analyse af flækkeindustrien i maglemosekulturen, ud fra en undersøgelse af seks bopladser på Sjælland.* Cand.Mag. speciale ved Institut for Arkæologi og Etnologi. Københavns Universitet. Copenhagen.

Sørensen, S.A. 1993. Lollikhuse – a Dwelling Site under a Kitchen Midden. *Journal of Danish Archaeology* 11, 19–29.

– 1996. *Kongemosekulturen i Sydskandinavien.* Egnsmuseet Færgegården. Copenhagen.

Sten, S., Ahlström, T., Alexandersen, V., Borrman, H., Christensen, E., Ekenman, I., Kloboucek, J., Königsson, L-K., Possnert, G. & Ragnesten, U. 2000. Barumkvinnan. Nya forskningsrön. *Fornvännen* 95, 73–87.

Sundelin, U. 1922. Råbelövssjöns och Nosabykärrets historia. *Geologiska Föreningens i Stockholm Förhandlingar* 44(5), 553–590.

Svensson, N.-O. 1989. *Late Weichselian and Early Holocene shore displacement in the central Baltic, based on stratigraphical and morphological records from eastern Småland and Gotland, Sweden.* Lundqua Thesis 25. Department of Quaternary Geology, Lund University.

– 1991. Late Weichselian and early Holocene shore displacement in the central Baltic Sea. *Quaternary International* 9, 7–26.

– 1999: Deglaciation och strandförskjutning i Norden. In: Burenhult, G. (ed.). *Arkeologi i Norden 1.* Stockholm, 168–169.

– 2001. Strandlinjer och strandförskjutning i Möre. In: Magnusson, G. (ed.). *Möre – historien om ett små-land*. Kalmar Läns Museum, Kalmar, 73–110.

of Scandinavia and its relationship with neighbouring areas. Acta Archaeologica Lundensia, Series in 8°, No. 24. Lund, 75–88.

Voss, O. 1961. Danske Flintægdolke. *Aarbøger for Nordisk Oldkyndighed og Historie* 1960, 153–167.

Taute, W. 1968. *Die Stielspitzen-gruppen im nördlichen Mitteleuropa. Ein Beitrag zur Kenntnis der späten Altsteinzeit*. Fundamenta. Reihe A. Band 5. Köln.

Troels-Smith, J. 1961. Et Pileskaft fra tidlig Maglemose-tid. *Aarbøger for Nordisk Oldkyndighed og Historie* 1961, 122–146.

Tromnau, G. 1975. *Neue Ausgrabungen im Ahrensburger Tunneltal. Ein beitrag zur erforschung des jungpaläolithikums im Nordwesteuropäischen flachland*. Neumünster.

Trönndahl, C. 1993. Rituell tradition och social förändring. Mesolitiska deponeringar med utgångspunkt från Hindby Offerkärr, Malmö. Unpublished seminar paper. Arkeologiska institutionen, Lunds Universitet.

Welinder, S. 1971. *Tidigpostglacialt mesoliticum i Skåne*. Acta Archaeologica Lundensia, Series in 8° Minore, No. 1. Lund.

– 1977. The Mesolithic Stone Age of Eastern Middle Sweden. *Antikvariskt Arkiv 65*.

Whittaker, J.C. 1997. *Flintknapping. Making and Understanding Stone Tools*. Austin.

Whitten, D.G.A. & Brooks, R.V. 1972. *A Dictionary of Geology*. Middlesex.

Wobst, H. M. 1976. Locational relationships in Palaeolithic society. In: R.H. Ward & K.M. Weiss (eds.). *Demographic evolution of human populations*. London, Academic Press, 49–58.

Wyszomirska, B. 1986. The Nymölla Project. A Middle Neolithic Settlement and Burial Complex in Nymölla, North-East Scania. *MLUHM* 1985–1986, Vol. 6, 115–138.

Vang Petersen, P. 1979. *Dateringsproblemer. Atlantiske bopladsfund fra Nordøstsjælland og Skåne*. Mimeo.

– 1993. *Flint fra Danmarks Oldtid*. Copenhagen.

Vang Petersen, P. & Brinch Petersen, E. 1984. Prejlerup-tyrens skæbne – 15 små flintspidser. *Nationalmuseets Arbejdsmark* 1984, 174–179.

Vang Petersen, P. & Johansen, L. 1993. Sølbjerg I – An Ahrensburgian Site on a Reindeer Migration Route through Eastern Denmark. *Journal of Danish Archaeology* 10, 20–37.

– 1996. Tracking Late Glacial reindeer hunters in eastern Denmark. In: Larsson, L. (ed.) *The Earliest Settlement*

Yesner, D. R. 1980. Maritime hunter-gatherers. Ecology and prehistory. *Current Anthropology*, Vol. 21, No. 6, 727–750.

Yu, S. 2004. *The Littorina transgression in southeastern Sweden and its relation to mid-Holocene climate variability*. Lundqua Thesis 51. Department of Quarternary Geology, Lund University.

Archive references

ATA 2584/1939. Hansen's excavation report and various correspondence pertaining to the Barum grave.

ATA 651/83. VA – Plan. Kiaby, Bäckaskogs slott. Gatukontoret, Kristianstads kommun.

Maps

Palmgren, K.-K. 1728. Geometrisk avmätning. Åby nr 1–15. Ivetofta socken. LMV Akt 17,1.

Topografiska Corpsens karta öfver Sverige 1869. Uppmätt 1862–63. Christianstad län. Skala 1:100 000.

Skånska Rekognosceringskartan. Uppmätt av fältmätningsbrigaden 1812 och 1815–20. Blad VIIÖ 200. Skala 1:30 000. Reproducerad 1985 av Lantmäteriet.

Personal communications

Claudio Casati, Saxo-Institute, Prehistoric Archaeology Section, University of Copenhagen.

Arne Sjöström, Department of Archaeology and Ancient History, University of Lund.

Lasse Sørensen, Saxo-Institute, Prehistoric Archaeology Section, University of Copenhagen.

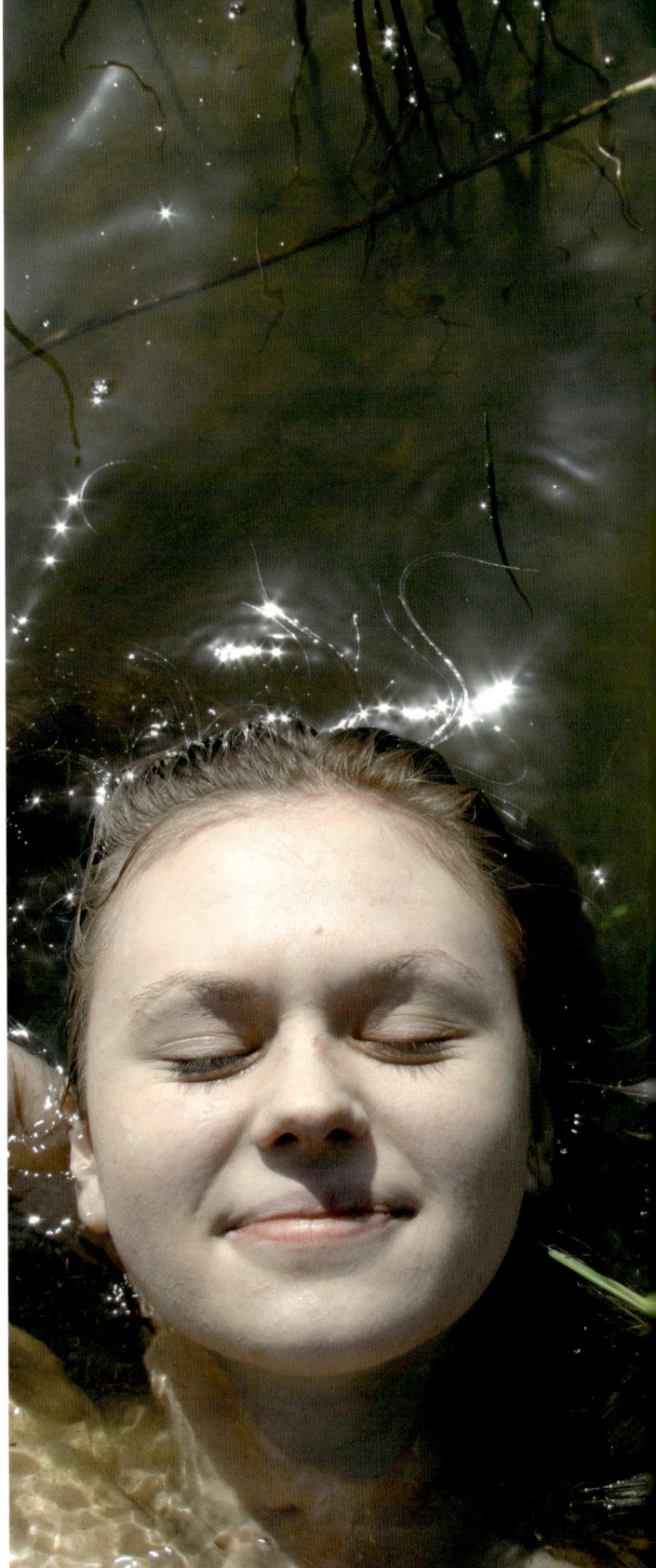